LINCOLN CHRISTIAN COLLEGE AND SEMINARY

Asian Church and God's Mission

Studies Presented in the International Symposium on Asian Mission in Manila, January 2002

P9-DIE-354

Wonsuk & Julie C. Ma
Editors

OMF LITERATURE INC.
PO Box 2217 Manila, Philippines

MWM, West Caldwell, NJ, USA
2003

The National Library of the Philippines CIP Data

Recommended entry:

Asian church and God's mission: studies presented
   in the international symposium on Asian mission
   in Manila, January 2002/ Wonsuk & Julia C.
   Ma, editors, – Mandaluyong City : OMF
   Literature Inc., © 2003
   1 v

   1. Missions, Asian — Congresses.
I. Ma, Wonsuk. IL Ma, Julia C.

BV2020   291.72   2003   P033000005
ISBN 971-511-784-8

Asian Church and God's Mission
Copyright © 2003, Mountain World Mission
54 W. Pond Rd. Hopelawn, NJ 08861
www.mtwm.org

*All rights are reserved. No part of this book may be reproduced
in any form without written permission from MWM, P.O. Box 1049,
West Caldwell, NJ 07006, USA.*

All Scripture quotations, unless otherwise indicated, are taken from the
HOLY BIBLE, NEW INTERNATIONAL VERSION®. *Copyright © 1973,
1978, 1984 by International Bible Society, Used by permission of
Zondervan Publishing House. All rights reserved.*

The "NIV" *and* "New International Version" *trademarks are registered in the
United States Patent and Trademark Office by International Bible Society.
Use of either trademark requires the permission of International Bible Society.*

ISBN 971-511-784-8

Cover Design by Nixon Na

Printed in the Philippines

CONTENTS

Preface   1
Editors' Note   2
List of Contributors   3

Wonsuk Ma and Julie Ma
    "Empowering the Asian Church for God's Mission":
    An Introductory Reflection   5

Part I
REFLECTIONS

Paul E. Pierson
    The New Context of Christian Mission:
    Challenges and Opportunities for the Asian Church   11

Melba Padilla Maggay
    Early Protestant Missionary Efforts in the Philippines:
    Some Intercultural Issues   29

Chin Do Kham
    Partnership Issues and Challenges in Asian Mission   43

Miguel Alvarez
    What Makes an Intercultural Program Effective?
    Lessons from Southern Hemisphere Experiences:
    Asia and Latin America   61

Jean-Daniel Plüss
    Empowering Asian Churches:
    How It Has Happened, and with What Consequences   79

Gratis

106016

Part II
CONTEXT

Eiko Takamizawa
A model for Presenting the Gospel to Pantheists   93

Veli-Mati Kärkkäinen
Doing Christ's Mission in the Pluralistic Context of Asia:
A Critical Dialogue with Some Asian Christologies   109

Julie C. Ma
"A Close Encounter with the Transcendental":
Proclamation and Manifestation in
Pentecostal Worship in Asian Context   127

Bal Krishna Sharma
The Mission of the Church in a Religious Pluralistic Society
with Special Reference to the Nepalese Context   147

Wonsuk Ma
Three Types of Ancestor Veneration in Asia:
An Anthropological Analysis   163

Part III
STRATEGIES

Byung-yoon Kim
Issues in the Short-term Missionary Strategy   181

David S. Lim
The Challenges of Empowering Philippine Churches for
Effective Missions to China (and Beyond)   195

Chiu Eng Tan
A Descriptive Study of Mission Programs of
Selected Philippine-Chinese Churches in Metro Manila:
Policies, Motives and Views of Mission   211

Contents

Junias V. Venugopal
Prolegomena to a Historical Perspective:
The Use of Education as a Mission Strategy in Asia   233

Elizabeth Ruth Peever
Asian Missionaries and Tentmaking   257

David A. White
Church Multiplication Coaching Networks   267

Scripture Index   275
Author Index   277

PREFACE

Perhaps, one simple way to define the mission of the church is to say that the mission of the church is a *transformed person*—one whose life is changed through encountering the Good News of Jesus Christ. The symposium held in Manila, Philippines is one humble way to affirm this belief. I believe that it has truly served its purpose to ignite the fire of visions for mission to many churches in Asia. Emil Brunner once said, "The church exists by mission as fire exists by burning." Churches without a vision for mission can hardly thrive. In fact, these churches only make vague impressions about Jesus Christ in compliance with the secular culture, but they can never make significant impacts that can transform secular culture. From this perspective, I hope that the Manila symposium served as a wake-up call to many people in Asia, thereby ushering the manifestation of God's reign in Asia. The Bible says, "Now is the time for salvation!" Yes, I truly believe that now is the time to proclaim the Good News. Now is the time to heed God's call for mission.

The Good News first spread from a corner of the Asian continent. I believe that the completion of world evangelism may also come in full when all the people in Asia have a chance to hear the Gospel and come before our Lord Jesus Christ. Therefore, we, all the members of Mountain World Mission, would like to see the Manila symposium become the first step toward this important task. We are also honored to be able to serve many hardworking pastors and evangelists as well as missionaries in the regions of Southeast Asia through this symposium by providing full financial support. We thank God for allowing us that opportunity!

On behalf of Mountain World Mission, I would like to express my heartfelt appreciation to all the presenters who shared their invaluable experiences and insights learned from their mission fields; and to all our friends from the Philippine Council of Evangelical Churches, especially Bishop Tendero, and Dr. Wonsuk Ma whose vision helped organize such a successful gathering. (We also thank his wife, Dr. Julie Ma, for joining him to make this book project possible.) We would like to extend our special thanks to our keynote speakers, Dr. Paul Pierson and Dr. Melba Magay, whose insights and challenges transcend beyond the boundaries of the Manila symposium.

Our continuous prayer and effort for world mission will not cease until the Good News of Jesus Christ reaches out to every corner and all the shores of the world.

Rev. Sun-young Joo
Chairperson, Board of Directors
Mountain World Mission

EDITORS' NOTE

This volume includes all the papers presented during the International Symposium on Asian Mission (Manila, Jan 2002). In this process of "translation" from the conference papers to a book, various people graciously assisted and they are precious "gifts" from the Lord for Asian mission. With a good chance of missing some important people, we may try to mention some of them.

The contributors not only participated in the Symposium, but also went through detailed revision processes to create this final product. Tosca Francesca Nathan managed the editorial process with her professionalism and dedication. Kathy Baxter proofread every chapter twice in the middle of her busy work caring for children in Visayan region of the Philippines. Barbara dela Cruz, my secretary, rendered her valuable help. The Mountain World Mission has demonstrated their generosity to undertaken this project and, more importantly, their keen interest in building fundamentals for healthy Asian mission in the future. We would like to thank Asia Pacific Theological Seminary, which both of us serve as faculty members, for their gracious suppoi: for this project.

It has been our joy to be able to encourage and facilitate our colleagues to be able to make an important contribution to the future of Asian mission. May the Lord continue to empower His church for His mission. Glory to Him alone!

Wonsuk Ma, PhD
Julie Ma, PhD

CONTRIBUTORS

Miguel Alvarez (D.Min., Ashland), a Honduran missionary; Vice President of the Asian Center for Missions; Adjunct Professor of Intercultural Studies, Regent University, Virginia Beach, VA, USA.

Veli-Mati Karkkainen (D.Theol. habil., Helsinki), a Finnish missiologist; Associate Professor of Systematic Theology, Fuller Theological Seminary, Pasadena, CA, USA; Docent of Ecumenics, University of Helsinki, Finland

Chin Do Kham (Ph.D., Trinity), a Burmese missiologist; Faculty member, Asia Pacific Theological Seminary, Baguio City, Philippines (1999-2002).

Byung-yoon Kim (Th.D., ABGTS), a Korean missionary, Professor of Missiology, Philippine Baptist Theological Seminary, Baguio City, Philippines; Director, Global Cross-cultural Missions Center, Inc., Manila.

David S. Lim (Ph.D., Fuller), a Filipino mission-theologian; Director, Philippine Missions Association and China International-Philippines; Contributing faculty member for Oxford Centre for Missions Studies, Oxford, UK.

Julie C. Ma (Ph.D., Fuller), a Korean missiologist; Faculty member, Asia Pacific Theological Seminary, Baguio City, Philippines; Editor, *Journal of Asian Mission*.

Wonsuk Ma (Ph.D., Fuller), a Korean missionary; Academic Dean and Faculty member, Asia Pacific Theological Seminary, Baguio City, Philippines; Co-editor, *Asian Journal of Pentecostal Studies*.

Melba Padilla Maggay (Ph.D., University of the Philippines), a Filipino Social Anthropologist; Director, Institute of Institute for Studies in Asian Church and Culture (ISACC), Manila, Philippines

Elizabeth Ruth Peever (Ph.D., Century), a Canadian missionary; Faculty member, Asia Pacific Theological Seminary, Baguio City, Philippines; TESL specialist in China, Thailand and Africa

Paul E. Pierson (Ph.D., Princeton), Former Dean and Senior Professor of History of Mission and Latin American Studies, School of World Mission, Fuller Theological Seminary, Pasadena, CA, USA

Jean-Daniel Plüss (Ph.D., Louvain), a Swiss Pentecostal theologian; Chair, European Pentecostal/Charismatic Research Association; occasional lecturer at various theological seminaries

Bal Krishna Sharma (Ph.D. cand., OCMS), a Nepali mission strategist; National director, ICI University, Nepal; Chair, Association for Theological Education in Nepal

Eiko Takamizawa (Ph.D., Trinity), a Japanese missiologist; Assistant professor of Missiology, Torch Trinity Graduate School of Theology, Seoul, Korea; Associate Professor, JTJ Mission Seminary, Tokyo, Japan; Visiting Professor, Londrina Biblical Seminary, Londrina, Brazil

Chiu Eng Tan (Ph.D., Trinity), a Chinese Filipino missiologist; Academic Dean and Faculty member, Biblical Seminary of the Philippines, Manila, Philippines

Junius V. Venugopal (Ph.D., Trinity), an Indian missionary; Dean, Asia Graduate School of Theology-Philippines

David A. White (M.Div., Talbot), an American missionary with OC International, church planter, trainer of church planters in the Philippines

"EMPOWERING THE ASIAN CHURCH FOR GOD'S MISSION" AN INTRODUCTORY REFLECTION

Wonsuk and Julie Ma

The changing paradigm of mission has been well recognized and discussed by the Western and non-Western Christian thinkers toward the close of the last century. This trend coincides with the steady growth of the churches in the traditional "mission field," while ironically the traditionally missionary countries have seen the weakening of Christianity and thus, of Christian mission. The missionaries from "non-traditional" missionary-sending churches, or simply "emerging churches" have rapidly joined the traditional missionary forces in the past several decades. It is particularly true with the Asian church.

As the new century dawned, Asian mission thinkers, often aided by Western friends, are assessing new challenges and opportunities. New paradigms are also emerging. For instance, many Korean churches now proudly have "mission" in their church names. One of the earliest cases may be found in the "Oriental Mission Church" in Los Angeles, CA, USA. Korean immigrant Christians perceived mission as their primary calling. However, this also reflects a changing paradigm. Traditionally, a "mission" church is a church that is not self-sustaining, thus, under another church's care. In this traditional usage, "mission" really means "someone's missionary work" or "mission-ed." However, the new Korean immigrants turned the word around and now redefined it as "a church that is doing mission," or "mission-ing." This may be an interesting evolution of the concept initiated by the traditionally "mission-ed" people.

This new change also challenges the traditional mission presuppositions. For instance, the indigenous church principle has been hailed as a genius conceptual driving force to bring success to Christian mission in the past two centuries. The assumed goal of mission in this scenario has been the establishment of local churches that would no longer require outside (or missionaries') help. This would allow the missionaries to move new "unreached" places to start new mission work. Seldom were the "mission-ed" churches taught to grow up to become "mission-ing" churches to join the missionaries. No wonder the old paradigm necessitates a constant flow of missionaries from the rich and white lands to the "uncivilized heathens." In fact, not long ago, a frustrated Asian missionary working in a neighboring Asian country challenged a group of Western missionaries and nationals who were engaging in seminary education: "I would not like to be 'up there' and be scolded by God for not preparing Asian churches for mission. Even if we missionaries do not teach them, God is already preparing them for missionary works." As a result, an academic journal on Asian mission was created. All the eight Evangelical seminaries in the Philippines have been producing this important academic journal since 1999. Some of the chapters in this volume present this "corrected" rule of mission.

The International Symposium on Asian Mission, under the theme of "Empowering the Asian Church for God's Mission," again represents this changing paradigm in several important ways.

First, a national church body (in this case, the Philippine Council of Evangelical Churches), an Asian-American missionary organization (i.e., Mountain World Mission, NJ, USA), an Evangelical seminary community (i.e., Asia Graduate School of Theology-Philippines through its Doctor of Missiology Program Committee), and a local church (i.e., Manila New Life Church) joined their resources together to bring about this historic meeting. What a network paradigm this is! This may be a visible demonstration of what Asian churches can do when they commit themselves to work together for God's kingdom.

Second (and equally significant), is that the mission thinkers and strategists came together from the West and Asia and demonstrated their shared conviction that the new era of partnership mission has come. As Asian churches are sending off their missionaries, suddenly new challenges and opportunities are before them. For instance, religious plurality is something the Western churches have not lived with, and yet Asian missionaries are constantly facing this issue. Both the Western and Asian scholars were able to put their thoughts together in strengthening the Asian church for God's mission.

Third, for this invitational symposium, a consensus has emerged rather powerfully: as much as popular type of mission conventions (for mobilization) and mission training should continue, conspicuously planned academic conferences are critical in laying a solid foundation for Asian mission. For this, the seminary community in each Asian country should grow beyond their denominational childhood and look beyond their churches. The historically and theologically unique tradition for each denomination and group is something we all need to strengthen in coming days, so that they will also function as unique gifts from the Lord to "edify the whole Body of Christ." However, this denominational or theological loyalty is within the kingdom principle. Asian churches are called to become truly "post-colonial" in their positive ecumenical orientation. This "ecumenical challenge" is well laid out by Pierson in a chapter.

Certainly, a one-day gathering is only a small beginning and could not possibly discuss many important issues that the Asian church is facing to become meaningfully "mission-ing" churches. More questions deserve serious attention. What will be Christian's (not just Evangelical's) response to poverty? How can we build meaningful and tangible solidarity with suffering Christians under totalitarian or oppressive rules? What is Christian's role in the wide spread corruption and injustice among Asian countries? Is there a good set of guidelines for inter-religious dialogues without compromising Christian conviction? What will be the role of the fast growing Pentecostal sort of Christianity in Asia? What are some traditional Asian values, such as family systems, that can be positively incorporated into the Christian life? What is our missiological approach to racial conflicts and issues? This array of untouched questions strongly suggests that this sort of contribution through a combined reflection through conferences and collected volumes is priceless.

The hope is for the Asian church to diligently learn from the past, and creatively chart the future of Christian mission through the empowerment of the Holy Spirit.

Part I

REFLECTIONS

THE NEW CONTEXT OF CHRISTIAN MISSION: CHALLENGES AND OPPORTUNITIES FOR THE ASIAN CHURCH

Paul E. Pierson

1. Changes in the Context

The context of Christian mission at the beginning of the twentieth century can be symbolized by the Ecumenical Missionary Conference, held in New York in 1900. Over 200,000 people attended its various sessions. President McKinley of the United States was a speaker, as were a former and future president. It symbolized an age of Western dominance, optimism and a close identification of the traditional Protestant churches, Western culture and even the missionary movement.

How things have changed! Two world wars, the end of Western political colonialism, the rise and fall of communism and the growth of secularism in the West have been accompanied by the striking growth of the church and the missionary movement in Asia, Africa and Latin America. Along with this we see new forms of the church growing rapidly. The paradox is that in an era in which ecumenism is stressed and embraced more than any time in recent history, we see greater diversity in the various forms of the church than ever before.

In this presentation, I want to examine a number of these trends and attempt to discover lessons which the Holy Spirit is teaching us and directions in which he seems to be leading us today and into the future.

1.1 Political Situation

Obviously, we have moved into a post-colonial era politically. In the two decades following World War II, scores of former European colonies in Africa and Asia became independent politically, if not always economically. It is generally perceived that European missionaries had maintained close relationships with colonial governments and at times benefited from their support. That was not always true. Frequently missionaries opposed the policies of their colonial governments, and at times those same governments prevented missionaries from serving in Muslim areas. Northern Nigeria was an example. However, to many it appeared that the Christian faith was simply the religious side of Western colonialism. Consequently, many believed that the church would cease to exist when the Europeans left. The fact that it did not disappear was clearly due to the vitality of the new churches established by missionaries and increasingly led by capable national leaders.

A second aspect of political change is that we now live in a post-ideological era. From 1917 to 1989, and especially after 1945, the world was divided into two ideological blocks, while a large number of nations, usually former colonies, attempted to remain non-aligned. Communism, of course, shut off much of the world from any overt missionary work and in most cases, severely persecuted the churches which already existed. That, of course, has changed in Eastern Europe and the former Soviet Union since 1989.

1.2 The Church

At the beginning of the twentieth century, the "mainline" churches were dominant both in their culture and in the missionary movement. These were churches with roots in the Protestant Reformation of the sixteenth century or subsequent renewal movements such as the Methodists, Baptists and Congregationalists.

Even though the latter three had begun as counter-cultural movements, they had all become strongly identified with their culture and its assumptions; along with the Anglicans, Presbyterians and Lutherans. In Europe, there existed a culture of Christendom in which the church was established and supported by governments, while in the United States these churches were widely respected even though not established by the government. They enjoyed a *de facto* Christendom status. Missionary movements had always arisen on the periphery of the ecclesiastical structures which we call churches, and at the beginning were led by visionaries. However, by the beginning of the twentieth century, the mainline churches and society as a whole had embraced the movement. In North America, for example, eighty percent of the missionaries served under the sponsorship of the mainline churches at the beginning of the century; but by the end of the century, the percentage had fallen to six percent. Those same churches were rapidly loosing members and influence in their societies.

The great changes in the missionary movement in the twentieth century came about because of three major factors. First, there was the rise of the more conservative, multi-denominational faith missions. The China Inland Mission, established by J. Hudson Taylor in 1965, was the prototype. The second factor was the growth of theological liberalism in the older churches, which, symbolized by the World Council of Churches, shifted the focus from world evangelization to social reform. The third and most important was the rise of the Pentecostal/Charismatic movement.

The latter now constitutes the most rapidly growing form of the Christian faith in the world. I will leave it to others to assess its strengths and weaknesses, but among the gifts it has brought to the whole church, three stand out in my mind. First, it has opened the way for a variety of new forms of the church, more closely adapted to specific cultural contexts. Secondly, it has rejected post-enlightenment Christianity which in both its liberal and orthodox forms often relegated God to the sidelines, encased in doctrine, but not active in human life today. And thirdly, it has been ardently missionary in nature, realizing that if the church is to be faithful, mission must lie at its very heart.

Even as secularism has grown and traditional churches have declined in the West, we have seen remarkable growth of Evangelical faith in the West and even more in Asia, Africa and Latin America. For example, Nigeria alone claims 20 million Anglicans and Uganda at least 8 million. And church attendance and participation are much higher than in England.[1]

In 1800, approximately one percent of Evangelical Christians lived in Asia, Africa and Latin America. In 1900 the figures were ten and ninety percent respectively. But by 2000, two thirds were found in Asia, Africa and Latin America, and only one third in the West.[2]

A few statistics illustrate this. Today, there are nearly four times as many Presbyterians in South Korea as in the United States. Seven of the largest Christian churches in the world are in Seoul. Nigeria counts seven times more Anglicans than the United States. In a number of

Latin American countries more people worship in Evangelical fellowships on any Sunday than in Roman Catholic churches. The number of Latin American Evangelicals has grown from 250,000 in 1900 to 50 million today. And the change in the shape of the church is shown by the fact that at least three fourths of those Latin American Evangelicals are Pentecostals.[3]

This brings us to two conclusions. First, while many in the West still think of the church in terms of traditional denominations with roots in the sixteenth century Reformation, we have now moved into a post-denominational era. Secondly, we see that the Christian faith, which began in Asia and moved both east and west, but was largely confined to Europe by the sixteenth century, is now a worldwide faith. Its center of gravity is no longer in the north and west; it is in the south and east. Thus, the church is much less identified with Western culture and its Christendom mentality. It is more sectarian, charismatic, flexible and independent of governments. Our challenge is to discover what these changes mean for us as we seek to be faithful to the worldwide mission of Christ today.

1.3 The Missionary Movement

Along with the changes in the political context and the church, we find significant changes in the missionary movement. Not long after Western missionaries arrived in a number of areas, the new churches began to send their own cross-cultural workers. In the mid-nineteenth century, Burmese Karens went to the Chins and other tribes within the country; South Sea islanders got in their long canoes and took the gospel to other islands and peoples. Korean Presbyterians went to Jeju Island beginning in 1907 and soon afterward, to China.[4] But the new phenomenon today is the extraordinary growth of the number of cross-cultural missionaries from Asia, Africa and Latin America. They do not always go to other countries; they are defined as those who cross a significant linguistic and/or cultural barrier to communicate the gospel. This often involves reaching a different ethnic/language group within their own country. Research done at the School of World Mission at Fuller Seminary illustrates this. The first project, done in 1972, documented 3,404 such missionaries. The second, in 1980, listed 13,000. The third, in 1989, found at least 35,924.[5]

The estimates of cross cultural missionaries from Asia, Africa and Latin America range from 100,000 to 120,000 today; and it continues to grow. Koreans alone account for 11,500, and it is estimated that over

20,000 Indian missionaries work in cultures and languages other than their own in that diverse nation. Increasingly Africans, Latin Americans and Koreans are planting churches in Europe and North America. Usually, they begin with persons of their own national and ethnic background, but often grow to include others, including persons of European descent. An interesting example is the Action Chapel, a Ghanaian group, which holds regular bible studies in the offices of the World Bank in Washington, D.C.

Significant numbers of missionaries from Asia, Africa and Latin America are now working in England and elsewhere in Europe. What is said to be the largest church in London, with 10,000 in attendance, was established by a Nigerian Pentecostal. About one half of its constituency come from forty African countries, the other half includes many other races, including many Caucasians.[6] The Anglican Church Missionary Society, established in 1799, has called twenty Anglican priests from India, Chile and Sierra Leone to come and invigorate dying parishes in England.

Thus, the shift in the makeup of the missionary movement gives us an opportunity, unprecedented since the third century, to communicate the gospel without all of its Western trappings. If we are wise, we will discover ways to experiment with new forms of the church, its leadership and its worship, which are more appropriate to the cultural contexts in which we work.

1.4 Cultural Diversity

There can be no doubt that we live in situations of great change and cultural diversity. Some are called to engage in mission in traditional cultures, some in modern and others in postmodern cultures. By traditional, I mean those cultures which look back, value the traditions of the past, give great emphasis to community and shun individualism. Thus, decisions are to be made by the group, and the elders are to be valued and respected. We are also called to communicate the Christian message in modern cultures. These are characterized by a more secular mentality, future orientation and individualism, quite different from traditional cultures. Increasingly, however, we confront postmodern culture. While definitions of 'postmodern' are elusive, this mindset is less rationalistic, more suspicious of traditional institutions, focused more on experience than on dogma, and tends to be relativistic regarding truth.

We will probably find all three groups in any country, or indeed in any city. I once had a conversation with a man in the airport in Pune, India. He was an entrepreneur who owned factories and traveled abroad frequently. He had a brother and sister-in law who were medical professors in the United States; but not far away were Indian villagers who lived much as their ancestors had lived. Today, in every country, there are pockets of very traditional groups living side by side with sophisticated modern and postmodern persons.

A second and related change is the great migration from rural to urban areas. The world is urbanizing with breathtaking speed as millions move from the countryside to the cities. This is especially true in Asia, Africa and Latin America. The statistics are staggering. Sao Paulo, Brazil had a population of nearly three million in 1956; today it numbers around 20 million. Mexico City adds 900,000 a year to its population, which already counts about 30 million; and one can hardly grasp the growth of cities like Manila, Bangkok, Jakarta, Lagos, Cairo, Calcutta and many others. Significantly, nearly all of the most rapidly growing cities in the world are in countries that have not had a strong Evangelical Christian presence historically.

Almost without exception these cities are multi-ethnic and multi-lingual. In many, if not most, of the great cities of the world, over one hundred languages are spoken. This suggests that we need to re-think our concept of unreached peoples. A former missionary to Guatemala told me that if you wanted to reach a certain people group of that nation, there were two places to which you should go. One was in the northern mountains of that country; the other was in a certain area of Los Angeles. Many were migrating, legally or illegally, to a specific barrio of that city. We may be sure that within a few years of their arrival, their culture had changed. They were not the same 'people group.'

Ralph Winter has suggested a typology of three eras of mission history and their representative leaders. The first focused on the coastlands (William Carey), the second, the inland areas (J. Hudson Taylor) and the third, the unreached or hidden peoples (Cameron Townsend and Donald McGavran).7 The first two involve geography, the third, culture. I suggest we are in a fourth era, that of the cities, which involves both geography and culture. They are the most challenging missionary frontiers for the present and future. Many of the unreached peoples in the hinterlands are moving to the cities. We need to consider this fact in our mission strategies.

The great majority of the newcomers to the cities, who hope to find jobs and opportunity, encounter only extreme poverty and terrible slums. I believe this calls some to form sacrificial Christian communities and live among the poorest of the poor in incarnational ministries. It also calls for holistic ministries which seek to help people begin to escape from the hopeless cycle of grinding poverty and in that context to communicate the gospel.

1.5 Changes in Technology

The changes in technology are so rapid and far-reaching that I will not comment on them here. It suffices to say that they have revolutionized communication, transportation and economic life in the last decades. Instantaneous communication around the globe is now a reality. The globalization of economic life means that Christian workers with technical skills will be welcomed in areas where professional missionaries are not. Technology also opens up new possibilities for leadership training. These are only a few implications of the changes.

1.6 Growing Persecution

Part of the reaction against Western cultural and economic domination coupled with the desire to rediscover cultural roots has led to the resurgence of religions such as Hinduism and Islam. This has become all too obvious in recent months but has been observed for a number of years. The fundamentalist Hindu party in power in India has led to increased persecution of Christians, especially in those areas where the church is growing. Christians are being attacked and killed and churches burned in Sudan, Indonesia, Northern Nigeria and elsewhere. The earliest missionaries had to confront diseases which took many lives, even though they often had the protection of Western governments. Today, missionaries and even more Christians in a number of countries face severe persecution by their own governments or are at least marginalized. While it is not always true that "the blood of the martyrs is the seed of the Church," often it has been the case. China and Ethiopia and now Cuba are contemporary examples. In other cases, the church seems nearly to have disappeared under persecution. North Korea is a recent example. We are called, not only to pray for the churches which live under the cross, but also to attempt to discover lessons to be learned from those which have survived and even grown under persecution.

1.7 Summary

These are some of the changes in the context in which we are called to carry out the Christian mission today. Others will describe more changes. To summarize, we note that the world in which we live and work is very different from the world in which the modern missionary movement began. Thus we are called to re-examine the assumptions with which we go about our task in the light of that changing context. Simply, to repeat the patterns of the past will not be sufficient. On the other hand, the new context opens an extraordinary array of new possibilities of mission, unprecedented in history.

Secondly, the church is being reshaped today to an extent not seen since the sixteenth century Reformation. What the reshaped church will look like, none of us can predict; but it will be more a church of the poor rather than the affluent. It will be less western, less traditional, more multi-cultural and much more diverse. We turn now to some of the characteristics of the newer churches.

2. Changes in the Shape of the Church

Obviously, the church always exists in specific historical/cultural contexts, and as the context changes, the church is called to change, even though the directions of change are seldom clearly defined. Nevertheless, I repeat my thesis that the church is being reshaped today to an extent not seen at least since the sixteenth century.

The churches of the Protestant Reformation were formed around certain issues: the doctrine of justification, authority, the sacraments and church governance. Congregationalists, Baptists and Methodists arose out of later renewal movements, primarily around the latter two issues. Christology, for example, was not questioned. All of these groups accepted that of Chalcedon and affirmed the authority of the scripture. They were dominated by the clergy, although not all began that way. However, while Christology and the authority of the scripture continue to be important, the other issues are of little interest to most people in the West, and even less so elsewhere. Furthermore, the churches in the West, which emerged from the Protestant Reformation and the subsequent renewal movements, have for the most part become institutionalized and have lost much of their vitality. There are exceptions, of course, but the decline in active membership and in missionary activity is a significant indicator.

Even as the more traditional churches are in decline in the West, but still growing in many areas of Africa, Asia and Latin America, we see new types of churches springing up and growing more rapidly. A number of books have been published, analyzing some of these new churches. *The Gospel People of Latin America* by Berg and Pretiz is one.[8] Berryman's work, *Religion in the Mega City*, examines one such church in Caracas, Venezuela.[9] A Ph.D. dissertation at Fuller by Joel Comisky, examined a number of cell based churches in Latin America;[10] and the sociologist, Donald Miller, has published *Reinventing American Protestantism*, which looks at three new, growing churches in the United States.[11] They are the Vineyard movement, Calvary Chapel and Hope Chapel. All three started in Southern California and have spread to other areas.

These works have discovered a number of common factors in the new churches. All can be characterized as "post-denominational," that is, they have been influenced by factors very different from those which shaped "mainline" Protestantism. Some still carry traditional labels. Others may be on their way to becoming structured denominations. But even those that bear a traditional label look more like the newer churches than older congregations of their denominations.

Let me outline some of the characteristics common to most of the newer churches.

2.1 Cell and Celebration

Most evangelism and nurture of believers takes place in cells of five to ten persons who meet weekly in homes. The value of this in modern society, which easily becomes impersonal, is obvious. These groups also provide an inviting, non-threatening context in which non-believers can discover Christian fellowship, then the gospel. The Charismatic Mission in Bogota, Colombia has grown to 50,000 in fifteen years, using this system. The Living Love Fellowship of Tegucigalpa, Honduras counts 7,000. The cell groups help believers to encourage each other in the Christian journey. They also recognize that each person, no matter how new or humble, has gifts to offer to the group. They are similar to the early Puritan conventicles, the Pietist "churches within the church," the Moravian choirs and the Methodist classes. It is significant that those four movements gave birth to the

Protestant missionary movement. It is also significant that in nearly every revival movement in history, small face to face groups have played a key role.

2.2 The Gifts Are Valued

Most of these churches are not classically Pentecostal emphasizing *glossalalia*, but they are open to all of the gifts. Unlike many traditional churches, they believe that all of the gifts are given today and are to be used for ministry by the whole body of Christ. Thus, there is a much greater focus on the gifts and ministry of the laity. Obviously, the small groups are led by laity, and in the Vineyard fellowships, for example, during the ministry time, lay believers gather around those who ask for prayer.

A few years ago I visited Brazil and stayed in the home of a Presbyterian couple—he a businessman, she a physician. I discovered that her mother, a former Methodist, not finding opportunity for ministry in her church, had started a new congregation in her city. Within a few years it had grown to 1000 members, mostly new converts.

2.3 Praise and Prayer

Normally, there is an extended time of praise and prayer. A worship team, using contemporary music, sometimes composed by the group, leads the praise. Worshippers do not sing so much about God, rather they sing to God, often using the body to express praise. There is little dichotomy between body and spirit. Worship is more a right brain than a left brain experience. Often worship and fellowship come first, then the theological reflection, quite differently from the way we have thought traditionally. But isn't that more the order of the New Testament disciples?

On that same trip to Brazil, I worshipped at two different venues of a Presbyterian church. The first was the traditional sanctuary downtown, with about 400 worshippers; the second was a former automotive garage, now a worship center. There we worshipped with about 1500 persons, many of them young, for about two hours, in a more praise oriented, contemporary service. Along with the period of praise, there was an extended time of prayer for the specific needs of those present.

2.4 Alternative Methods of Selecting and Training Leaders

Often these churches have their own training programs, but they are for those already in some form of ministry. That is, ministry comes first, then sometimes more formal training. I recently met a man who was converted while in prison for drug use. After his release, he became a part of Hope Chapel in Southern California, and began to lead small groups to help others get off drugs, alcohol, etc. Finally, his pastor suggested that he start a church in a neighboring city. He did so. The church meets across from a park where drug dealing and prostitution are common. It has become the largest Protestant church in the community, reaching out to those caught in such lifestyles.

Many of the pastors have had a dramatic conversion after a destructive life of drugs, illicit sex and even crime. They relate well to broken people and are living witnesses of the power of the gospel to transform lives. Often, they have been called through a vision, dream, or other kind of supernatural visitation. In some cases, there are women leaders, but mostly the leadership is male.

2.5 The Bible

Along with the emphasis on praise and prayer, there is strong emphasis on the exposition of the scripture. The conviction is that the Bible not only tells us what to believe, but how to live, and that God speaks to us personally through it. Sermons are longer, giving biblical teaching on various subjects. The focus is more on the scripture as narrative than doctrine. Thus people can find themselves within the biblical narrative and its personalities, and find the stories relevant to their own lives today.

These churches have also recaptured central aspects of New Testament teaching: a strong focus on the incarnation, the cross, the resurrection and the second coming. And along with this is a strong emphasis on the ongoing work of the Holy Spirit. This brings transformation of the lives of broken people, giving hope and meaning. Usually in worship there is a call to conversion and commitment.

2.6 Holistic Ministry

Often these churches are remarkably holistic in their ministries. I visited a church in a suburb of Rio de Janeiro, which in twenty years had grown from fifteen to 3400 members. It had all the characteristics mentioned above. It had also purchased homes (one for men and one for women, to help them get off drugs), had started two primary schools for poor children, and established a number of new churches. Other churches have feeding programs, work with street children and even offer job training. They do not usually get involved at the political level and are suspicious of politics.

2.7 Culturally Appropriate Communication

A major missiological issue is always that of culturally appropriate communication of the Christian message. This often includes the attempt to remove barriers which may prejudice the communication process. The new churches focus especially on the younger generation, both inside and outside the church. Often the buildings do not look like churches (e.g., the former garage in Brazil); they do not use traditional symbols, nor organs or hymnbooks, but project words on a screen. Many who are not attracted to traditional religion as they understand it are more open to hearing the message in a warehouse or home than in a building that looks like a church.

While these churches may be termed postmodern in the West and among urban populations elsewhere, in many cultures they are pre-modern. Remember, the worldview of most non-Western cultures is much closer to the biblical worldview than to the post-enlightenment modern worldview. Thus we find such churches in places as diverse as Budapest, Bangkok, Singapore, Lagos, Bombay and Bogota.

2.8 Summary

Donald Miller, the sociologist who studied the new American churches, is now directing a team examining similar churches around the world. He has been analyzing those which are growing rapidly and also have a strong social ministry. He told me that 80% of them were Pentecostal/Charismatic in nature. The three primary characteristics he found in such churches correspond to those we have observed.

They "mediate the sacred," that is, there is a profound experience of God. Lives are being transformed. They have a quality of community. That is, strong bonds are formed among the people, especially in the small groups.[12]

2.9 Issues to Be Faced

Lest we think these newer churches will not be subject to some of the forces of drift toward nominalism that other movements have experienced, I suggest there are at least five major issues they must face.

First, because most are started by charismatic leaders with a strong sense of call, transition to the next generation of leaders will be difficult. Will they develop adequate mechanisms for this? And will their successors be able to maintain the zeal and creativity into the next generations?

Second, after a beginning that is often the result of a powerful, transforming Christian experience, will they do the kind of theological reflection needed to explain, sustain and build on that experience?

Third, as they grow, will they develop the structures needed to nourish and maintain growth, without creating bureaucracies which begin to control and stifle the creativity?

Fourth, as they move into the second and third generations, will they be able to maintain the high level of experience and commitment, or will they lapse into routine?

Finally, will their methods of communication, tailored to a specific context, be adapted to still newer generations?

I do not predict the demise of the older churches. However, I am sure we will see a greater variety of worship styles compared with those of a few decades ago. And I agree with Miller, who suggests that the basic issue is the vitality of the experience with God. Those churches which lead people into a vital encounter with God, which transforms and orients their lives, will survive and grow. That is the key issue.

3. New Opportunities and Challenges

3.1 The New Ecumenism

One of the most positive factors today is the new Evangelical ecumenism. I believe that Evangelicals are now more functionally ecumenical than the World Council of Churches (WCC). The WCC deals primarily with theological issues of the sixteenth century (ministry, the sacraments, church government) which are not seen as relevant by most people, but pays less attention to social issues which are extremely important. The new Evangelical ecumenism is task-oriented, focusing on world evangelization. It is based on certain theological assumptions: the authority of scripture, high Christology, the necessity of conversion, justification faith, the church as central to

God's work in history, and mission and evangelism as central to the church's task. As a result of the Pentecostal/Charismatic movement, there is more explicit recognition of the role of the Holy Spirit. The Lausanne Conference of 1974 is seen as its beginning, followed by Manila in 1989. That was perhaps the most widely representative Christian gathering in history up to that time. Men and women from 150 countries, from older mainline churches, newer Evangelical groups, churches established by faith missions (e.g., the Evangelical Church of West Africa, established by SIM International), classical Pentecostal and newer Charismatic churches, were there.

Subsequently, the AD 2000 Movement focused on the purpose of planting churches in all of the world's unreached groups. It is also symbolic that while the leadership of the Lausanne movement was mostly from the Europe and the United States, Luis Bush, from Argentina, led the AD 2000 Movement. Both have encouraged sharper focus and greater cooperation in the worldwide evangelistic task. Thus, they have opened up the possibility of new forms of partnership between different mission agencies.

3.2 New Places for Mission

It is neither necessary nor possible to examine this subject in detail. A few examples will suffice.

3.2.1 Former Soviet Union

In Russia, nominal orthodoxy is in need of renewal. The scripture and the liturgy are in archaic Russian, which is not well understood. There is resistance to attempts to put them in modern language. There is also resistance against the few priests who have started small groups or worked for religious liberty. The Baptists and Pentecostals have been heroic but often have a ghetto mentality and easily fall into legalism, which makes it difficult for secularized people from outside to find a place. There is certainly a place for newer churches established by those from outside, often Koreans, but expatriate missionaries must think through their role with great sensitivity and care.

The former Soviet republics, e.g., Uzbekistan, are nominally Muslim but there are opportunities for evangelism and church planting. There is a great need to understand the culture, and the differences between Uzbeks and Russians. The church needs to be post-denominational. Missionaries should be careful not to import struggles in the West irrelevant to their culture. Missionaries must constantly ask, "What is essential if we are to have a viable, functioning church?" I believe that such churches must be open to all the gifts, to power encounter, and must seek theological as well as spiritual depth, going beyond the focus on experience. Also a major issue is the question of how leaders are to be selected and trained, and by whom.

3.2.2 Eastern Europe

There are some strong Evangelical churches, such as Baptists in Romania. At the same time, the traditional Orthodox churches, which have a strong ethnic identity, see themselves as the only true church. The question of how mission is to be carried out in such contexts requires careful prayer, dialogue and thought. I suspect that most Evangelicals will be called to plant new churches in such areas, while some may be called to attempt to work with the ancient churches.

3.2.3 Western cities

We need to recognize the importance of the multi-ethnic Western cities, as well as cities elsewhere. Some of the newcomers (e.g., Koreans and many Africans) have a strong Christian heritage, and can make a strong contribution to the life of the whole church. Other newcomers may see the church as part of the dominant culture in which they feel rejected. Asian missionaries have a key role to play as they build bridges between various groups.

3.2.4 Nominal Christians, or "Post-Christians" in the West

Leslie Newbigln said the secular West might be the most difficult mission field of all.[13] Could it be that vibrant Asian Christian communities in the United States and Europe might eventually reach out to Western secularized people and also become a source of new vitality in the older churches?

3.2.5 The Muslim world

This is such a critical issue that it deserves much greater consideration than I can give it here. We are all aware of the growing Islamic fundamentalism and militancy and some of the reasons for it. At the same time, there are positive movements toward contextualization of the gospel among Muslims with some success. Clearly, because of a number of historical and political factors, Asians have a key role to play here, probably more so than westerners.

4. Conclusion: Three Critical Issues for the Future

As we look at the history of the church, the people of God, certain issues arise constantly. Among them are the relationship between the gospel and culture; how the whole church is to be motivated and mobilized for mission; how to build and maintain the institutional church and at the same time, recognize the creativity of the Holy Spirit on the periphery; how to help the church discover and move to the new frontiers of mission in each generation,; and finally, how to devise methods of choosing and training leaders which are adequate to the challenges of the rapid growth of the Christian movement in our era.

In this concluding section I want to deal with three issues.

4.1 Cities

First, I believe the most crucial missionary frontiers are now the growing cities of the world. Every country, without exception, is urbanizing rapidly. In all of them, the urban culture is different from traditional rural cultures. There are now 500 cities in the world with over one million or more population, there are 25 with over ten million. And the characteristics and dynamics of life in the cities are very different from traditional lifestyles.

The factors behind this phenomenon are well known. Often the rural areas offer only subsistence farming, scarcity of land and help for agriculture, population growth and little educational or vocational opportunity. The cities are seen as places where there are jobs and educational opportunities for the next generation. More often than not, these hopes are tragically disappointed, with families living in terrible slums and without adequate employment.

One tragic result is often the breakdown of families, resulting in abused and abandoned children and prostitution. At the same time, there is often more openness to change as families migrate to the cities.

Certainly, the Holy Spirit will lead his people to plant many forms of the church in such places, from mega churches with numerous cell groups, to house churches in the midst of slums or in apartment buildings. The forms will be different, but the goal is the same: to communicate the Good News of Jesus Christ so that men and women will discover that they are called to become sons and daughters of God through the Son, and live as his disciples wherever he places them. Such discipleship will certainly include special concern for the poor and marginalized, helping them to escape from the cycle of poverty and abuse, and helping them to discover they are loved by God and called to new life.

4.2 Leadership

The second major issue, in my judgment, is that of leadership training. We estimate that there are two million functional pastors/ evangelists at work in the world today, who have little or no formal biblical or theological training. Yet they constitute the cutting edge of the church in many areas and are responsible for much of the growth. They are house church leaders in China; they work among slum dwellers in Latin America, in rural Nepal, among untouchables in India and in many parts of Africa.

I believe the primary reason for the rapid growth of Methodism in the early nineteenth century was a system of classes, which encouraged lay leadership, itinerant evangelists and leadership which came up from the "grass roots." The movement lost its vitality and began to decline when it moved to a more elitist model of leadership, leaving little or no place for the itinerant lay preachers who had led the movement earlier. A major reason for the rapid growth of the Pentecostal movement was that it, too, encouraged such grass roots leadership of both men and women.

Now, the major issue is this: How can we recognize and affirm the need for all of us to do serious biblical and theological study and reflection at the highest level, which is essential, and also encourage those two million pastors and evangelists who so often are on the cutting edge? Clearly, the challenge here is to constantly seek to discover appropriate ways in which we can stand alongside and help the two million. In other words, those of us who have the privilege of theological and biblical training are called, not to stand aloof, but to seek to become servants of the humblest pastor/evangelist and layperson. The church is always most effective when it encourages believers to use their gifts for ministry.

4.3 Renewal

Finally, as we confront the opportunities and challenges in mission today, we need to recognize that mission has always come out of renewal, both personal and corporate. This has always involved a new vision of God, a new realization of the depth of our sin and that of our society, and a profound experience of grace which has led us to hear again the call of God, "whom shall I send? Who will go for us?" (Isaiah 6:8).

---

[1] Philip Jenkins, *The Next Christendom: The Coming of Global Christianity* (Oxford: Oxford University Press, 2002), 58-59.

[2] Jenkins, *The Next Christendom*, 37, 61-63.

[3] Jenkins, *The Next Christendom*, 61-63.

[4] Timothy Kiho Park, "A Survey of the Korean Missionary Movement," *Journal of Asian Mission* 4:1 (2002), 113-16.

[5] Cf. E. Pentecost, J. Wong, and P. Larson, "Third World Mission Agencies" (M.A. thesis, School of World Mission, Fuller Theological Seminary, 1972); Lawrence Keyes, *The Last Age of Missions* (Pasadena, William Carey Library, 1883); Larry Pate, *From Every People* (Monrovia, CA: MARC, 1989).

[6] Interview with the Rev. Remi Lawanson of Nigeria in Pasadena, CA, May 15, 2002.

[7] Ralph D. Winter, "Four Men, Three Eras, Two Transitions, and Modern Missions," in *Perspectives on the World Christian Movement: A Reader*, eds. Ralph D. Winter and Steven C. Hawthorne (Pasadena, CA: William Carey Library, 1999), 253-61.

[8] Clayton Berg and Paul Pretiz, *The Gospel People of Latin America* (Monrovia, CA: MARC, 1992).

[9] Philip Berryman, *Religion in the Megacity: Catholic and Protestant Portraits from Latin America* (Maryknoll: Orbis, 1996).

[10] Joel Comiskey, "Cell-Based Ministry: A Positive Factor in Church Growth in Latin America" (Ph.D. dissertation, School of World Mission, Fuller Theological Seminary, Pasadena, CA, 1997).

[11] Donald Miller, *Reinventing American Protestantism: Christianity in the New Millennium* (Berkeley: University of California Press, 1997).

[12] Donald Miller, "MH 521 History and Theology of Evangelical Awakenings" (Unpublished lecture, Fuller Theological Seminary, May 17, 2001).

[13] L. Newbigin makes this comment in at least two of his books: *Unfinished Agenda* (Grand Rapids: Eerdmans, 1985) and *The Gospel in a Pluralist Society* (Grand Rapids: Eerdmans, 1989).

EARLY PROTESTANT MISSIONARY EFFORTS IN THE PHILIPPINES: SOME INTERCULTURAL ISSUES

Melba Padilla Maggay

1. Introduction

As a trained social anthropologist, I would like to present the findings of a three-year research on the early impact of Protestant missionary efforts at the turn of the last century. Some of these could be useful not only to Filipinos but also to other Asian churches as we reflect on the future of Christian mission in Asia.

It is important for us to grasp the fact that what we call Christianity is really a product of our interaction with the formal system, like the biblical *text*, and culture as controlling *context* in the process of translation. We are aware from the writings of Andrew Walls that Christianity is a vernacular faith.[1] Whether we are conscious of it or not, we are constantly contextualizing the Christian faith. This is in stark contrast with Islam where "translation" is not permitted, whether in language or culture. Muslims have to understand Arabic to be truly Islamic. It is not an accident that Christianity is always engaged in translation. The incarnational nature of the Christian faith demands it.

It is also important to realize that what we call "folk" religions or "popular" religions are actually products of this interface between text and context. In a setting where "translation" is done properly, Christianity more or less remains the same in substance, in spite of sometimes radically different perspectives on it. In the Philippines, we often say that our Christianity is not really "biblical" but "folk" Christianity. Positively, this is the result of a creative interaction between our understandings of Christianity as handed down to us and our own appropriation of it within the terms of our culture. Unfortunately, according to Jose De Mesa, a colleague within the Catholic tradition, it is not the indigenous religion that got Christianized but Christianity as a religion became Filipinized.[2] I assume that a similar process happens in many other Asian cultures.

2. The Static of Colonialism:
Iberian Catholicism and American Protestantism

"To civilize and Christianize" was the agenda of the early American missionaries who came to the Philippines at the turn of the last century. This was based on what they called their "manifest destiny." President William McKinley, speaking to a group of Methodist bishops just before the annexation of the Philippines, said he had this strange agonizing pain about what to do with the country. After much praying he said he finally came to the decision that it was God's will that America should come to Christianize and civilize the Filipinos.[3] Now, this talk of lofty intentions was more or less similarly experienced by many third-world countries where, along with the colonial powers, Christianity came as a handmaid to imperialism.

This is a fact that we need to face squarely: our sense of ambiguity towards the missionary as bearer of God's message and as culture-bearer of imperial power. We have seen this all throughout the influx of American Protestantism in this country. The same ambiguity was also felt about the convert. It was understood at that time that to be a Protestant was to be on the side of colonialism. During the early days of heated debates about independence from America, the converts themselves felt at a loss about their new-found faith and the fact that they were being identified as part of the colonizing power.

Also at the turn of the twentieth century, there was a massive movement called the Iglesia Filipina Independiente (Philippine Independent Church). It was a bulwark of the resistance against Spain and the vanguard of the movement towards secularization of the clergy. The movement, at the highest point of its popularity, was claiming that about five million Filipinos, or nearly two-thirds of the population, were with them during the first three or four years. They were consistently claiming three to four million Filipino followers.[4] The figures may have been exaggerated, but it was also true that it was a massive movement at that time.

It is said that the leader of this movement, Gregorio Aglipay, went to the missionaries and asked: "Why don't you teach and work with us? Your faith has something to do with the Bible, and we would like to go back to the Bible." But James Rodgers, the first Presbyterian missionary and first official American missionary to the Philippines, together with his colleagues, debated whether they should openly support the Iglesia Filipina Independiente or not. Eventually they decided not to endorse the movement, because they thought that Aglipay, who was an officer in Aguinaldo's army, was too political.[5] In the language of Frank Laubach, a Congregationalist missionary, the missionaries thought the movement was too Roman in ritual, too rationalistic in its theology and too Spanish in its morals.[6] Therefore, they felt they should shy away from being identified with this movement.

Now, a hundred years later, Filipinos like myself consider this to be a lost Reformation. We should remember that potentially, Protestantism could have influenced five million people with the Scriptures at the turn of the twentieth century. In a way I am glad this lost chance for a Reformation is taking place again with the advent of the Charismatic movement. We had to wait at least a hundred years before another massive movement approaching the proportions of a Reformation takes place in the Philippine church.

Also, it is noteworthy that quite early, there were schisms among the Protestants. Within the first decade of the Methodist history, Nicholas Zamora initiated a kind of rebellion among the ranks and founded a breakaway group, the Iglesia Evangelica Metodista en las Islas Filipinas. While we may understand the theological reasons why early Protestant missionaries refused to work with Aglipay, we wonder why there were schisms among those who shared the same faith tradition. Perhaps, it had to do with the tensions between expatriate missionaries and national leaders, as is often witnessed among two-thirds world churches.

There were also tensions with the old religions. One study conducted in the 1970s revealed that after 75 years of American Protestantism in the Philippines, only 1% of the population had crossed over to Protestantism.[7] The first three decades saw great growth, but soon plateaued. Indeed, by the 1950s and 60s, the mainline denominations began to decline or had a static church growth, while the Evangelicals registered the birth of many churches and organizations and grew within a strong pietistic and spiritualistic tradition. In sum, by

1974, only 1% of the Filipino population had made a move from traditional religions to Protestantism. What is behind this?

3. Tensions with the Old Religion

First of all, it is important to realize that the Protestant missionaries misunderstood the anti-friar sentiments of the Filipinos during the first three decades of the twentieth century. Although Filipinos were anti-friars, they were not anti-Catholic. The Spanish friars in the more than three centuries of Spanish occupation were quite hated, but they were also, in a way, harbingers of a European medieval Christendom. It is critical to recognize that Filipino Catholicism remains medieval in many ways. It never went through the crisis of the Reformation, the Age of Enlightenment and its liberalism, the social ferment during the industrial revolution, or the nineteenth century age of radical doubt which had influenced theology in the West. This is the reason why Cardinal Sin (current cardinal of the Philippines) still has great power in Philippine society, about as much as the Popes had in the Middle Ages. The most plausible explanation is found in the medieval nature of Philippine Catholicism. As a consequence, although the Spanish friars were badly hated, most Filipinos remained loyal Catholics.

The fact is that Catholicism, unlike Protestantism, had moved and grafted itself into Filipino hearts after a slow but steady inculturation process for almost four centuries. Catholicism had been extremely accommodative of the indigenous culture, thus, avoiding conflicts; which is very much a Filipino trait. It was a mistake of the early missionaries to expect that Filipinos would gladly embrace a religion that would free them from the friars, on the one hand, but also get rid of the old traditions, on the other.

Early Filipino Protestant converts often served as translators for missionaries, and this was both good and bad. Very early, they tried to contextualize Reformation themes such as *sola fide, sola gracia* and *sola scriptura*. Unfortunately, the missionaries and their early converts had a very polemical approach to Catholicism. It was almost a replication of the sixteenth century European Reformation which resulted in great persecution. In a similar way, the early Filipino Protestants were subjected to social and religious persecution as they squarely rejected the old Catholic religion. Their polemical attitude was in a way comparable to that of converts coming from this region's great spiritual traditions. Their (and consequently our) first response to the old religion was total rejection.

The old family religions, whether the indigenous ones or variations that have been accommodated within the Catholic tradition, ran against Protestantism as an individualizing faith. This is part of the problem: the faith that came from within American Protestantism was a faith that individualizes, whereas Filipino religiosity was operating in a culture where even one's identity is shared. I suspect that this is true with many Asian cultures that are communal and family-oriented.

One analogy used for the Filipino sense of self or ego is the multiple fried eggs. If you fry many eggs in one large pan, you will notice that while the yolks are still distinct, the egg whites are seamlessly connected. Our sense of self is like this, we are so connected with each other, with the family or *sakop* or the group that we do not think as individuals. The Protestant missionaries came with a faith that was so individualistic that the converts were immediately rejected by their families. Protestantism was soon viewed as a threat to the family tradition.

This individualizing and its perceived threat to family unity remains true even today. I remember how my father reacted very strongly when I crossed over from Catholicism to the Protestant faith. It took me some time to realize that he was not really reacting to my faith, but to the fact that my new faith took me away from communal celebrations like fiestas, novenas, family rosaries, *pasiyam*, *Todos los Santos* and all other rituals that we used to do as a family. I was, in a sense, extracted from the family heritage. So it took a long time before my family would come around to some kind of Evangelical faith. Similar struggles happen all the time.

Also, there was a perception that Protestantism has come to us as a cold and highly intellectualized religion, whereas the indigenous religious consciousness is highly mystical as are all other Asian spiritual traditions. In a sense, we are very much right-brained, whereas Protestantism as it has come to us, with its emphasis on propositions, apologetics, and inductive Bible study, is left-brained. Some of the non-converts complained about the poverty of color and of symbols (such as candles) in Protestant churches. It was just too barren. This was another barrier to many. On the other hand, among the Protestant converts themselves, many were attracted by the intellectual clarity of Protestantism, leaving what to them was a highly obscure, mystical and ritualistic Catholicism and embracing a faith that wed reason to revelation.

From all this we begin to understand what the failure to cross over was all about. We have, as Protestant Christians, lost the richness of the indigenous mysticism as often seen in the passion narratives in our Holy Week pageants. According to one art historian, Filipinos like to have celebrations, with rituals as a kind of performance, things related to the body.[8] This is one reason why the Charismatic movement has become a strong religious movement here, with its emphasis on dancing, supernatural gifts and healing. It has a strong appeal to feeling, to the postmodern consciousness, as well as to the indigenous mind which has been largely shaped by images and incense. The shift from Catholicism to Protestantism here is analogous to that of the Reformation in Europe: there was a shift from a highly visual, highly dramatic culture centered around the altar to the abstract perorations of the pulpit. By the time Protestantism came to us, it had become very propositional and so wordy that it repelled our people.

Protestant spirituality, which was highly dualistic and divided between the secular and sacred, also stood directly against traditional holism and communal spirituality and worldview. The *cañao*, for instance, a ritual in the Cordilleras of the northern Philippines, is not just a spiritual tradition but a social celebration. A pig is killed and its meat is distributed to the community. If one does not get a piece of the meat, it is a sign that he or she is not part of the community. The *cañao* is a way of defining who belongs to the community. That is how our indigenous religions compare and contrast with the highly individualized and dualistic Christianity that has come to us.

Also, there was a study made some decades ago among the Four Square churches, where there is not as great a divide between secular and sacred, and between natural and supernatural gifts as is often found in the Western theological tradition. Consequently, in the 1950s and 1960s, the Four Square Church together with the Assemblies of God registered the highest growth rate. It was reported that at least 80% of converts among the Four Square churches revealed that the manifestation of various supernatural experiences, particularly healing, was the primary factor in their attraction towards the Four Square Church in the Philippines.[9] I assume that the same is true during the last two decades within the Charismatic movement, both Catholic and Protestant.

Still another part of the problem is the concept of guilt stressed so strongly in Protestantism. A Filipino anthropologist argues that Filipinos are not interested in salvation; it is the least of our problems.[10] Like most Asians, Filipinos believe that individuals after death will continue their existence in the afterlife, with about the same kind of life they have lived before. This idea is a direct contrast to the modern understanding of death as an existential threat or as the end of life. That is why in Tagalog, death is called *sumakabilang buhay* (literally, "went to the other side of life "). That is, one just went across to the beyond and into another world or life. Consequently, many Asians, including Filipinos, are not really interested in salvation understood as having a ticket to heaven or an afterlife. Our real interest is in potency and inner power for this life. Salvation is in the present tense.

A faith which stresses or talks about sin, guilt and so on will have difficulty connecting with the Filipino mind. Even in the sixteenth century, during the Spanish conquest, the natives had difficulty in understanding the concept of sin as individual personal accountability before God. The high god, Bathala, is never described in our folk tales as angry over human wickedness. At most, he is described as depressed when faced with human malfeasance. We do not feel that we are "sinners in the hands of an angry God," as Jonathan Edwards put it. At best, we feel we have lost our way, *naligaw ng landas*, or made a mistake, *nagkamali*. Or we have offended some spirit who got overlooked in our ritual celebrations, or caused *sama ng loob* (literally, "ill feelings") in someone, resulting in disharmony and disturbances in the natural order of things. One should remember that in much of Asia, sin is understood in a communal context. Sin is more like a state of disharmony, whether social or cosmic. This posed a great difficulty among the missionaries who saw sin mainly as an individual transgression of some abstract law rooted in the character of God.

4. A Clash of Cultures

Along with the tension between the religious consciousness and the kind of Christianity that was introduced at the turn of the twentieth century, there was also a clash of cultures. Some of the early missionaries found it striking that Filipinos always looked so playful, like children. For instance, the old YMCA made a rule in volleyball that teams playing should only pass the ball three times and throw it over the net. The rule was made because apparently, when Filipinos played with the American team, they just kept passing the ball to each other. At one point they passed and dribbled the ball to each other fifty-two times before they shot it over the net! The Americans became very frustrated. The Filipinos were interested in the play itself, but not the goal. [11] Missionaries concluded that Filipinos do not know how to focus. The fact is that we enjoy having fun. We derive a great deal of energy and enjoyment just in being together. When traveling abroad, you can single out a group of Filipinos: they laugh together every three or four minutes!

Also, there was a great disagreement between the Filipino's accommodative nature—the harmonizing instinct is very Asian—and the boundary-keeping of the American missionaries. Some of the converts kept complaining that Protestantism had too many rules. The Filipinos chafed at being kept within the boundaries of creeds and rules, because the Westerners wanted their boundaries well kept. To them, religion was mostly boundary-keeping. By a creed, one can define who is excluded and who is to be included. However, Filipinos are not like that: we like everybody to be included. There is even a word for it, *salimpusa* ("cat included"). It is a word we use for a child who is allowed to play in a game among older children, or someone who does not quite make the grade or the terms of membership but is included anyway. This inclusive and harmonizing instinct and behavior was unfortunately viewed as syncretistic by the missionaries. Filipinos do not operate by officially sanctioned ways, but by fuzzy borders, not sharp sets. This was a great barrier to the American missionaries entering the Filipino mindset.

Also, Filipinos tend to be loose, flexible and non-linear, in contrast to the very highly structured Western ways. We call rather fixed and regimented ways of doing things *de kahon* ("boxed" or "box ways") in the Filipino language. Filipinos like to improvise, experiment and be free-flowing. A national cultural historian said that Filipinos do not like to do anything the same way twice, including jeepneys. If you look closely, no two Jeepneys really look the same; one is always different from the other, with a dash of color and a bit of curlicue here and there that is different from the others. A standardized, assembly-line way of doing things is not part of the Filipino worldview.

5. Implications to Mission

What then are the implications of this discussion to mission in Asia?

It is important that we understand ourselves as God's church. Unfortunately, in the Philippines, there is such a cultural divide that those of us who have been so influenced by the elite culture do not know how the masses think. We operate by the Western ideal of modernity. Even though we no longer regard English as our national language, we still laugh at a president who does not speak English. After higher education in Western countries, one comes back out of context and alienated, and consequently of not much use any more. It is important, in spite of our differences, for us to ponder hard and attempt, from out of our culture, to bring to the surface theological themes that will truly penetrate the Filipino heart.

Filipinos have had five centuries of Christianity, and yet, deep down, we have resisted the forms of Christianity brought to this country by Western missionaries. It appears that the Philippines is a good case study on the failure and success of Christianity in Asia. While Christianity has been around for five centuries, one can ask hard questions such as, "Why is our level of public justice and of private morality much lower than that of our neighbors?" In Japan, 80% of its criminals are likely to get caught and prosecuted. In the Philippines, if one is famous and important, like our former president, there is no way that he or she would go to jail. In fact, one can even arrange for hospital accommodation and have parties during a prolonged trial. What has Christianity been doing here?

My contention is that the Filipino culture can be very misleading. We all have a very warm, accepting face to outsiders. We welcome outside influence, we have embraced Christianity wholeheartedly, but changes occurred only on the surface structures of our culture. We simply exchanged dark wooden *anitos* [12] for plaster saints with Caucasian features. But the deep structures remain the same. Christianity has not changed us.

This takes us to the critical issue of contextualization. We talk of contextualization almost too much, but we often do not have a clear understanding of what this process means. I suggest, first of all, that we look at the experience of the Eastern churches with a fresh historiography. The truth is that we know little about the Eastern churches, while we are well aware of figures like Constantine, Augustine, Luther and so on. We barely know what happened to the Mar Thoma Church, the Coptic churches or the Syrian churches. Christianity came to Asia quite early but it has not flourished. This is something that anyone teaching mission history should take seriously. Moreover, for those who teach Asian mission history, this is the major agenda. We need to be able to describe to ourselves our own story as churches. History will aid us greatly in understanding the struggle of

Christianity to take root in Asia, and the reasons that account for its lack of success.

Genuine contextualization is contextualization from within, not from without. It is the kind that begins with the categories of the culture, and constructs a message that will make sense from within its meaning system. It is not simply adapting a fixed message from outside the culture. This is what people often mean by contextualization, but it is an inadequate definition. It is what I call contextualization from without. Instead, we should look closely at the cultural themes, or the root metaphors by which a culture describes itself.

Each culture has a set of root metaphors which very rarely change through time. In the Filipino culture, there is the metaphor of the "multiple fried eggs," a fact about us that has not changed and has been with us for centuries. I do not think it is likely to change. We need to engage this root metaphor by surfacing biblical themes that are important in either changing or affirming it. This in turn forms the basis for formulating a new theology. The reason the gospel is not seen as "good news," but just a Westerner's religion, is because we have not deeply engaged the root metaphors in this culture. We have not deeply identified with indigenous spirituality, and how Christianity interfaces with that. So this is a major agenda for all of us. Contextualizing from without has some value, but it is fairly limited and does not really scratch where it itches. The grand theological themes that have surfaced in Western cultures are certainly a part of our historical heritage as the body of Christ. However, this does not substitute for the task of engaging with our own context such that we come up with a fresh text that surfaces another face of the work of Christ.

For instance, Filipinos are sensitive to disturbances in the natural world. They think of calamities as God's wrath at work. Unfortunately, most pastors have been modernized, and simply dismiss such notions. Instead, they should affirm these thoughts and explain how this came about, elaborating on it as a consequence of the fall and our alienation from God.

We start from and affirm an indigenous concept and deepen it biblically. This is called "concept fulfillment." We do the same when speaking about sin. Filipinos in general have difficulty understanding it, because *Bathala,* the high god, is seen as good and tolerant. Besides, he is above everyone else, so high that, according to the natives in the sixteenth century, nobody speaks to him. As a result, he was perceived as distant and rather indifferent. He just gets depressed but not get angry when people sin. That is why Filipinos are happy people. They are not guilt-ridden. They do not have a sense that sin is a serious thing. It is merely *sala,* the word the Spanish friars used to translate the concept. In our language *sala* is just to make a mistake, it is a minor infraction. To deepen this understanding, we begin with the people's sense of wrath creationally and move it towards the biblical idea of disharmony, whether social or cosmic, as being caused by the alienation between us and God.

There is an anthropological notion that there are "shame" cultures and "guilt" cultures in this world. I think this is oversimplified. The fact is that we just have different understandings of sin, especially in Asian cultures; but we all have an understanding of sin. It is not true that a shame culture does not have a sense of sin. We have a sense of sin, that is why we are ashamed. It is just important to find out what we consider as sin in various cultures.

One of the challenges to those of us who are engaged in mission is to put together a theory and practice from an incarnational rather than a multinational model of mission. We have all seen in our experience mission organizations and denominations opening branches like McDonalds does. The gospel is treated like hamburgers, the same size and shape everywhere. I think we need to stay away from this unholy universalizing. True, there is only one gospel. But our understanding of this one gospel is always mediated through culture—first through the Jewish, then through the Greek, through the Germanic tribes and so on. The latest massive translation of what the gospel means is American. Because of its economic power, it spreads. If we want to be truly diverse in our understanding of Christianity, about all we need to do is put our own understanding as Asian peoples on the common table.

Also, I think it is important to realize that we must begin a new model of mission: mission that comes not with imperial power, nor with economic power, but from a position of powerlessness. It is a documented fact that the overseas Filipino workers (OFWs) are one of the most vital mission forces in the world today. OFWs are in 181 countries, and most of them are Christians. In fact, I heard one of my colleagues say that there are probably more Filipino Christians scattered all over the world than all the Western missionary movements put together. In addition, I am told the good news quietly emerging from the Arab peninsula is that Filipinos are some of the most adept cross-cultural missionaries to the Muslims precisely because they come, not with power, but as a vulnerable community.

It seems to me that the Holy Spirit continues to speak to the churches. We need to hear collectively what our culture is saying to us, what the Spirit is saying to us, and what the text is saying to us. These together—the text, context and the Holy Spirit—form a kind of hermeneutical circle. We are able to hear what the Spirit is saying as we engage with our context in the light of our text and the illumination given to us as a community of believers.

---

[1] Andrew F. Walls, "Old Athens and New Jerusalem: Some Signposts for Christian Scholarship in the Early History of Mission Studies," *International Bulletin of Missionary Research* 21:4 (Oct. 1997), 146-53.

[2] Jose M. de Mesa, "Hispanic Catholicism and Lowland Filipino Culture," in *Conversion to Protestant Christianity Track II Report*, vol. 2 (unpublished report, Manila: ISACC, 1995-1999), 4.

[3] From an account of Gen. James F. Rusling, "Interview with President Mckinley," *The Christian Advocate* 78 (January 27, 1903) and as quoted by Mariano Apilado, *Revolutionary Spirituality, A Study of the Protestant Role in the American Colonial Rule of the Philippines, 1898-1928* (Quezon City, Philippines: New Day, 1999).

[4] See Mary Dorita Clifford, "Iglesia Filipina Independiente: The Revolutionary Church," in *Studies in Philippine Church History*, ed. Gerald H. Anderson (Ithaca and London: Cornell University Press, 1969), 234. Also Howard Stuntz, "A Letter to Rev. A. B. Leonard, Secretary of the Methodist Society in New York, February 15, 1905 (New York: Methodist Archives), 484-90.

[5] See James B. Rodgers, *Forty Years in the Philippines: A History of the Philippine Mission of the Presbyterian Church in the United States of America 1899-1939* (New York: Board of Foreign Missions of the Presbyterian Church in the USA, 1940), 22.

[6] Frank Laubach, *The People of the Philippines: Their Religious Progress and Preparation for Spiritual Leadership in the Far East* (New York: George Duran, 1925).

[7] James Montgomery and Donald A. McGavran, *The Discipling of a Nation* (Manila: Global Church Growth Bulletin, 1980), 45.

[8] "Rod Paras Perez's Interview on Filipino Myths, Symbols, Icons: What They Tell Us About Religious Consciousness, September 8, 1995," in *Conversion to Protestant Christianity Track II Report*, vol. 1 (Manila: ISACC, 1995-1999), 30-31.

[9] Montgomery & McGavran, 45.

[10] Prospero Covar, an anthropologist in the University of the Philippines, in a private conversation with the author during the "Philippines Studies" class, Manila, Philippines in 1991.

[11] Melba P. Maggay, "A Clash of Cultures," in *Conversion to Protestant Christianity Track II Report*, vol. 2, 172.

[12] Anitos are wooden statues representing either ancestral or nature spirits

PARTNERSHIP ISSUES AND CHALLENGES IN ASIAN MISSION

Chin Do Kham

1. Introduction

Partnership has become a popular concept in many segments of human society today. It seems as if the secular world has popularized and implemented this concept ahead of the church and its mission. In recent years, various segments of business organizations such as airlines, banks and other companies formed partnerships to build synergy through networking and intentional cooperation, so that they might enhance their effectiveness and productivity to benefit all participating parties. William Taylor describes it this way, "There is a cluster of terms which are related to partnership. Some of these include cooperation, teamwork, networking, joint ventures, and strategic alliances."[1] Since the 1980s, many international businesses have formed strategic alliances even between those who were formerly competitors.

Since the early 1990s I have traveled often on airlines that are members of Star Alliance.[2] Their member airlines are: Thai, Singapore, United, Nippon, Lufthansa and a few others. As business partners they recognize and respect one another, and provide privileges to their mileage plus members. They were not newborn companies when they joined. They all have their own philosophy, goals, form of governance, basic guiding principles, values and organizational culture. But they formed an alliance to mutually benefit from one another. In order to build and maintain genuine partnership, they developed shared values and philosophies before they signed a memorandum of agreement. After the basic agreement was reached, they implemented their agreement to make the partnership concept a reality based on mutual trust and respect.

Within Christian mission, partnership has been seriously thought of only in recent years with the maturing of national churches. The emergence of mission work run by Asians brought mixed feelings among some expatriate missionaries and foreign mission organizations. On one hand, mission organizations are happy to see their children becoming adults. On the other hand, some of them seem to struggle with the fear of losing control and significance or lack of trust in the young Asian missionary forces. Mission organizations and national churches have come to a realization that business cannot be done as usual. We need to move beyond superficial partnership to biblical, genuine partnership.

When we look back the last two hundred years of modern mission history, the first one hundred or more years were primarily the pioneering and groundbreaking stage in many new and hard places in Asia. During this stage, missionaries who were predominantly from Western and European countries engaged themselves in meeting basic human needs, teaching how to read and write, and even in inventing the written form of tribal languages. Many missionaries were effective in helping people in Asia improve their living conditions while sharing the love of God in word and deed. While the intentions were good, some Western missionaries did not differentiate between civilization and evangelization. Instead of helping local people see Jesus in their own context, they had a misconception of importing Jesus just like foreign goods. Because of the lack of such sensitivity, many Asians perceived Christianity as an imported Western religion. This became a major hindrance to evangelization. In the eyes of many Asians, missionary work became Christianized Western imperialism.

During the twentieth century, the gospel took deep root in many Asian soils. God blessed the labors of missionaries to bear much fruit. The seeds they have sown in remote areas of Asia have become trees, and now they are in turn bearing fruit. Many of the national churches did not become missionary sending churches themselves until the late twentieth century. With modernization and the growth of the Asian economy, today a number of Asian countries are sending their own missionaries to other countries with a significant amount of financial contribution. However, Asian churches and missionaries do not have a long enough history to learn from. Consequently, they are facing many challenges today.

Some Asian local churches are sending their own short-term and long-term missionaries to other countries without much coordination with other mission agencies or even their national headquarters. As a result, there is unintended duplication and competition among groups and individual missionaries. Unless serious and careful attention is given, there could be undesirable consequences in the near future. As individual local churches function independently from other organizations or missionaries, they tend to lack pre-field orientation, missionary care and educational programs for missionary children. While Western mission models might not work for the twenty-first century Asian churches, there is a need for Asian church leaders and missionaries to seriously and honestly look at the challenges they are facing in the current state of Asian mission. Leadership should look ahead and develop a kingdom-centered Asian mission model to ensure the mistakes of past missionary efforts are not repeated. To meet this challenge, Asian Christian leaders from all denominations and organizations need to come together to pray and develop strategic plans for new century mission in Asia.

To fulfill the biblical mission mandate, local churches must be educated regarding basic biblical teaching on missions. Unless the grass-roots level local churches understand, become mission minded, and committed to fulfilling the Great Commission, annual international conferences on the leadership level with a handful of individuals alone will not accomplish the task of mission in Asia. Even though most local churches may not have much resources, they can become a mighty force of prayer warriors for revival in their lands, region and the world. We should always be aware of the fact that doing mission has multiple dimensions, including the spiritual and physical dimensions. Unless the Holy Spirit is at work through believers and our missionary efforts, finance and human skills alone will not accomplish God's mission. I have seen two extreme emphases in missions: 1) unconsciously equating mission with money, and 2) overly emphasizing the spiritual dimension at the cost of ignoring human and financial aspects of mission. We should avoid dichotomization but develop a holistic view of mission, so that the significance and role of all believers can be recognized, regardless of their nationality and economic status.

The current condition of relationships between Western mission agencies and non-Western nationals is characterized by a lack of trust and suspicion. Some mission agencies and missionaries see Asians as adolescents or young adults, and do not fully trust them to take leadership role yet. They have known them since childhood, and in some cases, raised them and watched them grow up before their own eyes. The organized and well established mission organizations and veteran missionaries want to see proven leadership and accountability especially in the area of finance. At the same time, Asians cannot truly exercise God-given leadership potentials until and unless they are given the chance to do so.

Some Western mission leaders have the mentality that says, "We brought the money and we have our own goals for certain countries, and we must be in control over the money." This is the so-called "golden rule" in South America, which means the one who has the gold sets the rule. Though this has been the case in most part of the world, it is an unbiblical and unhealthy philosophy and practice. At the same time some Asians are saying, "We used to be babies, children, and young adults but now we have become adults by God's grace and through your help. Let's relate to one another as adult to adult." In some extreme cases, Asians are saying, "After all, this is my country and you have to work with us or under us." This may be called "unhealthy territorial spirit." With this kind of reaction, Asians might be guilty of what they have blamed the expatriates for.

What are the underlying issues with which we are struggling? They are issues of power and control, ownership, trust, finance, etc. These hinder biblical partnership. Asians should never forget or discredit the sacrificial efforts made by Western mission agencies in the past and present. God never sees us as East and West. He sees us as his children and as one body, belonging to him. Asians and non-Asians, as the people of God, need to change their attitude.

Only in a few instances is transition taking place, but with much pain and cost. Unless a clear philosophy is developed and understood by both parties the transition can cause more harm than growth. In fact, unhealthy or poor transition will result in more misunderstanding. As much as Asian churches need to learn from established Western missions, Asians also have a lot to offer to world missions. Those who have learned in the past need to relearn and re-educate themselves to be relevant in today's world, and those newly emerging missions also need to learn from those who have walked the path longer. Unless we are willing to learn we are not ready to teach. I remember Ted Ward saying in a personal conversation, "During my whole career as an educator, my students are my best teachers. They taught me how to teach them."[3] A true missionary at heart is always a learner.

This is a defining moment for Asian mission. How the transition and partnership issues are handled will impact the future of mission in

Asia significantly. We need to humbly and prayerfully, with utmost care, handle the process of transitioning, restructuring, reorganizing and facilitating our changing roles. In this period of transition, partnership is even more crucial. The financial resources and living expenses for Asian missionaries (which is less than those of Western missionaries) should also be a consideration in developing new strategies.

Mission leaders and national church leaders are trying to make partnership a reality. Though most Christians agree in principle that unity in diversity is a must, mission agencies and local churches are still facing many unanswered questions. Some are having healthy and effective partnerships, but to many mission organizations and national churches in Asia, the concept of partnership is still an ideology. Before we seriously rethink what we mean by partnership there is a need to develop a clear definition. This topic is so delicate that, in many Christian circles, people do not even talk about it openly.

2. Defining Partnership

The word partnership has different meanings to different people. Often times, a particular group wants the other group to agree with their predetermined agenda and join them in the implementation of it. In this instance one group is using the other to accomplish its goal. In order to accomplish this, the group may even make an attractive offer of material benefits. Unless the predetermined goal is achieved the missionary or mission agency will not be able to face the donors at home. Because of such practices, nationals often feel being bought or used. As a result, unhealthy attitudes and uneasy feelings can develop easily.

Christian partnership in mission begins with the lordship of Jesus Christ over all of humanity, particularly over the people of God to whom the missionary mandate is given. As a community of the redeemed, whether we recognize it or not, we are one family and partners in the harvest. In order to have genuine, healthy and God-honoring partnership among Christians, there must be a clear understanding of our identity and the purpose for our existence regardless of our denominational affiliations, nationalities or economic status. All nationals, as well as mission organizations, must follow God's agenda. No one should work independently apart from God or the body of Christ.

In the secular business world, the goal in partnership is to build synergy so that combined efforts will benefit all member organizations with measurable results and protect them from competition. They have only the horizontal dimension in their commitment and relationship. For Christians the primary goal of partnership should be to bring glory to God by fulfilling his mandate. At times, this may mean losing money and even lives. There may be no visible or tangible gain or result in one's life time. Following two simple diagrams, one for a secular partnership model and the other for a Christian partnership model, will help us differentiate the two and embrace the model to which we belong.

Secular Partnership Model

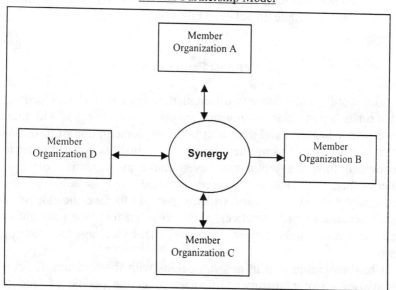

In the secular partnership model, each member joins the alliance after it has established its own self-identity. Each member can join or disconnect itself based on circumstances. They are in contract with terms and conditions. In the secular model of partnership, each independent organization decides to join with others to pursue a specific goal with the ultimate purpose of self-benefit.

Biblical Model of Partnership

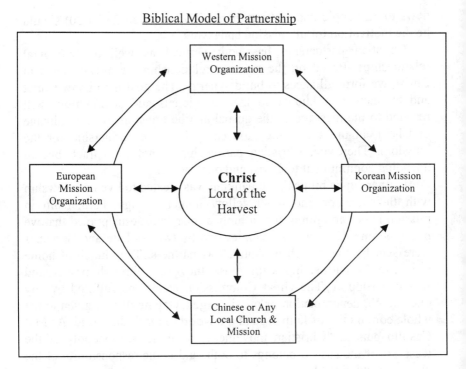

In Christian partnership, the biblical mandate is the same for all believers. God has planned for partnership from the beginning. Therefore, mission strategists and church leaders did not invent partnership in mission; it is God's idea. In Christian partnership there are three dimensions: 1) Our commitment to Jesus Christ; 2) our commitment to one another; and 3) our commitment to the task of mission. In the above biblical partnership model, all partner organizations as well as local churches, in which the missionaries minister, must pledge their allegiance to the lordship of Jesus Christ in whom "we are heirs—heir of God and co-heirs with Christ" (Rom 8:17). Each missionary organization's commitment and obedience to the Great Commission should be its primary reason for partnership. Long before the individual organizations were formed, they belonged to God's family. Joining hands and hearts in partnership with other members of the universal body of Christ, especially with those who are in our immediate context, will enhance our effectiveness. Therefore, the biblical mandate of going into all the world and preaching the good news to all people and making them disciples (Matt 28:19-20) should be the motivation for all mission endeavors.

Christian partnership has both vertical as well as horizontal relationships. Based on the existing relationship we already have in Christ, we form alliances to build synergy. The goal is to know Christ and to make him known so that individuals and communities will respond to the message of the gospel and be transformed to the image of Christ, in order that they too can join us in partnership for the kingdom. Therefore, Christian partnership is not a contract, but an unending commitment to Christ and one another.

Partnership is biblical. Humankind was created to live in fellowship with their creator and other fellow human beings. Partnership in mission is not an option. It is a biblical mandate. Jesus prayed that we might be one. He sent his disciples two by two, as Paul and Barnabas were sent by the church in Antioch as partners. The church at home was also in partnership with those they sent through prayer and financial support. The Great Commission cannot be fulfilled by any one church, denomination or mission agency alone. It was given to the whole community of faith around the world to reach the world. As Met Castillo puts it, "Christian movement...is neither a monopoly of the west nor of the east. It belongs to both, and is the responsibility of the church worldwide."[4]

Most writers define partnership in terms of task-based relationship. Fulfilling the Great Commission is what brings Christians together for partnership. While we need to have partnership to do the task of evangelization, we must not forget the fact that Christian partnership is not based on tasks or projects only. It is not the task that makes us one, but it is the oneness we have in Christ that causes us to work for the Lord hand-in-hand. If our partnership is brought about by tasks or projects only, then the partnership will no longer exist or be needed, when projects are accomplished. Since Christian partnership is based on being a part of the body of Christ with one hope, one Lord and one baptism, partnership must continue until Christ returns.

Luis Bush defines partnership as "an association of two or more autonomous bodies who have formed a trusting relationship, and fulfill agreed-upon expectations by sharing complementary strengths and resources, to reach their mutual goal."[5] This definition should be understood in terms of short term and long term goals, but more so in fulfilling God's ultimate goal. The moment we are born into the kingdom of God we belong to one another. If Christians will grasp this kingdom concept it will be much easier to overcome the evils of Christianized colonialism or a nationalistic over-reactionary attitude. True partnership must be kingdom-oriented so that our human differences can be overcome. God's agenda will supercede organizational agendas. As people of God, the specific task is not what makes us partners. For we all serve one Lord, and the missionary mandate given by the Lord is for all the people of God in every nation to communicate and demonstrate the message of salvation by all possible means. Mission is no longer only from the West to non-Western countries. It is from all nations to all nations. As Castillo said, there is a great need "to move beyond superficial fellowship to true partnerships—cooperative ventures, strategic alliances, mutually engaged projects, and the sharing of material and human resources."[6] This will happen if we actualize the song we often sing as doxology: "Praise God from whom all blessings flow." Having a deep conviction of the truth that "all that we are and all that we have comes from God and belongs to God" will help us implement true partnership. Therefore, partnership is not only a functional issue, but a biblical and theological issue as well.

One of the most obvious places of partnership in Asia is seen in some theological seminaries where Western missionaries are working together with national/local and other Asian faculty members. At the Asia Pacific Theological Seminary in Baguio City, Philippines, the faculty represented nine different nationalities at one point. They all were appointed, sent and supported by their respective national churches. Another example of partnership among theological seminaries is the consortium programs of Asia Graduate School of Theology (AGST) where the AGST-Philippines is offering postgraduate programs. Though these institutions represent various theological views and denominations, all are working together in partnership to train Asian leaders through theological education. Each member school contributes to the consortium programs. At the same time, each member school also benefits from the consortium programs especially in the area of faculty development. In the end, Christ will be glorified, as the graduates of AGST train many in Asian countries and beyond to extend God's kingdom.

3. Multidimensional Partnership in Asian Mission

Partnership in Asian mission must be multidimensional to be credible and effective. Typically people think of partnership in terms of relationships between Western mission agencies and non-Western churches or missionaries and nationals. Though that is a significant part of it, it is broader in scope. True kingdom partnership in Asia should involve the following: 1) partnership between different Western mission organizations working in Asia; 2) partnership between different Asian mission organizations and local churches; and 3) partnership between Western mission organizations and national agencies or local churches. Instead of competition among individual missionaries serving on the same field (whether Asian missionaries or non-Asian missionaries serving in Asia), there needs to be intentionally coordinated networking, information sharing, resource sharing and regular fellowship in the country where they serve.

The time has come when all mission organizations and churches should consider one another as equal partners. God has blessed the hard and long sacrificial labors and love of the Western missionaries, and now Asian churches are emerging. In many places within Asia, there are strong national churches, mission agencies, as well as a number of mission training institutions. As the Spirit of the Lord is moving in an unprecedented way across Asia, both Asian churches and non-Asian missionaries must realize the reality that business cannot be done as usual in the twenty-first century Asia.

In order to implement genuine partnership between Western missionaries and Asian churches, we must ask ourselves some hard but practical questions.

3.1 Questions for Western Missionaries:

- Will the Western missionaries and mission agencies recognize the rapidly changing Asian context and emerging missionary movement in order to make major adjustments in philosophy and methodology?
- Will the Western mission agencies and missionaries be willing to revise or adjust their basic concept of mission from one way (West to non-West) to multi-directional missions (from all nations to all nations)?

- Will the Western mission agencies and missionaries be willing to adjust and reorganize their basic structures to be relevant in contemporary Asia and to facilitate the changing roles?
- Will the Western mission agencies and missionaries honestly recognize emerging Asian leaders as equal partners, and allow them to take on leadership responsibilities including the handling of finances?
- Will established Western mission agencies and missionaries be willing to admit mistakes, and if needed, even apologize for their colonial attitude?
- Will Western mission organizations still raise and share resources after leadership transition has taken place?

3.2 Questions for Asians:

- Will Asian church leaders and missionaries be willing to humbly and honestly acknowledge with sincere hearts their thanks to Western mission agencies and missionaries for their incredible love, sacrifice and investment in Asia in the past and present?
- Can Asian Christians overcome their inferiority complex and avoid a reactionary attitude and false pride and admit their need for one another now and in the future as in the past?
- Will Asian Christians be willing and able to forgive and forget the mistakes of Western missionaries, but learn from them?
- Will Asian Christians be willing to admit their own limitations and unhealthy attitudes toward expatriates?
- Can Asian Christians prove themselves to be accountable and reliable if the funds and resources from the West are entrusted to them?
- Will Asian Christians/churches/organizations survive without the resources from the West?
- How soon will Asian churches be able to generate the necessary funds from within their own community to do missions?
- How soon can Asian churches move from dependency to interdependence?

In order to build genuine partnership we must honestly address issues such as trust, control, ownership, lack of biblical understanding of mission and partnership, and financial matters.

3.3 How Long Should Partnership Be Maintained?

In light of emerging Asian mission endeavors in recent years, many Western mission organizations are seriously considering transferring leadership to the nationals. At the end of the leadership transition, they will evaluate whether they are still needed, wanted or invited to stay. Considering this new trend, should partnership have a time limit? Should Western missionaries leave or stay after the transition? What are the criteria to measure the level of maturity in national churches? What should be the process of healthy transitioning? In what attitude should the transition be done? These are additional important questions we must address.

I have seen seasoned missionaries who are sensitive to the move of the Holy Spirit, carefully reading the signs of the times, and responding in humility and flexibility, knowing that it is God's kingdom that we are building. On the other hand, I have also seen some missionaries who are not ready to let go of their control, and who see potential national leaders as threats. Expatriate missionaries in the latter category do not consider nationals as equals and, therefore, do not trust them to do the work they have been doing. Overstaying can have the same affect as leaving too soon. Looking at this issue objectively, if reliable local church leaders have not been trained after so many years of working in a certain context, it could be said that it has not been a fruitful and sustainable work. It is essential to build a healthy and trusting working relationship between expatriate missionaries and nationals and local churches. Met Castillo saw the importance of considering the issue carefully. To him,

> The issue is not whether we still need expatriates in view of the fast emergence of missions in many churches here in Asia, but whether expatriates are willing to commit themselves to work with national Christian leaders.... It is no longer justifiable for expatriates to continue to plant and carry out evangelism and church planting without the involvement of the churches in both the planning and doing.[7]

Even if we have accomplished a certain mission-related project or even if a significant amount of church planting is already done, true kingdom partnership will remain until Christ comes. It will be unbiblical and unhealthy if Asians ever say, "We don't need Western missionaries anymore." Or if Western missionaries say, "Our work in

Asia is totally done, and we have no part in the life of the church in Asia anymore." We all need one another though we might have to change the specific role we play.

After thoughtfully looking at several models on the changing missionary role and developmental stages in mission and national relationship, some mission leaders developed a plan to totally relinquish leadership responsibilities to the local churches in the next few years. At that point, they could withdraw their structure and any remaining missionaries would be there at the invitation and under the supervision of local leadership.[8]

At the outset, this plan seems appropriate and relevant. However, if the national leaders will not extend their invitation for the missionaries to stay, there is no plan or concept of ongoing partnership. In this particular case, like many other situations, partnership is defined and needed based on the task at hand. Ideally it would be best if kingdom partnership continued through mutual encouragement, prayer for one another and sharing resources and information. This would illustrate the truth that we belong to one another and genuinely love one another whether missionaries remain on the field or not.

After the leadership transition process is completed and the mission organization is relocating themselves to a new field, a new form of partnership between the Western mission organization and the emerging missionary sending Asian church should develop a new form of partnership. From this point on, the partnership should be between two missionary sending organizations, Western and Asian, in partnership with a third party Christian community in the new field. In this way, the partnership is not based on the working relationship for a specific project in a given locality only, but is ongoing until Christ returns. By implementing this concept, we can overcome the spirit of independence as well as over-dependence, but develop the spirit of interdependence. This will be like a father raising his children up and when the children become adult they work together in the field as equal partners.

There is a need to make a careful evaluation on the practices of partnership in the past and present, and the outcomes of these in the Asian context. We will certainly find some encouraging, as well as a few discouraging facts. While expatriate missionaries might have made some mistakes, some Asian church leaders and young Asian missionaries might have overreacted and experimented with their system and effectiveness, instead of learning from the pioneers. In fact, at present there are only a handful of mission organizations in Asia that are systematically structured and organized. We must have a teachable spirit before we can critically assess any system. Otherwise, we will be assessing other systems with our own biases.

In recent years, mission awareness in local churches has been rapidly increasing. As a result, many Asian Christians go on short-term mission trips. Some have responded to God's call and are now in long term commitments to missions. A significant number of Asian Christian professionals are leaving their professions and go to other countries as missionaries or tent-makers. As encouraging as this trend may be, however, my frequent observations of national mission leaders in Asia indicate that there is a lack of cooperation among sending local churches even within the same denomination. Only a few missionary candidates come through the national church office. The consequences might be duplication, competition, a lack of steady support, a lack of missionary care and a lack of fellowship with other missionaries in the field.

4. Proposed Stages of Building Genuine Partnership

Healthy partnership will require the following stages:

4.1 Building a Biblical Basis for Partnership Together

All parties involved in the partnership should understand and believe that they are one family in Christ, and that it is God's will to work together. The general and specific goals must be clearly defined by all parties. The biblical and theological basis for partnership must be clearly communicated and understood.

4.2 Making an Honest Assessment of the Field Together

Both insiders and outsiders should do felt-need and real-need assessment. No one should write prescriptions without a proper diagnosis. Incoming mission organizations should never assume that they know the needs of a people and that they have the answers without consulting with the local churches and mission agencies. At the same time, the local churches also should recognize the fact that their felt needs may not necessary be their real needs, as we all have our own blind spots. Therefore, insiders' perspective and outsiders' perspective must be brought together for objective and honest assessment.

4.3 Praying and Planning Together

With the understanding that it is God's mission in which we are instruments, all parties involved in the partnership should pray together all the way through. All parties should together be setting priorities and making short-term and long-term planning. The basic questions of "what, why, how, when and who" should be honestly discussed and agreed upon by everyone before the actual work has started to make sure, as much as possible, that everyone is on the same page.

4.4 Doing the Actual Work Together as a Team

No party should just sit and watch others work. The missionaries and local Christians should work together hand in hand. Though the specific role each person plays may be different, everyone involved must have servant attitude, and do the work as doing it unto the Lord.

4.5 Evaluating the Effectiveness and Outcome Together

At different stages there should be honest evaluations done by nationals and missionaries together. The criteria for assessment and evaluation should be based on the previously agreed upon goals and processes. Based on the findings, an affirmation of the strengths as well as a recommendation for further improvement should be made.

4.6 Giving Credit to God and Others

Although the mission has grown through the combined efforts of all involved, often certain groups want to get all the credit. Credit must be given where it is due. Paul said, "I planted the seed, Apollos watered it, but God made it grow. So neither he who planted nor he who waters is anything, but only God, who makes things grow" (1 Cor 3:6-7).

5. Conclusion

Obviously, twenty-first century Asian mission is taking a different form. If Asian church and mission leaders do not address this critical issue of partnership at this juncture of Asia's young missionary sending history, the effectiveness of the missionary effort will be limited for lack of synergy. Though Asians might not want to fall into an overly structured, tightly controlled traditional Western mission model, a proper financial system, and more informed, organized and careful planning and network are needed.

When the missionaries move on to a new field, they should still work with the new missionaries from their previous field and form a new set of missionary alliances. If not, the message they are sending is: "we are done with you, we have raised you up, you are adult now so you do your own thing and we will do our own thing somewhere else." Unlike Western culture where old people are put in nursing homes and young people go about their own business, among Asians the children and parents become mutually responsible to take care of one another as long as they live.

If mutual accountability is not in place, mission agencies will be hopping from one field to another, implementing their own agenda without cooperating with existing and newly emerging mission organizations. Thus, we must ask ourselves: "Whose mission are we doing? Whose kingdom are we building?" The church is engaging itself in an unfinished task in mission. We must watch our own attitudes and check whether or not we are faithful to the Lord of the harvest. Though there are signs of maturity, no church is fully mature. It has to reach out to each contemporary generation which has new issues and challenges constantly.

Kingdom partnership begins with total submission and obedience to the lordship of Jesus Christ, and commitment to one another as the people of God. Genuine partnership in Asian mission will result in glorifying God and edifying the church as the lost are won and believers are nurtured through the combine efforts of his people from all nations called and empowered by God to reach Asia for Christ.

---

[1] William Taylor, ed., *Kingdom Partnership* (Pasadena, CA: William Carey Library, 1994), back cover page.

[2] For more general information, see www.star-alliance.com/cgi-bin/sa.storefront/979016791/UserTemplate/17 (checked Feb 25, 2003).

[3] On Nov 8, 1998 in Deerfield, IL, USA.

[4] Met Castillo, "Issues and Trends in Christian Missions in Asia," in *World Missions: The Asian Challenge. A Compendium of the Asia Missions Congress '90* (Singapore: World Evangelical Fellowship, 2000), 94.

[5] Luis Bush and L. Lutz, *Partnering in Ministry: The Direction of World Evangelism* (Downers Grove, IL: InterVarsity, 1990), 46.

[6] Castillo, back cover page.

[7] Castillo, 96.

[8] Richard Schlitt, "Final Stage Transitions from Mission to National Church: An OMF/ABCCOP Case Study" (a paper presented at the tenth William Menzies Annual Lectureship at Asia Pacific Theological Seminary, Baguio, Philippines, January 2002), 14.

WHAT MAKES AN INTERCULTURAL PROGRAM EFFECTIVE? LESSONS FROM SOUTHERN HEMISPHERE EXPERIENCES: ASIA AND LATIN AMERICA

Miguel Alvarez

1. Introduction

This document offers a comparative review of current mission trends in Asia and Latin America. It also expands on current issues related to regional and intercontinental missionary efforts. With this framework in mind, I would like to introduce this debate from the point of view of someone who was born and raised in Latin America. Having served in the Central American region, and later on, in the Asia-Pacific region, I would like to think of myself as an apprentice in the intercultural field of service. Based upon that, I will attempt to compare some historical patterns and current trends observed in most missionary activities in Asia and Latin America.

In this presentation, I am also committed to fairness. I believe our generation must appreciate those servants of God who actually gave their lives in the mission fields of Asia and Latin America. Consequently this debate will also offer due honor and respect to those men and women who unselfishly brought us the good news of the gospel, even beyond their limitations. By no means will I attempt to undermine their historical input due to cultural or educational differences or their methodology in comparison to the current trends of missionary ministry today. On the contrary, it is with a spirit of gratitude that I submit the following review.

This effort also deals with the issue of *intentionality*.[1] It is only with this attitude in mind that any negative missionary experiences of the past may be overcome. It deals with situations and circumstances related to attitudes, actions and even the methodology of service.[2] My line of reasoning is that if the missionary endeavor is to be improved this must be done intentionally. With all of these facts in mind, let us consider some important lessons learned from the field.

1.1 Lessons Learned from the Asians

In the early 1990s, just after I arrived in Manila, I had the opportunity to participate in several mission meetings, particularly in the Philippines. The aim of the message was always the same: to "encourage the nationals to fully participate in mission service," particularly in those areas of the so-called 10/40 Window. They always referred to the fact that Asians and particularly Filipinos were the right people to meet most missionary needs in Asia and beyond.

On the contrary, however, one may argue, "Of course, there are more than a thousand Spanish words, and may be another thousand English words in the Filipino language, which makes us indeed international people linguistically speaking. Moreover, are we not very similar to most Southeast Asian people physically? The color of our skin and our black hair makes us close. Besides, like most people in the region, we also eat rice. With such a natural similarity we must be the right people to reach out to them." However, after a few doses of reality in the field, they soon realized there was something more required to become a true missionary. Indeed it was necessary to select carefully and later train and equip in the proper way. They are now approaching the field more adequately and with long-term assignments in mind.

1.2 Lessons Learned from the Latinos

Similar situations took place in Latin America. The discourse was basically the same: "This is the time for us Latinos. Are there not about three thousand Arabic words in the Spanish language? Aren't we physically very similar to the people of North Africa and the Middle East? Due to our color of skin and hair we could go in and move among them unnoticed. 10/40 Window, here we come." Well, it also took a few doses of missionary reality for them to realize there was something more required to become true missionaries—adequate training and equipping was necessary.

2. Current Mission Trends in Asia

Consequently to be able to understand and approach objectively the current trends in world evangelization that have originated in Asia and Latin America, one must evaluate some patterns observed in recent history. These events occurred among churches, denominations and Christian leaders of both regions. Let us take a look at some of them.[3]

2.1 Inherited Patterns

The issue of the historical "colonial" mentality was evident in the beginning, and today continues to be one of the most significant elements of discussion in the mission strategies that affect Asia and Latin America. This colonial mentality has been observed in both the sending and the receiving parties involved. Of course, more research will also register that this colonial mentality has also been observed in other regions of the world. During most of modern history, this has been the most predominant characteristic observed in the relationship between the sending and receiving parties. Hence, it was in a recent publication of the *Journal of Asian Mission* that Wonsuk Ma clearly described how this vicious attitude was historically developed:

> It is true that in the past, missionary-sending nations and missionary-receiving countries were clearly divided. That division also coincides with rich versus poor, developed versus underdeveloped, white versus non-white or even western versus non-western nations. The missionary culture and lifestyle that was always viewed as superior to their national counterparts was not entirely the missionaries' fault. Realistically, as far as Christian practices were concerned, missionaries were expected to lead nationals, particularly in evangelistic and training situations. Moreover with the missionaries' financial capability, it is common to see an "inherited" pattern of dependency.[4]

Indeed "colonialism" was not only practiced culturally, economically, politically and sociologically, but eclessiologically as well. Incidentally, this was the context in which most current missionary efforts were initiated. Unsurprisingly this context also initiated other natural sequels like the following.

2.2 "Dependant Forever"

I lived in the Philippines for almost a decade and I suppose that was enough time to get a glimpse of what goes on in the relationship between foreign missionaries and the nationals. Historically most local leaders assumed a secondary role in the administration and leadership of the church. The nationals were expected to submit to the authority of those sent from overseas to manage them, without protest. Of course there have been some outstanding exceptions, but these have not been the norm.[5]

The problem has its roots in the denominational individualism and competition of the West. Denominationalism eventually became the greatest obstacle in the development of strong and efficient national leaders. Denominations only cared for the preservation, maintenance and continuity of the institution. Thus the role of an overseer or a denominational leader was to provide those said elements on behalf of the organization. Therefore people were never seen as the object of their service. On the contrary, people were used as instruments to protect and preserve the system. So if an individual or a group of people were not willing to submit to the rules and regulations of the establishment, they were disciplined or simply separated from the organization.

In some cases national leaders were regarded with suspicion. In the worst scenario, the goal of the foreign overseer was to keep them feeble or inferior, and therefore, dependent on the mother denomination.

On the other hand, in some countries of Asia the quest for a legitimate national pride threw them into the other extreme. This is very much the same with most Latin American countries. Strong oppression from the past gave birth to a strong national pride that eventually broke all ties with the founding mission agencies in the region. At the end of the twentieth century there was an overwhelming thrust for national pride and self-determination. A new generation of leaders arrived with a new mentality and strong commitment to the national values of their culture and society. They saw the previous generation of church leaders as oppressors and for that reason their responsibility was to break with all of those sources of archaic leadership. This attitude provoked innumerable church splits and the establishment of numerous new independent ministries.

2.3 "Colonizers Forever"

Most missionaries arrived in Asia as church planters, which was a justified need at that appointed time. But later on they became well-established and powerful—financially and politically. They conveniently failed to build new and capable leaders to replace them. Consequently they became indispensable; no one could actually replace them. They built their own kingdoms and became irreplaceable. They did not trust the nationals or their fellow missionaries. Hence, they have continued to think of the nationals as inferior and incapable of assuming such high responsibilities as pastoring the congregation that they have established. This cycle has been observed in Asia, particularly in the countries where English is spoken. This experience obviously denies the nature and purpose of cross-cultural service.

3. Current Mission Trends in Latin America

Unlike Asians, Latinos speak either Spanish or Portuguese. However, it would be a mistake to affirm that because of the common language there are not cultural differences among them. As a matter of fact in each country people keep their own customs and traditions to preserve their identity. Many times this is only used as a way of self-protection or as an opportunity to communicate their needs among friends. With this framework in mind, let's take a look at some of the most observable significant issues that affect the missionary efforts in Latin America.[6]

3.1 Unhealthy Interaction

Most Western missionaries arrived in Latin America under the same premises of those who went to Asia. Here they planted "their" congregations in the midst of persecution, primarily from the Roman Catholic Church. Catholicism had been imposed on the local cultures since the times of the colony. On the other hand the new missionaries, mostly North American and European also brought their own culture with them. They taught the nationals to submit to the foreign spiritual authority without any complaint. Moreover, only the foreign overseer had the right to exercise ecclesiastical authority such as appointing the necessary subordinated authority.[7]

Another element that perpetuated dependence was the financial component. Since most missionaries established their congregations among underprivileged communities, the congregation and the local leaders were at a financial disadvantage in their relationship to the foreign leader. As a result they had no choice but to submit to him. As a consequence this relationship created a continuous cycle of economical, spiritual and political dependency.[8]

3.2 The "Transnational" Model

Most denominational missionaries were sent to Latin America following the same pattern of the transnational brands of the region. For most Christian denominations from the United States, this was the natural American way of providing leadership overseas and the church was no exception. They carried the title of "missionary," but some of them were only international administrators or representatives at the service of the denomination. Their "ministry" was to oversee as administrators the local interest of the denomination in every country where they were established. In addition this leadership succeeded by way of forming local leaders shaped with the same mentality—the most important leader in the denomination was the overseer. His most important responsibility is to preserve and maintain the system that he represents. Moreover his position is the most desired by the nationals and some of them would endure the system until they were considered as candidates for such a privileged position. Of course not all nationals followed this way of service. On the contrary this attitude was mostly observed in those who thought they had the gift of administration.

3.3 The "Golden Rule"

The transnational mentality based its success upon the need for financial support. The denomination provided the financial sustenance or maintenance of the work in the field. Hence the financial crisis of the local people, particularly during the second half of the twentieth century. They were forced to remain submitted to the foreign missionary whose primary responsibility was to preserve and maintain the denominational system that he represented. In most places of Asia and Latin America today one can still observe this financial dependency, particularly among most denominationally bound congregations and ministries. This dependence is mostly observed through the leadership selection process, where denominational boards will only appoint the leaders they trust.

3.4 The "Institutionalized Terrorism" Syndrome

Institutionalized terrorism is used by the social sciences to define the oppressive relationship used by an individual in authority over a subordinate. The person in authority uses any mechanism that represents a threat, rejection or discipline against the subordinate, who in this case, is in a disadvantaged position and consequently is unable to defend himself.

In plain missionary language this comparison may seem awkward, nevertheless if one digs a little deeper in recent church and missions history, there are sufficient cases that confirm a certain level of abuse in the exercise of authority by those in privileged positions in the denominational structure. There are a number of people who have been hurt by authoritarian leaders. Most of those cases are not well known or documented due to the obvious inferior position of the hurting party. Historically the church "overseas" has lost innumerable outstanding people at the hand of untouchable authoritarian "missionary" leaders.

4. Missions in the Asian and the Latin American Context

The question is, "How do Asians comprehend cross-cultural missions?" Of course one must be careful not to generalize the issue. The same principle should be applied to the Latinos. However most Asians live in monocultures and therefore each culture has its own understanding and commitment to the Great Commission. In light of that, allow me then to propose some of the most pressing issues related to the missionary communities of both Asia and Latin America.

It is obvious that God yearns for all persons to have the opportunity to become true disciples of Jesus within their own social, cultural and linguistic context. Therefore, as the church enters the third millennium, missionaries must work together in order to build a worldwide missions movement. This development should grant every person in every segment of the human mosaic an opportunity to hear, understand and respond to the gospel during his or her lifetime. Once they accept Jesus, they should also have the opportunity to be incorporated into the life of a local congregation; to grow in intimacy with the Holy Spirit;[9] to manifest the life of Christ and exhibit the fruit of the Spirit as salt and light in the world; and to be spiritually empowered to minister effectively both in the church and in the world.

4.1 The Right Options

As the gospel reaches more places and peoples and the church grows in numbers, missionaries must seek to build up believers in nurture, discipleship, faith and knowledge. Missionaries should support every effort that provides various levels of training so that every church may have equipped and mature leaders and that every mission endeavor may have adequate pioneering leadership.[10] Asians and Latin Americans must recognize and promote the importance of a solid missiology in the context of world evangelization. Consequently churches, organizations and institutions must place cross-cultural missions at the very core of the total curriculum of Christian education and missionary training. It should be understood that the church must include not just congregational structures, but also missiological and educational structures at all levels.

4.2 Regional Partnerships

Contemporary partnerships are an important part of world evangelization. Asians and Latin Americans must build relationships of trust so that they can work together in partnership. They must build and foster fellowships of believers in Christ among all peoples that worship him.[11] A fundamental question in missions must change, from "What can I do?" to "How do we fit, in relationship to what others are doing?" Partnerships can help us answer this question and provide a forum for practical collaboration.[12] These partnerships will not emerge or operate without people who have the vision, skills and commitment to both the partnership purpose and process. In this way they must encourage the church to identify, recruit, train and support partners and facilitators.

4.3 National Initiatives

At this point it is crucial that in both Asia and Latin America, nationals assume their responsibility as leaders and mobilizers. Current missionary initiatives must emphasize the importance of mobilizing indigenous resources and church structures to find and reach every unreached people group within their own countries and beyond.[13] This is the future of missions. Along these lines several models of missionary mobilization have been established in both regions.[14] Undoubtedly these efforts are already establishing a new paradigm for the new order of world evangelization. However, every effort must be strategically planned and all missionaries should receive the appropriate training. There will be no excuse for making the same mistakes as the previous generations.

4.4 Networking

As a missionary educator and mobilizer, I have had the opportunity to visit with different missionary leaders and agencies in both regions of Asia and Latin America. Most of them have shown the same pattern—the only perfect program is theirs. They do not talk to other agencies or to other missionaries. They talk about partnership and cooperation but in actuality deny them. Some of them refuse to share information and even to sit down with fellow organizations. Missions work has been permeated by selfishness. There are certain individuals who only seek after their own gain. Obviously this report represents the reality of the old paradigm.

The new paradigm however focuses on the ability to *intentionally* network and cooperate. Relational leadership must have the ability to serve as a catalyst to bring the mission community together to cooperate and coordinate toward a common goal and thereby boost the effectiveness of the overall mission force. Building networks and partnerships to accomplish this will be an essential part of the process.

Regional missionary organizations and ministries should be brought together to form specific "tracks, task forces and resource networks."[15] These ministries with similar areas of outreach should network, cooperate and coordinate their efforts. For instance, specific tracks should be formed for those involved with prayer, translation, Gospel recordings, mobilization, church planting, women, youth and more. Hence networking leadership will bring together the adequate use of contemporary technology that will foster better communication within and between the various networks and tracks. These networks and task forces will force a much needed networking attitude among the different Christian organizations. The language and the spirit of cooperation will enfold the Christian movement.

4.5 Information: Gathering and Distribution

At this time in history the missionary movement is faced with one of the most urgent situation—the proper use and distribution of information. It is no secret that the power of communication begins with the collection of the best information available in the field. Today missionaries are sent out to collect the best information available on whom the unreached peoples are and what God was doing to reach them. This information is necessary to mobilize churches and mission agencies and to help focus their efforts on reaching those unreached peoples.[16] Another benefit of networking is the use of information to convene national, regional and intercontinental gatherings with specific missionary purposes. Equally beneficial is the power of fairness in the distribution of missionary resources available in the body of Christ. Of course this new paradigm points toward a new order in the mobilization of the church for the purpose of world evangelization.[17]

5. Pressing Issues on Current Missionary Training

I must admit that even the term, missionary-training, has already been abused, and therefore we need to establish some conceptual foundations in order to understand which kind of training we are talking about here. By missionary training we mean the ability to provide instruction in cross-cultural disciplines, including spiritual foundations or practices designed to impart the necessary proficiency to undergo cross-cultural tasks. This training is intended to develop missionary skills, such as behavioral and spiritual habits and mental attitudes. Likewise, missionary training should cause change; it should be action- and involvement-oriented. [18]

It is based upon my Asian and Latin American experiences that I introduce this discussion for the sake of a sustained and long-term missionary program initiated in the Southern Hemisphere. I believe Asians and Latinos need to establish a sustained dialogue focused on common grounds of understanding and interpreting the missiological task of the church in the South.[19] Indeed there are a number of issues that remain constant in the missiological universe of both Asia and Latin America.

5.1 Planning

There is a legitimate concern among mission agencies on the need to establish clear objectives and reachable goals, which will determine the expected level of success in a long-term assignment. Missionaries must offer clear evidence and justify why they have chosen a particular country or culture as an object of their ministry. Of course the said planning process will also include obvious organizational relationships, and sound direction, coordination and supervision.

5.1.1 Team work and interpersonal relationships

There is one element that makes Asians and Latinos similar. Both are capable of working as a team, unlike the individualistic attitude of some missionaries from other latitudes. However, Asians and Latinos need to learn the benefits of teamwork and how to relate properly to teammates, family, sponsors, churches and even missionary agencies. They need to develop theological and pastoral foundations that will enable them to carry these issues adequately.

5.1.2 Spiritual discipline

Missionary training must focus on the development of a sound individual and collective spirituality. This must be observed in the lifestyle of the missionary. The love of Christ must be the final object in all their efforts.[20] Only a solid relationship with the Holy Spirit will guarantee successful long-term missionary service. It is no secret that the most outstanding missionaries in the history of missions evidenced a powerful passion in their love of Christ.

5.1.3 Pastoral care

A successful long-term missionary assignment will be associated with qualified pastoral care and counseling services provided to the worker in the field. This service must be planned and intentionally organized. If a missionary agency is incapable of providing pastoral care for its missionaries, it has failed to provide for one the most urgent needs in the mission field.

5.1.4 Strengthening the mission agency

The first priority of the national churches is to strengthen the missionary agency. In most negative cases of frustrating experiences the local mission agency has been identified as the weak link. This is due to lack of support from the local church. Most churches use their resources for local development thus neglecting their missionary responsibility. When this trend continues the missionary agency is forced to neglect its primary responsibility due to lack of resources. Churches have no excuse to restrain their support to the mission agency. To do otherwise only evidences lack of commitment to the Great Commission.

5.2 Synergy from Partnership and Cooperation

It is the purpose of this dialogue to continue to affirm that partnerships are an important part of world evangelization. Christian organizations must build relationships of trust so that they can work together in partnership, to enhance fellowships of believers in Christ among all peoples that will worship him. Partnerships will provide a forum for practical missionary collaboration.[21] Recently there have been signs of a new day dawning among God's people everywhere to worship and work together with God's people from everywhere. There are already several dozens of international missionary partnerships emerging and operating among and for the good of the unreached peoples. Undoubtedly this effort is pleasing to God. It is true to his character and to the mission of the church. However, a major challenge is still before us. These partnerships will not emerge or operate without people who have the vision, skills and commitment to both the partnership purpose and process. Therefore this kingdom of partnership must continue to encourage the church to identify, recruit, train and support partnership facilitators.[22]

It was William D. Taylor who initiated this concept of partnership at the meeting of the Missions Commission of the World Evangelical Fellowship in Manila in June 1992. In his book *Kingdom Partnerships for Synergy in Missions*, he upholds that the church and the missions community must move beyond superficial fellowship and simple networking to true partnership—cooperative ventures, strategic alliances, mutually engaged projects, and the sharing of material and human resources. The expected result is synergy—a phenomenon where the output is greater than the sum of the individual components.[23] Later he adds that one draft horse can pull four tons; and two draft horses harnessed together can pull twenty-two tons! Are the church ready to sacrifice self-identity and unilateral control for the possibility of such a huge playoff?[24]

A simple definition of partnership would be "using mutual gifts to accomplish tasks."[25] However the essential components of partnership are laid out in a broader definition offered by Luis Bush. He helps us to understand the idea of partnership in the context of missions as "an association of two or more autonomous bodies who have formed a trusting relationship, and fulfill agreed-upon expectations sharing complimentary strengths and resources, to reach their mutual goal."[26]

5.3 Partnership with Mutual Respect and Acceptance

Recently churches in many countries have developed national strategies and processes for mobilizing the body of Christ toward completing the unfinished mandate within and beyond their borders.[27] Visionary servant leaders have facilitated national initiatives that affirm existing structures and foster cooperative commitments to church planting and to the goal of a pioneer church planting movement within every ethno-linguistic people.[28] It is encouraging to observe that united missionary efforts among the unreached people groups have already borne much fruit. And yet much work remains. Therefore, the church must continue to pray for the hastening of the day when all persons will have a valid opportunity to experience the love, truth and saving power of Jesus Christ in fellowship with other believers among their own people. Missionary leaders must continue to encourage God's people everywhere to do their part in establishing a missions-minded church planting movement within every unreached people group, providing every believer the opportunity to seek and discover God's missionary purpose for his or her life regardless of the cost.

5.4 Servant Leadership

This issue also must be addressed with an objective attitude. It is obvious that Asians and Latin Americans are becoming more and more sensitive to the holistic needs of the poor. In a way the Asian and the Latin American church represents one aspect of the body of Christ for which Jesus showed deep concern. His followers were among the poor. Today the majority of the church is itself poor. Consequently ministry to the poor will be a ministry *by* and *with* the poor. It is encouraging that missionary organizations and fellow Christian networks are now promoting holistic, incarnational and community-transforming ministries, especially in the economically deprived areas of the world.[29] However, missionary agencies are keenly conscious of the enormous social and spiritual ills affecting millions of the poor and needy. It is also true that both the rich and the poor are guilty of covetousness, injustice and indifference leading to sins of commission and omission. Missionaries are then confronted with an overwhelming demand to join with the poor in breaking the chains of injustice and oppression, sharing with all the resources that God has given them, and spreading the gospel of the kingdom, which is good news for the rich and the poor alike.

6. Women in Missions

Today, women all over the world are experiencing God's most outstanding visitation. They are rising to their birthright and inheritance, as they trust God to fulfill all his purposes in and through them. They are committed to follow the leading of the Holy Spirit, as they realize their intrinsic value, not in cultural, geographical and generational imperatives but rather in knowing that they are made in the image of God.

The Creator, who designed both male and female to reflect his likeness and glory, calls men and women to serve together as equal partners in his purpose. Missionaries therefore must continue to strengthen and pursue the ministry of reconciliation[30] and justice extending it not only to race and class but to gender as well. Consequently men and women should learn to walk and work together in the mission field with mutual and godly respect.[31]

7. Conclusion

In this paper I have attempted to highlight some of the most observable elements considered as negative in recent missionary service. Likewise I also offer some possible options that can be considered as potential solutions. There may be other indicators that could be used to demonstrate whether a missionary program is implementing the proper method for success or not. At this point what matters is that those committed to missionary service, and particularly to training missionaries, should take a closer look at those indictors and determine whether they are helpful or not.

It is also important that missionary service in the twenty-first century be carried out in a cooperative and networked basis. This is especially important as more and more new missionaries and mission agencies are arising from the four corners of the world. Indeed, times have changed. A new generation of missionaries and mission agencies has arisen. This generation is facing a fascinating and fast changing world. Current technology has made life different and this will continue to evolve even faster.[32] Thus, more adjustments will have to be made.

What makes a missionary program successful? There is no simple answer to this question. The success of a missionary program cannot be found in the pages of an outlined handbook. We all wish that were the case. Instead, we are faced with a dynamic and ever improving process.

I would like to see it continue that way—a process. It must be progressive. There are many different contexts of people and societies in the world. The generation of the twenty-first century will have the opportunity to interact with missionaries of different cultural backgrounds—e.g., race, color, language, nationality, etc. Indeed the Holy Spirit has been able to mobilize his people all over the world to reach out to those who are lost. This is the new context of world evangelization today.

---

[1] On the issue of intentionality in missions, see William L. Isley Jr., "A Spirituality for Missionaries," *Missiology: An International Review* 17:3 (July 1999), 302.

[2] C. René Padilla, "Toward the Globalization and Integrity of Mission," in *Mission in the Nineteen 90's*, eds. Gerald H. Anderson, James B. Phillips and Robert T. Coote (Grand Rapids, MI: Eerdmans, 1991), 30-32.

[3] The following Asian authors offer a clear picture and understanding of the new context of missions in Asia. Julie C. Ma, *When the Spirit Meets the Spirits. Pentecostal Ministry among the Kankana-ey Tribe in the Philippines* (Frankfurt am Main: Peter Lang, 2000); Ken Gnanakan, *The Pluralistic Predicament* (Bangalore, India: Theological Book Trust, 1992), 26-38; Joseph R. Suico, "Pentecostalism: Towards a Movement of Social Transformation in the Philippines," *Journal of Asian Mission* 1:1 (March 1999), 7-19; Choan-Seng Song, *Christian Mission in Reconstruction: An Analysis* (Maryknoll, NY: Orbis, 1977); David S. Lim, "A Critique of Modernity in Protestant Missions in the Philippines," *Journal of Asian Mission* 2:2 (September 2000), 149-177; Ajith Fernando, *The Christian's Attitude toward World Religions* (Wheaton, IL: Tyndale, 1987); Rodrigo D. Tano, "Toward an Evangelical Asian Theology," in *Biblical Theology in Asia*, ed. Ken Gnanakan (Bangalore, India: Theological Book Trust, 1995), 46-76; John Gnanapiragasam and Felix Wilfred, eds. *Being Church in Asia*, vol. 1, *Theological Advisory Commission, 1986-92* (Quezon City, Philippines: Claretian, 1994); Wonsuk Ma, "Mission: Nine Hurdles for Asian Churches," *Journal of Asian Mission* 2:1 (March 2000), 103-124; Jose M. De Mesa, *Solidarity with the Culture* (Quezon City, Philippines: Maryhill, 1987); Melba P. Maggay, *The Gospel in the Filipino Context* (Manila: OMF Literature, 1987); Emerito P. Nacpil, "Philippines: A Gospel for the New Filipino," in *Asian Voices in Christian Theology*, ed. Gerald H. Anderson (Maryknoll, NY: Orbis, 1976); Bong Rin Ro, "Urban Missions: Historical Perspective," *ATA Journal* 3:2 (July 1995), 30-48; Hwa Yung, *Mangoes or Bananas?* (Oxford: Regnum, 1997); Titus Loong, "Equipping the Next Generation of Missionaries," *Asian Mission* 1 (July 1998); Met Castillo, "Missiological Education: The Missing Element in Mission Strategy," *Asia Pulse* 1 (1973), 2-5; Met Castillo, ed., *The Asian*

Challenge Compendium of the Asian Missions Congress '90 (Singapore: World Evangelical Fellowship, 1991).

[4] Wonsuk Ma, "Mission: Nine Hurdles for Asian Churches," 107.

[5] See Samuel Escobar, "The Promise and Precariousness of Latin American Protestantism," in *Coming of Age: Protestantism in Contemporary Latin America*, ed. Daniel R. Miller (Lanham, MD: University Press of America, 1994), 31.

[6] The following authors offer a clear picture and understanding of the new context of missions in Latin America. C. René Padilla, "The Future of Christianity in Latin America: Missiological Perspectives and Challenges," *International Bulletin of Missionary Research* 22:3 (July 1999), 105-112; C. R. Padilla, *Bases Bíblicas de la Misión: Perspectivas Latinoamericanas* (Grand Rapids, MI: Nueva Creación, 1998); C. R. Padilla, "Toward the Globalization and Integrity of Mission," in *Mission in the Nineteen 90's*, pp. 30-32; Rodolfo (Rudy) Girón, "COMIBAM: Three Independent Partnerships in Latin America," in *Kingdom of Partnerships for Synergy in Missions*, ed. William D. Taylor (Pasadena, CA: William Carey Library, 1994), 197-204; Darío López, *Pentecostalismo y Transformación Social. Más Allá de los Estereotipos, las Críticas se Enfrentan con los Hechos* (Buenos Aires, Argentina: Kairos Ediciones, 2000); D. López, *La Misión Liberadora de Jesús. Una Lectura Misiológica del Evangelio de Lucas* (Lima, Perú: Ediciones Puma, 1997); Alexandre Araujo, "Confidence Factors: Accountability in Christian Partnerhips," in *Kingdom of Partnerships for Synergy in Missions*, 119-130; Samuel Escobar, "Latin America," in *Toward the 21st Century in Christian Mission*, eds. James M. Phillips and Robert T. Coote (Grand Rapids, MI: Eerdmans, 1993), 125-135; Federico Bertuzzi, "A Latin American Response to Patrick Sookhdeo," in *Kingdom of Partnerships for Synergy in Missions*, 93-99; William D. Taylor, "Hispanic American Models of Missionary Training," in *Internationalising Missionary Training: A Global Perspective*, ed. William D. Taylor (Grand Rapids, MI: Baker, 1991), 121-131; Guillermo Cook, ed., *New Face of the Church in Latin America, Between Tradition and Change* (Maryknoll, NY: Orbis, 1994); Enrique Dussell, ed., *The Church in Latin America, 1492-1992* (Maryknoll, NY: Orbis, 1992); Pablo Alberto Deiros, ed., *Los Evangélicos y el Poder Político en América Latina* (Grand Rapids, MI: Eerdmans, 1986).

[7] On the issue of historical "colonialism" in Latin America, see Enrique Dussel, *A History of the Church in Latin America: Colonialism to Liberation* (Grand Rapids, MI: Eerdmans, 1981).

[8] See for instance, Claudio Veliz, ed., *The Politics of Conformity in Latin America* (London: Oxford University, 1967), 7.

[9] On this subject see for instance, L. Grant McClung, Jr., "'Try to Get People Saved': Revisiting the Paradigm of an Urgent Pentecostal Missiology," in *The Globalization of Pentecostalism. A Religion Made to Travel*, eds. Murray W. Dempster, Byron D. Klaus, and Douglas Petersen (Oxford: Regnum Books, 1999), 31-51.

[10] For a comprehensive coverage on the current worldwide missionary mobilization, see David Shibley, *A Force in the Earth: The Move of the Spirit in World Evangelization* (Lake Mary, FL: Creation, 1997).

[11] See for instance, Steve Hoke, "A Glorious Pursuit: Reflections on God's Passion for Worshipers from All Peoples," *Mission Frontiers* 23:1 (March 2001), 20-27.

[12] "The Millennial Manifesto: Covenanting for the 21st Century," *Mission Frontiers* (http://www.missionfrontiers.org/2001/02/200102.htm), checked on December 2001.

[13] See Emilio Antonio Núñez and William David Taylor, *Crisis and Hope in Latin America and Evangelical Perspective* (Pasadena, CA: William Carey Library, 1996), 496-498.

[14] See for instance, Samuel Escobar, "Latin America," 125-135.

[15] See Gerald H. Anderson, "Christian Mission in A.D. 2000: A Glance Backward," *Missiology: An International Review* 18:3 (July 2000), 284.

[16] At GCOWE '95 in Seoul, Korea, the AD2000 Movement released, in cooperation with the Peoples Information Network, a list of unreached peoples under the title, "The Least-Evangelized Peoples of the World." See Keith Butler, "Joshua Project 2000: Unreached Peoples List," *Mission Frontiers* 18:5-8 (May–August 1996), 38-52.

[17] Following GCOWE '95, the AD2000 Movement launched Joshua Project 2000 with a focus on reaching the unreached peoples with a population of 10,000 or more. Shortly after the launch of Joshua Project 2000 in November 1995, the first Joshua Project list of 1,739 unreached peoples was released in Keith Butler, "Joshua Project 2000: Unreached Peoples List," 38-52.

[18] For a broader discussion on missionary training, see Miguel Alvarez, "Missionary Training: A Discipline," *Journal of Asian Mission* 2:1 (March 2000), 95.

[19] The term "Southern Hemisphere" has been used recently to refer to parts of the world other than Western Europe, North America, Australia and New Zealand, traditionally known as "Northern Hemisphere" nations due to their common cultural, political and economical background.

[20] Cf. William L. Isley, Jr., "A Spirituality for Missionaries," *Missiology: An International Review* 17:3 (July 1999), 299-309.

[21] Phil Butler, "Do Strategic Partnerships Really Make a Difference," *Mission Frontiers* 18:9-10 (Sept-Oct 1996), 29-30.

[22] See for instance William D. Taylor, ed., *Kingdom Partnerships for Synergy in Missions*, 1-8.

[23] A thorough exposition and analysis on current trends and models of partnership can be found in Taylor, *Kingdom Partnerships for Synergy in Missions.*

[24] Taylor, *Kingdom Partnerships for Synergy in Missions*, 241.

[25] Taylor, *Kingdom Partnerships for Synergy in Missions*, 4.

[26] Luis Bush, *Partnering in Ministry: The Direction of World Evangelism* (Downers Grove, IL: InterVarsity, 1990), 46.

[27] See Luis Bush, "The Unfinished Task," *Mission Frontiers* 17:3-4 (March–April 1995), 12.

[28] A good example of cooperative strategies in church planting is found in David Garrison, *Church Planting Movements* (Richmond, VA: International Mission Board of the Southern Baptist Convention, 1999), 7-10.

[29] A scenario of servant leadership in the context of a Latin American society can be found in Darío López, *Los Evangélicos y los Derechos Humanos: La Experiencia Social del Concilio Nacional Evangélico del Perú 1980-1992* (Lima, Perú: Centro Evangélico de Misiología Andino-Amazónica, 1998).

[30] Cf. French L. Arrington, *Ministry of Reconciliation: A Study of 2 Corinthians* (Grand Rapids, MI: Baker, 1980).

[31] For a broader discussion on the issue of women in missions see Ruth A. Tucker, "Women in Mission" in *Toward the 21st Century in Christian Mission*, 284-293. Also in the context of Brazil, see Benedicta Da Silva, *Benedicta Da Silva: An Afro-Brazilian Woman's Story of Politics and Love* as told to Medea Benjamin and Maisa Mendoca (Oakland, CA: A Food First Book, 1997), 193-201.

[32] A thorough research of facts and trends on current world evangelization can be found in L. Grant McClung, Jr., *Globalbeliever.com: Connecting to God's Work in your World* (Cleveland, TN: Pathway, 2000).

EMPOWERING ASIAN CHURCHES:
HOW IT HAS HAPPENED, AND WITH WHAT CONSEQUENCES

Jean-Daniel Plüss

1. Introduction

If you search the Internet for the word "empowerment" you will find a multitude of entries relating to social, psychological, political and economical subjects. Then, if you are lucky and patient, you will find a few references to empowerment in a theological sense. On the other hand, if you ask a Pentecostal to explain empowerment, he or she is likely to focus on the power of the Holy Spirit being manifested in the believer's life.

Although I am a Pentecostal believer, in this presentation, I will focus on different forms of empowerment. Furthermore, because I am a Swiss and not an Asian Pentecostal, I intend to approach the topic indirectly, that is, I invite you to look at some aspects of the work done by the Basel Mission Society that has been present in India, China and Kalimantan for a long time. Furthermore, I would like to invite secular reflection to join us in the discussion, and ask, among other things, about non-religious resources of empowerment.

2. The Basel Mission in Crisis

The Basel Mission was the third missionary society to be founded in German-speaking Europe. It was established in 1815 and became well-known and respected in West Africa and South India. It played a pioneering role in establishing schools, medical facilities and other infrastructures on the mission field. In Switzerland, the Basel Mission was instrumental in founding a cooperation of Evangelical churches and missions which is called KEM.[1] Suddenly, however, in the fall of 1999 it withdrew its partnership from the KEM not only because the associated societies, as well as the Basel Mission, experienced severe losses of financial support, but more importantly because and the strategies envisioned by the other societies were not wide enough for the administrators of Basel.[2] Many Evangelical and Reformed Christians in southern Germany and Switzerland were wondering if this was not only going to be the end of a cooperation but also the end of the Basel Mission, the well-known, well-established and appreciated Christian agency. Others, perhaps among them more conservative Christians, were tempted to argue that the Basel Mission had forsaken its Pietistic roots and had become too liberal, too syncretistic, too this-worldly and that the crisis was tantamount to a judgment from above. It had lost the power by which it was driven for almost 200 years. Is such an argument valid? What was the power behind Basel? In order to find out more, I invite you to look at the beginnings of the Basel Mission.

2.1 The Beginning

The end of the eighteenth century saw the beginnings of the British missionary societies. It was a response to the Methodist revival, a new attitude toward slavery and colonial relations. In a sense, the missionary work could be understood as a form of reparation for the injustice created through the slave trade.[3] The reports of these new religious projects were translated into German and widely circulated among the Pietists who also had experienced a profound revival and were motivated to serve the Lord wherever he would lead them. A handful of Christian businessmen were among the interested parties. It must not be forgotten that the Swiss city of Basel with its strategic location on the Rhine River and bordering both the French Alsace and the German Black Forest had been an important center of trade long before any industry developed there in the nineteenth century. The mix of religious conviction and economic know-how in that city was the catalyst for the birth of this missionary enterprise that in a few years would reach out to the farthest ends of the earth. Paul Jenkins, the archivist of the Basel Mission, put it like this: "People with the necessary knowledge and self-confidence to create a trading business, a corporation, or a bank would also be capable of organizing a religious enterprise, a hospital, a school or a missionary society."[4] Of course, the twentieth century has repeatedly illustrated how the mix of religious dedication, financial strength and economic know-how has been the motor for much missionary work emanating from the United States of America. On the other hand, the crisis of the Basel Mission a few years ago illustrates what can happen if financial empowerment suddenly diminishes.

2.2 Human Assets

The early missionaries were recruited from the Pietistic following that was willing to go anywhere, even under the risk of death, to proclaim the good news they had personally experienced in an encounter with Jesus Christ. Concretely, this meant the first candidates for the mission work were farmers, masons, carpenters, weavers and the like. Besides a spiritual experience and conviction, they brought along their skills, abilities and gifts. One would not find theologians, medical doctors and other highly trained individuals on the mission field in the early days. In a picture taken in 1890 at the training center of the Basel Mission, one can see the seminarians dressed in their work clothes proudly holding their tools,[5] thus identifying their professional background. Among them were farmers, loggers, tanners and builders. This was human empowerment at work. People were prepared for the mission field with the very abilities they brought along.

Pentecostals are reminded that their early missionaries were not people of high standing in society either.[6] They were for the most part working people and artisans. Early mission activity was empowered by willingness and obedience to God and the natural gifts at hand. There is another striking parallel between the early days of the Basel Mission and the beginnings of the Pentecostal movement. The willingness to be part of the great commission was more important than the allegiance to a particular creed. There was an ecumenical generosity.[7] In other words, what was important was not primarily a certain denominational affiliation but the calling to missions work. Empowerment to the ministry was by the Spirit not by the letter.

Another aspect of human empowerment is illustrated in the work of the Basel Mission involving women. Originally, the wives of the missionaries were to support their husbands emotionally and create an appropriate atmosphere at home on the mission field. No actual missionary activity was expected from them, with perhaps the exception of being a witness in the background.[8] However, it was the contact among women that opened many doors. They seemed more gifted in communicating essentials and discovering common concerns. Soon the training of "Bible women" working in the neighborhoods and in small groups was encouraged and began to be an important element in the South Indian work of the Basel Mission.

Michael Bergunder, a Lutheran who studied South Asian Pentecostalism intensively, also devotes a section on the role of women in his book on South Indian Pentecostalism.[9] He argues that, although in the public scene, both leadership and the pastorate are dominated by men, women play an essential role in the spread of Pentecostalism in India. There are two reasons for this: women play an important role in church life and they are boldly practicing charismatic gifts. According to Bergunder, a good number of pastor's wives have taken on the important functions of evangelists, counselors and teachers in women's meetings so that the theoretical division between male and female ecclesial roles is being broken up. This challenges a new generation of believers to re-think the role of women in the church. An important form of empowerment is taking shape. Officially, the ordination of women to the ministry is not yet accepted by a majority of Indian Pentecostals. However, the fact that the South Indian Assemblies of God are now granting a "Bible Women's Certificate" (whence does the name come from?) does constitute an encouraging step in that direction.[10]

3. Power and the Clash of Civilizations

It is a common assumption that the group which has the money is also the one who calls the shots, i.e., has the power to implement or stop any project. The fact that money is equated to power seems to be even truer in the context of globalization; but as global power increases so does apprehension to it. The recent terrorist attacks[11] are a clear sign that sheer power meets resistance. Pressure will create counter pressure. Hence, it is appropriate to reflect on the way one defines power in the context of our empowerment discussion. Samuel P. Huntington, professor of international relations at Harvard University, in his book *The Clash of Civilizations and the Remaking of World Order,*[12] addresses two issues in his discussion on indigenization and the resurgence of non-Western cultures: one is the use of power and the other is the role of religion.

First, as far as the use of power is concerned, Huntington makes clear that there is an important link between culture and power. As European colonialism is over, and American hegemony is receding, non-Western cultures reassert themselves.[13] In the past, non-Western cultures were impressed by the economic and military power of the West and thought they had to imitate their cultural values in order to be on the road to similar success. Now, however, as the world can no longer be divided into "the West and the Rest" categories, different civilizations compete with each other and they are discovering resources that go beyond economic and military power. Huntington adopts Joseph Nye's distinction "between 'hard power' which is the power to command resting on economic and military strength, and 'soft power,' which is the ability of a state to get 'other countries to *want* what it wants' through the appeal of its culture and ideology."[14] If cultural and ideological expressions are attractive and represent avenues of success, they become just as important as the commanding type of power we are acquainted with. In missiological terms, this means that flaunting Western power, success and materialism is likely to be a hindrance to winning and empowering people for a life in Jesus Christ. Non-Westerners do not want to copy a life style that increasingly looks one-sided and incapable of addressing their specific cultural issues. On the other hand, ideological empowerment, e.g., reaching the people of Asia with Asian Christian values represents "soft power" with an attractive and winning face. However, it would be naïve to assume that "soft power" alone would bring the desired effects. "Soft power" is most convincing if it rests on a bed of "hard power." In the end, people will be convinced if the gospel not only brings them peace of mind and solace of soul, but also comfort for the body. That, I am afraid, is the bottom line.

Let me again illustrate this point with an example taken from an experience of the Basel Mission and its work in South India. The caste system made it difficult for Hindus to convert to Christianity, because a conversion would immediately mean expulsion from the caste, and thus loss of occupation. Work in this society is a caste related activity, and according to tradition one is bound to the caste-related profession. As a result, the missionaries of the Basel Mission began to make good use of their original skills and started small business enterprises like farms and cotton mills.[15] Best known is a brick factory in Jeppu that employed several hundred Indian Christians at the beginning of the twentieth century. In the beginning, some of the administrators in Basel thought that providing an occupation for the converts was no longer the business of missionary work,[16] but it soon became obvious that providing sustenance was a necessary part of the gospel. Creating Christian industries in India was also an exercise of soft power accompanied by robust financial backing that was possible at that time. The second aspect that Huntington mentions is the role of religion in the clash of civilization as we are witnessing it. In the middle of the twentieth century, it was believed that secularization would put an end to traditional religious values and at best accommodate them within a this-worldly value system. However, there has been a remarkable resurgence of the religious, a new search for sacred foundations. Whereas Pope John XXIII spoke about a necessary *aggiornamento* of Christianity as he called for the Vatican II Council, we hear today far more about the second evangelization of Europe. Whereas a few decades ago, Western-educated Islamic thinkers advocated a modernization of Islam, many more voices today call for an Islamization of modernity.[17] Is it surprising that the very elements that supposedly would bring the death of religion are now responsible for its resurgence? As people move from the countryside into the cities, as the social net is disrupted, as economic factors command flexibility, and people are uprooted from their traditional value systems, they are faced with a void and are looking for a new identity, community and moral directives. Religion meets this need. Lee Kuan Yew puts it like this:

> We are agricultural societies that have industrialized within one or two generations. What happened in the West over 200 years or more is happening here in about 50 years or less. It is all crammed and crushed into a very tight time frame, so there are bound to be dislocations and malfunctions. If you look at the fast growing countries—Korea, Thailand, Hong Kong and Singapore—there's been one remarkable phenomenon: the rise of religion.... The old customs and religions—ancestor worship, shamanism—no longer completely satisfy. There is a quest for some higher explanations about man's purpose, about why we are here. This is associated with periods of great stress in society.[18]

Perhaps the most convincing illustration of this is the conversion from Buddhism to Christianity of more than 30% of South Korea's population in the last 50 years. Asia is also a good example of the resurgence of competing religious ideologies. The influence of Islam in Asia is a formidable force to contend with. Christianity is not alone in the religious market place providing meaning to societies that are experiencing massive change and turmoil. In terms of the empowerment of Asian churches for God's mission this means on the one hand, that Christianity has an answer that can reconcile, heal and empower people and that the people long for this message and the reality it represents. It also means that people hearing the gospel are comparing it with other messages they hear. In other words, empowerment in Christ must go beyond spreading the good news if it is to restore people and set them free. The word and the Spirit work hand in hand.

In closing this section on power and the clash of civilization let me cite a negative example from the activity of the Basel Mission in China. An early German missionary to Hong Kong had the financial means to employ a handful of Chinese he thought were Christians and paid them to preach the gospel and spread Christian literature. The messengers came back regularly with optimistic reports and demanded more literature. They also received their pay. Only later when a Swedish missionary came to Hong Kong and learned to speak the messengers' Chinese dialect was it revealed that the emissaries simply dumped the literature, spent their money in town and came back with tales of success in order to receive more money.[19] The early work of the Basel Mission in China in the 1840s is a sad example of naïve, culturally insensitive and obviously ineffective approaches of evangelizing. Money may be power, but power does not equal empowerment. Empowerment has to do with people, with economic and human resources (as we have seen), with the power of the Holy Spirit changing human lives (as we know) and with communities (as we shall see).

4. The Role of the Local Church

For the last 200 years, Western missionary societies have been known to provide resources. The recent crisis of the Basel Mission has been mentioned, but there are other crises that suddenly changed the plans and expectations of missionaries as well as those of the congregations on the field. A major crisis was the outbreak of World War I. Work in Ghana, Cameroon and India, to mention just a few, came suddenly to a halt, because those fields were all located in colonies governed by European nations then suddenly at war against each other. Of course, the rise of National Socialism in Germany made missionary work nearly impossible in the 1930s. Hitler had no interest in allowing national assets to leave the country. The communist revolution in China and the subsequent expulsion of Westerners is another instance where the missionary impact was apparently quenched.

Hence, in view of the unexpected taking place, true empowerment for God's mission will need to focus on the local church. If a national or local church is empowered to have a life of its own, then it will survive any crisis that may arise from the secular, political and economic structures that shape our existence. The survival of the Chinese church for decades after the revolution is a good example of that.

Hong has nicely elaborated why the church and missions are closely related.[20] His basic argument is that mission activity is inherently church centered, for the church is an image of the triune God. As communion is a symbol of God's love, the relational nature of God is best expressed in the church as the body of Christ acting through the power of the Holy Spirit. This empowerment is the clearest expression of the *missio Dei* and must always stand above all other interests such as expanding a denomination or the globalization of Western values. [21] Neither triumphalism nor elitism, nor the exercise of hard power (and with it the love of power) can be allowed to express itself, but rather the power of love expressed in stewardship and service. As the Spirit energizes believers in the church to serve in the name of Christ through acquired skills, personal talents and various charismata, the community is able to share this empowerment so that others may come to have abundant life in Christ. Hong summarizes, "The Holy Spirit is expected to work effectively through the interpersonal relationships of a community made up by the contribution of each believer."[22] This Pentecostal vision of the church can only be maintained if the focus on community life is strong and the expectancy for God to work through his Spirit in us is actively upheld.

The Basel Mission took over the work of the Rhenisch Mission Society in Indonesia at the end of the First World War. It concentrated its activities in southern Kalimantan. From the period between 1947 and 1950, we have two reports that were published by the Basel Mission.[23] I mention these at this point because they illustrate, firstly, the role of the clan or family and, secondly, the role of the local church. It was clear to the missionaries that the gospel really spread through the social net of the family. Their efforts were focused on that idea and in turn bore fruit as the first eye witness account illustrates. The other thing that is interesting to notice is the fact that the Basel Mission did much toward early independence of the Reformed Church there. The

Dajak Church was basically given independence in 1935.[24] None too soon, it seems, for the Indonesian struggle for in the middle of the twentieth century, independence forced the churches to survive on their own. This is the topic of the second narrative in that brochure.

So in theory, the Basel Mission did all the right things. Power to the churches and to the families that constitute them! Without wanting to be condescending, I would still like to be Pentecostal enough and partisan in saying that empowerment does not automatically follow if one does the right things. Otherwise, the Basel Mission would have been far more successful than other Christian groups, which I do not think to be the case. I believe it is not only important to do the right things (preach the gospel, concentrate on social welfare, building medical facilities, starting schools and sustaining communities), but it is also important to have the right attitude of expectancy before God: faith that God will intervene through the power of his Spirit in the very lives of those that call upon him.

5. Conclusion

"Not by might nor by power, but by my Spirit, says the Lord Almighty." This quotation from the prophet Zechariah (4:6) was the first reading at the founding of the Basel Mission in 1815 and it subsequently became the Mission's motto. It is also the motto of many Pentecostals. It reminds us that empowerment is self-transcending. It is a gift from above, and it is an action that reaches out to the community. Our discussion on empowerment has shown that it takes place within the context of life. The available assets are human abilities, economic and political help, and professional training. If these are available and the people involved are aware of their dependency on the Spirit of God, then they may take the promise in Phil 2:13 personally and say, "God who works in you to will and to act according to his good purpose."

We have also learned that empowerment has to do with power and that it is important to evaluate power structures in our churches and in our organizations with prophetic care. Power should never be mistaken as a means to gain and retain influence and force personal agendas. In the same way, we should allow our institutional structures to be tested by eschatological and prophetic questioning. An eschatological outlook is a gift that allows us to change our point of view critically and refocus on the biblical mandate. If we do not do this, the next crisis will do it for us.

Finally, I would like to focus once more on the issue of indigenization. Michael Bergunder, who studied the South Indian Pentecostal movement in detail and compared it, for instance, with popular Hinduism, is convinced that in Pentecostalism there is a quite indigenous version of Indian Christianity.[25] Although there are phenomenological parallels between the two faiths, such as miraculous healings, the communal reality makes all the difference. The congregations care for their families, and it is within that familial web that the good news reaches Christians as well as non-Christians. Similarly, Allan Anderson, who grew up in a missionary context in South Africa and now teaches about intercultural Christianity at the University of Birmingham, praises the ability of Pentecostalism to indigenize and incarnate Christianity in local churches. These experiences will, according to Anderson, help in the development of a theology of religions in modern mission.[26] This indigenization is only possible if empowerment is taken seriously, if it is encouraged by the institutional powers rather than thwarted for reasons of fear or expediency.

Perhaps I should end this paper with a "grace note." I have used the Basel Mission as a vehicle to illustrate a few issues. The Basel Mission has a rich tradition from which we are invited to learn. To many Christians, however, this mission society has now drifted into a preoccupation with partnerships promoting some sort of social gospel with liberal and syncretistic points of view. Who knows that perhaps there is another crisis looming in the background—one that will be brought forward by the indigenous Christian churches of the East and the South and will bring a fresh awareness of God's mission to the world. I believe it likely that Pentecostals could be a catalyst to that effect. After all, wouldn't that simply be what Huntington calls the second evangelization of Europe?

---

[1] KEM stands for Kooperation Evangelischer Kirchen und Missionen.

[2] C. W., "Mission 21—Aufbruch nach der Krise Zusammenschluss fünf evangelischer Missionswerke," *Neue Zürcher Zeitung*, December 18, 2000, 9.

[3] Paul Jenkins, *Kurze Geschichte der Basler Mission*, Texte und Dokumente Nr. 11 (Basel: Basler Mission, Mai 1989), 4. The text is also available in English und the title: *A Short History of the Basel Mission*, Texte und Dokumente Nr.10.

[4] Jenkins, *Kurze Geschichte*, 10.

[5] Jenkins, *Kurze Geschichte*, 2.

[6] L. Grant McClung, Jr., "Missiology," *Dictionary of Pentecostal and Charismatic Movements*, eds. Stanley Burgess, Gary McGee, and Patrick H. Alexander (Grand Rapids: Zondervan, 1988), 608.

[7] Hans Anstein, *Nicht durch Heer oder Kraft: 125 Jahre Basler Mission 1815-1940* (Basel: Missionsbuchhandlung, 1940), 11.

[8] An informative book on the role of women in the Basel Mission has been written by Waltraud Ch. Haas, *Erlitten und erstritten. Der Befreiungsweg von Frauen in der Basler Mission 1816-1966* (Basel: Basileia Verlag, 1994). See for example the testimony of Liselotte Velan, 158.

[9] Michael Bergunder, *Die südindische Pfingstbewegung im 20. Jahrhundert*, Studien zur Interkulturellen Geschichte des Christentums 113 (Frankfurt a.M.: Peter Lang, 1999), 241-45.

[10] M. Bergunder, *Die südindische Pfingstbewegung*, 244.

[11] The attacks on the World Trade Center in New York on September 11, 2001 are a clear illustration of a revolt against Western economic power. The symbolism of the two towers collapsing needed no interpretation. Similarly, the suicide bombings in the Near East display a flagrant disregard for Western values by relativizing the importance of an individual and, consequently, easily instill terror to people of Western cultures. People that may have considered themselves privileged and unique, but in fact experience the loss of commonly held values in postmodern societies.

[12] Samuel P. Huntington, *The Clash of Civilizations and the Remaking of World Order* (London: Simon and Schuster, 1996).

[13] Huntington, *The Clash of Civilizations*, 91.

[14] Huntington, *The Clash of Civilizations*, 92 (italics his), referring to Joseph S. Nye, Jr., "The Changing Nature of World Power," *Political Science Quarterly* 105 (Summer 1990), 181-82.

[15] Jenkins, *Kurze Geschichte*, 7-8.

[16] Anstein, *Nicht durch Heer*, 44.

[17] Huntington, *The Clash of Civilizations*, 96.

[18] Huntington, *The Clash of Civilizations*, 97, quoting Fareed Zakaria, "Culture Is Destiny: A Conversation with Lee Kuan Yew," *Foreign Affairs* 73 (March/April 1994), 118.

[19] Anstein, *Nicht durch Heer*, 52-53.

[20] Young-Gi Hong, "Church and Mission: A Pentecostal Perspective," *International Review of Missions* XC, no. 358 (July 2001), 289-308.

[21] Hong, "Church and Mission," 293.

[22] Hong, "Church and Mission," 295.

[23] R. Kurtz, ed. *Stark und Treu. Die Kraft des Evangeliums auf Kalimantan,* Vierteljahresheft für die Mitglieder der Quartalskollekte der Basler Mission (Basel: Basler Mission, 1951/3).

[24] Anstein, *Nicht durch Heer,* 98.

[25] Michael Bergunder, "Miracle Healing and Exorcism: The South Indian Pentecostal Movement in the Context of Popular Hinduism," *International Review of Mission* XC no. 356/357 (January/April 2001), 111.

[26] Allan H. Anderson, "The Gospel and Culture in Pentecostal Mission in the Third World" (a paper presented at the 9th Conference of the European Pentecostal Charismatic Research Conference, Hamburg 1999, available at http://www.epcra.ch/papers/Hamburg99/allenhanderson.html).

Part II

CONTEXT

A MODEL FOR PRESENTING THE GOSPEL TO PANTHEISTS

Eiko Takamizawa

1. Pantheism and World Religions

Among various religious traditions and emerging religious groups, Judeo-Christian religions are distinct in their belief in the absolute and personal God.[1] In other words, the denial of the absolute and personal Being is the common fundamental belief of other religions. For example, Hinduism among some Upanishads observed a basic view that the universe is one entity. In this monistic view, all the gods and objects in the universe were conceived to be elements derived by self-distribution from one originative source, a cosmic person or cow, sacrificing itself by self-dismemberment.[2] There are billions of deities in Hinduism, but they hold little distinction from all other creatures. George Braswell points out that the pantheistic nature of Hinduism is that "God, principle, humankind, animals and nature are all basically one. A primary goal of Hinduism is union or absorption of all the parts into the whole."[3]

Buddhism too, especially in the Hinayana sect which has been influenced less by the Judeo-Christian worldview, demonstrates little concern for life beyond this world.[4] Buddha's primary teaching was centered on life philosophy, and does not emphasize the concept of eternity or that of creator God.[5] Confucianism is basically the religious and ethical code that teaches the importance of "xiao," honoring parents, ancestors and elders. Confucius did hold to a concept of heaven. However, it was influenced by the primal Chinese worldview which they called *shangdi*, "the ruler on high." David Noss and John Noss explain its pantheistic nature as follows,

This Ruler on High...was a sort of ancestral figure, a vaguely conceived being located in the upper regions of the sky; he was far from being the Almighty God of Western religions, it seems , for he had no clearly defined character and sent down no messages preserved in scriptures.[6]

Taoism is regarded as one form of pantheism in its belief in the impersonal being. *Tao*, "the way," is a name for the "absolute cosmic law," or the "order of the universe." *Tao* is the path the whole universe flows out of and follows, and all things evolve from it. *Tao* is at once immanent and transcendent; it includes and pervades all that exists. Yet Taoism denies that *Tao* is a personal being. This denial of personality in the supreme being is identical with that of pantheism.[7] Communism, which can be regarded as a religion, for it has religious elements, such as a founder, believers, a belief system, eschatology, organization and so forth, belongs to the same category. Communism is based on the materialistic worldview of history, which also denies the absolute God, the Creator. In this sense, Communism shares the common worldview with pantheism.

As observed above, pantheism provides the fundamental worldview to a variety of religions. This inclusive nature is expressed in the introduction of the World Pantheist Movement,

But almost all of what we say applies to all the spiritual orientations that find shelter in the WPM [World Pantheist Movement]. They include scientific pantheism, religious humanism, religious naturalism, religious atheism, deep ecology, nature-worship, philosophical Taoism, modern Stoicism, Gaian religion, as well as to those forms of wicca and paganism that see magic and the gods as symbols rather than realities, also Western forms of Buddhism that celebrate nature and everyday life, and to those in Unitarian Universalism or paganism who do not believe in supernatural beings, organizational structure, doctrine, salvation, eschatology and so forth.[8]

Thus, to understand pantheism and to develop effective strategies to meet the pantheistic worldview is a crucial and urgent task for Christian mission today.

2. Pan-Theology

Varieties of pantheism exist. There is the ancient form of Taoism and transcendental pantheism represented by Spinoza, logical pantheism represented by Hegel, Panentheism as a distinct form of pantheism, and the postmodern version of the New Age movement.[9] In spite of the variety of streams and forms, one common feature is observed; the denial of a personal and absolute god. Theists believe god is self-sufficient, non-contingent and the prime mover with personality. Pantheists also believe in the cosmic being as god. However, they do not recognize the personality of the deity. Because of this difference in worldview between pantheism and Christianity, the pantheistic cosmology, anthropology, soteriology, eschatology and other areas of theology are different from biblical ones. In the following section, the nature of "pan-theology" will be discussed with a focus on primary areas of theology.

2.1 Pan-Theology Proper

Pantheists believe in a divine being called the "divine unity" of the universe. Even though they use the term "being," they deny the personality of the divine being. This pantheistic position shows an internal conflict in its term and concept. The term "theism" presupposes God, but the pantheists deny a god who has personality. Michael Levine explains the confusion,

> [P]antheism is non-theistic, but it is not atheistic. It is a form of non-theistic monotheism, or even non-personal theism. It is the belief in one God, a God identical to the all-inclusive Unity, but pantheists (generally) do not believe God is a person or anything like a person.[10]

They explain the logic by creating the concept of god as an impersonal being, which is also a composition of two conflicting concepts. Considering the fact that the term "god" generically implies the personal being, pantheists' denial of the personality of God seems logically inconsistent.

In addition, to discuss God at all, the definition of the term needs to be clarified. The existence of God, for instance, is determined only when the definition of the term is identified. In order to avoid confusion, some pantheists substituted the term pantheos with the impersonal expression, "divine unity." However, there is no one common definition of the term "god" among the diverse pantheistic groups. Therefore, there is also no attribute articulated for the term "divine unity." In this regard, pantheists face two problems at the outset of developing their theology. The first is their belief in the divine being and their denial of its personality. The second is their ambiguous definition of the term *theos*. Without any clarification of the definition, not even the existence of such a being can be identified.

2.2 Pan-Anthropology

By refusing the idea of a creator and his creation, pantheists also deny the origin of humans as God's creation. Humans, for pantheists, are a mere part of the universe. All existence is explained in the model of raindrops that fall into the ocean and become one with it.[11] Edward Pace elucidates this: "Human personality is a mere illusion: what we call the individual man is only one of the countless fragments that make up the Divine Being; and since the All is impersonal no single part of it can validly claim personality."[12]   In pantheism, the value of one person or one element in the universe does not carry any value of its own. Thus, pantheism, contradictory to its emphasis, degrades the value of nature and its members.

2.3 Pan-Soteriology

Pantheists consider evil as a product of God's laws. When God is not considered as a moral standard, there is also no evil. Due to the lack of a moral standard, such as God's law or his righteousness, pantheists recognize as evil that which disturbs the divine all-inclusive "unity" of the universe. Thus, pantheists do not see the necessity of salvation from sin or punishment. They regard the term "salvation" as applicable only to a theistic concept. The ultimate achievement for them is to fulfill the "essential nature." Happiness is determined by how well one fulfills the "essential nature" in the harmony and in the order of the "divine unity."[13]

Another significant soteriological point for pantheists is the denial of life after death. Pantheists deny God as the cosmic personal being; they also reject the idea of personal immortality. Levine states,

> Historically, the denial of personal immortality is one of pantheism's most distinctive features. This is partly because it is in clear opposition to the theistic view. But, it is primarily significant because it is constitutive of the pantheist's world-view and ethos, and so has implications for pantheistic practice.[14]

Because of these points pantheism is often put in the atheistic circle. Pantheists actually believe in immortality, but in an impersonal sense. They assert that it is natural for humans to long for impersonal immortality, just as theists and atheists desire to be remembered or remain as another part of matter after their physical death. For pantheists, death is the time for them to return and merge back to God. Levine furthers explains the idea, quoting Jeffers:

> What is distinctively significant is the recognition of the individual as a part of the Unity—what Jeffers calls "the one organic whole...this one God." The parts "change and pass, or die, people and races and rocks and stars," but the whole remains.... All its parts are different expression of the same energy, and they are all in communication with each other, influencing each other, therefore parts of one organic whole.[15]

2.4 Pan-Christology

If sin is not acknowledged, no savior is expected by pantheists. In the denial of the personality of God, there is no possibility of any one (e.g., his Son) coming to earth. Since pantheists do not expect a savior to come, any who would claim to be one may be seen as arrogant and controlling.

2.5 Pan-Ecclesiology

The structure of the organization in pantheism is not as developed as other religious organizations. This is due to the fact that pantheism is spread more as a worldview than as a religious organization which would have scriptures, doctrines and organizations. Without having an organizational structure, pantheism has been increasing its influence and its membership today especially as folk practice within the formal religions. Stephen C. Neil estimates that 40% of the world's population bases their lives on animistic thinking which eventually denies the absolute transcendent being. Van Rheenen even considers the number that Neil counts as a low estimate.[16] This means that almost a half of the total population holds pantheistic worldview. This is possible because of the doctrinal ambiguity of pantheism. Pantheism also offers a broader invitation to potential followers, presenting its inclusive and flexible nature. The WPM exposes the inclusive nature as follows:

Do you find it impossible to believe in supernatural beings, and difficult to conceive of anything more worthy of reverence than the beauty of nature or the power of the universe? If you answered yes to these questions, then you will feel thoroughly at home in the World Pantheist Movement. Our caring and celebratory approach focuses on nature rather than the supernatural, on what we can see and do and live out rather than on invisible entities that we can only imagine.[17]

2.6 Pan-Eschatology

Pantheism holds to a monistic cosmology, and does not concern itself beyond the universe. The universe itself is divine. Therefore, heaven is not of interest for pantheists. The universe was there from the beginning, just as the biblical God claims, "I am that I am." Eschatology is not related to the end of time when God will consummate all evil or the material universe. The ultimate goal for pantheists is the state of mind, that is, to be in perfect harmony with the "divine unity."[18] There is no concept of judgment, nor concept of evil as theistic religions hold. There is no heaven that God rules, other than the present universe. There is no God who judges the sinful. Thus, entering heaven is not of interest for pantheists. Rather, the ultimate goal is to attain perfect peace of mind, which can be possible when one has a right relationship with the "divine unity."[19]

Pantheism thus described is contrasted with Christian theism. Some of the points have totally different perspectives from one another, while others seem just to substitute the theistic terms with pantheistic terms. These similarities and differences make it difficult for pantheists to pursue Christian truth, according to Christian scripture and doctrine.

3. Gospel Presentation to Pantheists

In this section, the key points and an example for presenting the gospel to pantheists will be introduced.

3.1 God as the Absolute Transcendent Being and the Creator

The pantheists identify God with the universe or the "divine Unity" within the universe. In their denial of the creator, pantheists discard all the personal attributes of God. Consequently, the definition of the pantheistic "god" becomes obscure, which allows pantheists to identify god with nature itself. Therefore, clarifying the identity of God as the creator and articulating all his personal attributes is a crucial initial step for presenting the gospel to pantheists (Diagram 1). God, the creator, the "prime mover," and the "first cause," and his sovereignty over all his creatures need to be clearly addressed.

Most pantheists take the monistic position which holds the universe is the only reality. In order for them to understand the Christian gospel, creating the mental realm for the reality beyond the universe is an imperative step. As the Scripture declares, God's realm is beyond the material universe.[20] Secondly, God's personal attributes should be clearly discussed. God's action, disposition and sovereignty are needed to emphasize his personality: 1) Action: God creates, rules, communicates, acts, performs miracles, reveals and has fellowship with humans; 2) His dispositional attributes: loving, righteous, holy, caring, merciful, gentle, bold, jealous and many others; and 3) His sovereignty: omnipotent, omniscient and omnipresent. God himself is infinite, thus, his attributes should be understood as unlimited.

Diagram 1

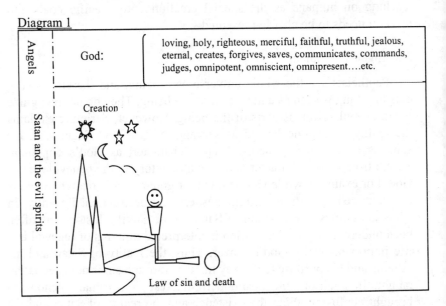

3.2 Human as Heirs of the Creator

Christian teaching on the origin of humans renders the highest value to humanity. While pantheists do not recognize the individual value of each person, the Scripture teaches that each individual is created in the image of God. Carrying the image of God implies that we inherit God's life and his attributes and that we are heirs of God. Just as children resemble their parents, the fact that humans retain the image of God suggests that humans are God's children. While pantheists hold that humans are not different from other creatures, the Scripture teaches that humans are a special creation in *imago Dei*. God commissioned humans to name and administrate all other creation. Thus, they are not a mere part of the universe, but ones who are to administrate the universe. This view on humans and their position and task is not observed in pantheism.

Not only is the origin of humans different in pantheism and Christianity, but the purpose for which humanity was created is different. As pantheism denies the personal God and creator, the purpose of the existence of the universe is not certain. Just as the universe is something that "flows forth" without a specific reason, humans do not find the purpose and goal of their existence in the pantheistic view. In this outlook, a possible goal for humans is to maintain the divine Unity of the universe, which the pantheists call their god. The scriptural teaching on humans as the special creation with specific goals and mission needs to be clearly presented.

3.3 Angels and Satan

Pantheists see the whole universe as a being, and therefore every existing thing is seen as a mere part of the being. They do not recognize Satan or evil spirits as parts of the being. However, Scripture explains the reality of angelic beings as servants of God and Satan with his subjects as God's opponents. Satan's character, as God's opponent, differs from God's character and is contradictory to the benevolence of God. For example, while God is loving, righteous and creative, Satan is characterized by hatred, unrighteousness and destruction. Recently, in Christian circles, the position of Satan in the salvific history has often been underemphasized. Salvation is interpreted in terms of renewal and life improvement by God's power. Thus, the reality of Satan and his scheme and his purpose to destroy humans through sin is not adequately taught. In addition, the postmodern interest in spiritual phenomena brought confusion about the existence and the reality of Satan and the evil spirits. The New Age movement as a contemporary expression of pantheism is one of the phenomena related to this. The biblical worldview, articulating the reality and position of angels, Satan, and evil spirits needs to be explained. In order to avoid the animistic perspective that views Satan and God in conflict with similar power, Christian should identify Satan as a part of God's creation, and yet he rebelled against God. The Satan's rebellion will result in the final judgment. Thus, God's salvific plan for humanity is to be clearly understood from the "spiritual" perspective.

3.4 Sin and Salvation

Pantheists do not have concern for sin; they consider sin as an outcome of theistic belief.[21] Scripture describes the origin of sin as the first human's disbelief and disobedience to God's word, and the consequential separation between God and humans. When the first humans chose to believe Satan's words and follow his suggestions, they came under the control of Satan. At this moment humanity lost its relationship with God and all his inheritance. The restoration of the relationship between the created humans and the creator is thus possible only by the worshipper's absolute submission to his word. The fall degraded the human position from heir of God to slave of sin.

Eternal life is one of God's attributes (upper level in the Diagram 1). Once humans were separated from God, their immortality was also lost. Therefore, sin became the cause of death for humans. Paul calls this "the law of sin and death" (Rom 8:2). Satan causes death, but he was not wrong in bringing death to the sinners. The only person who does not deserve death is the sinless Son of God. Thus, the fallen creation needs a savior to come for the restoration of the original states of *imago Dei*.

3.5 The Word of God

The pantheistic "god," as an impersonal being, does not communicate with humans in the same way as the biblical God communicates with them. Scripture characterizes the biblical God. He created the whole universe with his word; He commanded the first humans not to take fruit from one tree in the center of the garden. The sin of humankind as studied above was disbelief and disobedience to God's word. Therefore, in God's salvific plan, the word played a significant role in the restoration of the broken position of the human beings. Noah was chosen to be God's vessel of salvation, for he believed what God spoke about the flood and prepared the ark despite the ridicule of his neighbors. Abraham believed in God who commanded him to leave his own land. Abraham followed without knowing where he was going. Abraham's whole life, including his willingness to sacrifice Isaac for the Lord, was a test of his belief and obedience to God's word. God made a covenant with those who listened and obeyed him. Therefore, as a covenant people, Israel was given his word as an opportunity to demonstrate their belief and obedience.

Diagram 2

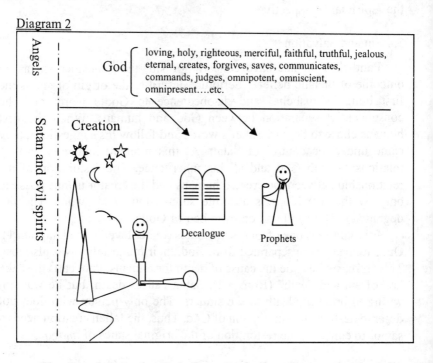

The Decalogue, the Ten Commandments, is not merely a list of prohibitions or religious commands for God's pleasure. The Decalogue has significance in reminding Israelites of their identity as God's people. It reminded them of God's absoluteness as an almighty God (the first commandment); his sovereignty and distinctiveness over all the creation (the second); his nature with all the authority as God, the sovereign Lord for all the creation (the third); the purpose of human existence to glorify and worship God (the fourth); respecting parents would eventually reminds the Israelites of God, the creator (the fifth); the prohibition of murdering, adultery, stealing, false witnessing and coveting—all to remind the Israelites that they were originally created in the *imago Dei*, and that they are not supposed to do what Satan would do.

The Israelites, therefore, as witnesses of God and priests for fallen humanity, were to demonstrate God's character. The list of sinful acts in the latter part of the Decalogue was to bring the identity of *imago Dei* back to the covenant people. However, the Israelites continued to fail in fulfilling the law. Their history was rebellious. The Israelites lost the ark of covenant and the tablet of the Decalogue written by God's hand.

The word of God was the means for God's revelation and the means for the Israelites to show their faith and obedience to God. When the law was neglected and lost, God sent prophets to his people to communicate with them. Prophecies were/are not merely the foretelling of future events. These are the words of God which encourage, direct, help, correct and rebuke his people. When prophets confronted the sin of the Israelites, they were rejected and persecuted by them. Thus, hopeless humanity needed the savior, the Son of God to come down to the earth.

3.6 Jesus Christ, the Son of God

Diagram 3

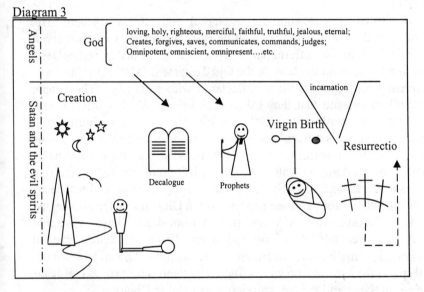

In pantheism, no savior is expected for they do not recognize the need for salvation. To the contrary, the newly emerging religious cults often advocate their own messiah figures, who claim to be the representatives of God.[22] It is important to know the uniqueness of Jesus Christ as the true Son of God and also as the Messiah for humanity. The uniqueness of Jesus is first observed in the Old Testament prophecies about him. Scholars have identified more than 300 Messianic prophecies in the Old Testament.[23] Being the Son of God cannot be sustained just by self declaration. Jesus Christ fulfilled all the messianic prophecies given throughout the Old Testament period, and by doing so, he proved to be the one whom God promised for the redemption of mankind.

The virgin birth of Jesus Christ needs to be understood as the evidence of his divine origin. If Jesus Christ was born of human parents, he is not distinct from any ordinary human being who is under the curse of sin. If Jesus came directly from heaven, he cannot be the incarnated savior. Just as human life starts from an egg, Jesus' life was conceived in Mary's womb, but without the human paternal element. Thus, Jesus' divine origin is demonstrated in his virgin birth.

His sinless life is another proof of his divinity. Nobody could find any crime, nor any charge for punishment in Jesus (Matt 27:4; Luke 23:4, 14, 22; John 18:38, etc). The only charge against Jesus was his claim to be the king of the Jews. The centurion who witnessed Jesus Christ's crucifixion also declared that Jesus is the true Son of God (Mark 15:39).

His teaching was supreme by moral and ethical standard. His morality and moral teaching cannot be easily criticized. Criticism about Christians is to be differentiated from that of Jesus' teaching. His teaching fulfilled all the laws in the Old Testament (Matt 5:17), and was different from others for it was declared with authority. "The people were all so amazed that they asked each other, 'What is this? A new teaching—and with authority!'" (Mark 1:27). This authority was demonstrated in his miraculous deeds. Jesus controlled nature in various miracles such as transforming the water into wine, calming the storms by commands, walking on water, the multiplication of two fishes and five loaves of bread, and so forth. These miraculous deeds proved that Jesus is the one who is above nature (upper level in Diagram 3). He also healed the sick, forgave sins and raised people from dead. These prove that Jesus is above "the law of sin and death" (Rom 8:2, upper level in Diagram 2). Finally, Jesus overcame the temptation of Satan and cast out evil spirits from those who were afflicted by them. This proves that Jesus is beyond Satan and the evil spirits (upper level in Diagram 3).

His death was the mission from Father God. It was prophesied in the Old Testament at different times in history and fulfilled in Jesus' death on the cross. It is interpreted in various ways: Jesus died to propitiate God, to satisfy God's holiness, to redeem human life, and to be the substitute for the human punishment for their sin. Another perspective is that Satan, the accuser and the principality and power of this world, has brought death to sinful humans throughout history. However, if death is the result of sin as explained in the law of sin and death, Jesus' death should not have occurred for he was sinless. Satan, by killing the sinless Son of God, made the greatest mistake. Satan lost his right and dominion and power over this world. Thus, Jesus could win the victory over Satan only through his death. His death propitiated God's wrath against sin, substituted humans punishment, and at the same time he deprived Satan of his power over this world.

Jesus died physically. However, he, as the sinless one, did not have to remain dead, as Acts 2:24 reads: "But God raised him from the dead, freeing him from the agony of death, because it was impossible for death to keep its hold on him." He was resurrected from the dead, and appeared to his disciples. His resurrection is the evidence and promise for the victory over "sin and death." His resurrection is not a mere supernatural phenomenon or mystery of nature, as pantheists may interpret. It was one of the primary purposes of his incarnation; and it is the means for God to save fallen sinners from eternal punishment. Therefore, various critiques were brought forth by those who wanted to deny the Christian belief: the swoon theory, the stealing theory, the wrong tomb theory, the phantasm theory and others. However, they were proven to be false accusations against the biblical records.[24] Pantheists are faced with this proven fact that Jesus Christ historically resurrected.[25]

3.7 Pentecost and the Holy Spirit

Diagram 4

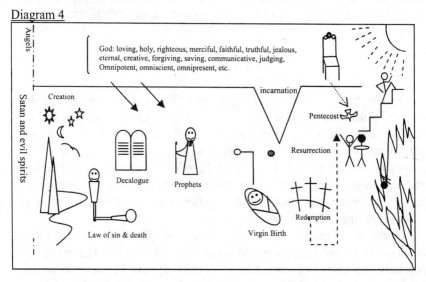

Since the bondage of sin and death was broken, humans may receive the indwelling Spirit of God. The immanence of the transcendent God was made possible in the experience of Pentecost recorded in the book of Acts. Pantheists, who believe in the immanence and perfection of their god, cannot still deny the fact of evil in the present world. Pantheists need a solution for the reality of evil in the world. Logically, the belief in the immanence of God leaves no further expectation for God's intervention. To the contrary, Christian teaching on the descent of the Holy Spirit and his indwelling the believers gives the assurance of salvation through Christ, his presence in them, and the hope of eternal life as proven by his resurrection. The Holy Spirit is not an unknown spiritual entity, as pantheists may believe. The Holy Spirit gives life, reveals the divine truth, works on human conscience, convicts humans of sin, helps bring humans to repentance and faith, teaches what the Scriptures say, heals the sick and comforts the hurt, empowers believers in witnessing, and seals believers with the promise of eternal life. Thus, the transcendent God can indwell the believer through the presence of the Holy Spirit.   The immanence of the transcendent God is what the pantheists pursue, while their concept on crucial issues such as evil and life after death remain eluded. Christians can present the truth revealed by the living God, encompassing all aspects of human life and history to the pantheists, as being comprehensive and coherent. Talking to the Athenians, Apostle Paul said, "He [God] is not far from each of us. For in him we live and move and have our being" (Acts 17:27b, 28).

4. Conclusion

Today, people live according to two different values: one is the spiritual phenomenon of postmodernity, and the other is secularization, the persisting influence of the Age of Enlightenment. In this setting, pantheism has the potential to increase its influence because of its charming mixture of these two values. People who cannot believe in God and the gospel   of Jesus Christ are exposed to the temptation of pantheism more and more; and pantheism's acceptance of various religious forms makes it very attractive.

Christian churches in Asia, in the very heart of the pantheist territory, must hold firmly to the uniqueness of the Christian truth and proclaim the gospel of Jesus Christ, as the only way revealed to people by the true living God. Then pantheists will see the truth which human wisdom and speculation cannot attain. By restoring the *imago Dei* offered by Father God, through the way that Jesus the Son prepared, and with the help of the immanent Spirit of God, humankind will see the true beauty of nature and the value of the whole creation revealed to bring glory to God, the creator.

---

[1] Islam is included in this category for it also shares the Judeo-Christian heritage.

[2] David S. Noss and John B. Noss, *A History of the World's Religions*, 9th ed. (New York: Macmillan, 1990), 101.

[3] George W. Braswell, Jr. *Understanding World Religions: A Christian Perspective* (Nashville, TN: Broadman, 1983), 193.

[4] The fact that Mahayana Buddhism and Pure Land Buddhism were developed in the Tang Dynasty in China provides a possibility of Nestorian influence, for Nestorian Christianity as well as other foreign religions were active in Siang, the capital city. Thus, their less strict approach to the Buddha's teaching as Hinayana Buddhism is explained.

[5] The primary teachings of Buddha include the "four noble truths" and "eightfold right path" that focus on mental discipline and ethical actions for attaining Nirvana.

[6] Noss & Noss, 280.

[7] David Burnett, *Clash of Worlds: A Christian's Handbook on Cultures, World Religions and Evangelism* (Nashville, TN: Oliver Nelson, 1992), 92.

[8] "World Pantheist Movement" (www.pantheism.net/index.htm), checked: Jan 16, 2003.

[9] Edward A. Pace, "Definition of Pantheism" (www.ourladyswarriors.org/dissent/defpanth.htm), checked: Nov. 15, 2002.

[10] Michael Levine, "Pantheism," *Stanford Encyclopedia of Philosophy*, ed. Edward N. Zalta, winter 2002 ed. (http://plato.stanford.edu/entries/pantheism), checked: Aug. 14, 2002.

[11] Ernest Valea, "Critical Considerations Regarding Pantheist Religions and Philosophy" (www.comparativereligion.com/pantheism.html), checked: Nov. 15, 2002.

[12] Pace, 4.

[13] Levine, 11-12.

[14] Levine, 13.

[15] Ibid., 14.

[16] Van Rheenen, *Communicating Christ in Animistic Context* (Grand Rapids, MI: Baker, 1991), 25.

[17] "World Pantheistic Movement" (www.pantheism.net/index.htm).

[18] Ibid.

[19] Levine, 18.

[20] What to call this realm can differ according to the audience. For pantheists as a contrast with a material universe "spiritual universe" can be one way of conceptualization.

[21] Levine, 8.

[22] The Unification Church in Korea and the Science of Happiness in Japan are some examples of this category.

[23] Herbert Lockyer, "Prophecy," *Nelson's Illustrated Bible Dictionary* (Nashville: T. Nelson, 1986) contained in *PC Study Bible*, version 3.0 (Biblesoft, 1993-1999) identifies over 300 Messianic prophecies in the Bible fulfilled in the life of Jesus Christ. Specific details given by these prophecies include his tribe (Gen 49:10), his birthplace (Mic 5:2), dates of his birth and death (Dan 9:25-26), his forerunner John the Baptist (Mal 3:1; 4:5; Matt 11:10), his career and ministry (Isa 52:13-53:12), his crucifixion (Ps 22:1-18), his resurrection (Ps 16:8-11; Acts 2:25-28), his ascension (Ps 2; Acts 13:33), and his exaltation as a priest-king (Ps 110; Acts 2:34). The kingly magnificence of his second coming is also graphically portrayed. Ps 2; 45, and Ps. 110 picture his conquest and dominion over the nations. His kingdom is characterized in Ps 72. Events leading up to and including the first and second advents of Christ are described in the two burdens of the prophet Zechariah (Zech 9-11; 12:1-14:21).

[24] Murray J. Harris, *Three Crucial Questions about Jesus* (Grand Rapids, MI: Baker, 1994) discusses more on this in his.

[25] Harris, 31-64.

DOING CHRIST'S MISSION
IN THE PLURALISTIC CONTEXT OF ASIA:
A CRITICAL DIALOGUE
WITH SOME ASIAN CHRISTOLOGIES

Veli-Matti Kärkkäinen

1. The Critical Asian Principle

There is a quiet determination among Asian Christians that their commitment to Jesus Christ and their words about Jesus Christ must be responsible to the life they live in Asia today. Such theology is called a living theology.... Asian theology seeks to take the encounter between life in Asia and the Word of God seriously.[1]

With these words Kosuke Koyama, one of the most well known Asian theologians from Japan, introduces an anthology of essays focusing on the themes of emerging Asian theologies. While Asia is the cradle of most major religions in the world, with regard to Christian theology it was not until the last part of the twentieth century that major contributions began to emerge on a larger scale. What is distinctive about the Asian context is the continuous correlation between Christian theology and the pluralism of Asian religiosity. Recently, many Asian churches have been on the forefront of ecumenism both with regard to other churches and to other religions. The groundbreaking work of the Ecumenical Association of Third World Theologians (EAOTWT), founded in 1976, has especially fostered both interreligious and ecumenical activities.[2]

During the years I lived and taught in Bangkok, Thailand, I used to go jogging early in the morning to avoid the deadly heat of the sun.

Most often, the route I took passed three different worship centers: first a huge Thai Buddhist temple, then an Islamic mosque, and finally a little bit further down the street, a Catholic church. The Buddhist monks were collecting morning offerings from grandparents, from the houses along the street, and the owners of small businesses who set up their shops around five a.m. and went first to burn incense to the spirits. As devoted Buddhists they knew that spirits or gods did not exist, but for a pluralistically oriented Asian, paying homage to powers like that did not pose a problem. Their attitude toward me, a theologian and teacher of a foreign religion was always friendly and affirming. After all, promoting religion, most any religion, contributes to the well-being and safety of the community.

In any Asian country, Christians live in a minority position. This fact has implications for Asian theologies when compared to European and U.S. theologies, which are often written from the standpoint of Christianity being a major force in the society. The thrust of Asian theology is to inquire into the identity of Christianity *vis-à-vis* other religious confessions. Kosuke Koyama aptly notes the various forces that shape Asian Christianity as Asians are addressing the question, "but who do you say I am?" (Matt 16:15):

> This question comes to Asian Christians, who live in a world of great religious traditions, modernization impacts, ideologies of the left and right, international conflicts, hunger, poverty, militarism, and racism. Within these confusing and brutal realities of history, the question comes to them. Here the depth of soul of the East is challenged to engage in a serious dialogue with the Word of God. Jesus refuses to be treated superficially.[3]

Now the question comes to us, as urgent as ever: How do we do Christ's mission in an environment as pluralistic as this? What are the theological and pastoral parameters? What is the content of our proclamation? Since no single presentation is able to address all of these questions and the many corollary issues (such as the challenge of contextualizing Christian mission for Asians), I will limit my discussion to exploring the meaning of the person of Jesus Christ in the context of the pluralism of Asia. I will engage in a critical dialogue with one of the leading Asian theologians, Stanley J. Samartha, who has written extensively on the challenge of pluralism in Asia from a Christological perspective. Ordained in the Church of South India and involved in theological teaching in his earlier years, Samartha has exercised considerable influence through his post as Director of the

Dialogue Programme of the World Council of Churches, which he initiated. Throughout his life, Samartha has advocated dialogue among world religions as the demand of our age. There are three main reasons why I have selected Samartha as my dialogue partner. First of all, he represents a moderate, mainline pluralistic approach and as such is a representative figure. Second, through his extensive ecumenical activities his ideas are well known and influential. Third, he has spoken extensively on this relationship. On the basis of this dialogue, my aim in this discussion is to put forth a number of theses for the development of a responsible Evangelical theology of mission.

2. "The Unbound Christ"

One of Samartha's major areas of interest in the beginning stages of his career was the study of an unprecedented interest in the person of Christ in the so-called Indian Renaissance or Neo-Hindu reform. During the nineteenth century and the first part of the twentieth century, various Hindu personalities came to acknowledge Christ in relation to their own religious background and context. Samartha describes the Christ acknowledged by Neo-Hinduism as an "unbound" Christ. What he means by that is that while many attach themselves to the person of Jesus Christ, they usually detach that person from the institutional church, which for them does not represent the quintessence of Christ's religion. They often complain that the church of Jesus' followers is either a hierarchical institution or a Western, even colonial power system:

> The Christ acknowledged by Hinduism is often a churchless Christ. For that matter, the Christ acknowledged by Hinduism is often a Christ delivered from the encumbrances of numerous "bonds" with which he is laden by traditional Christianity—whether it be a matter of applauding his message while rejecting the Christian claim to his person, or of receiving from him as one divine manifestation among others in a catalog of divine descents (*avatara*) as varied as it is extensive.[4]

Samartha has become more and more weary of the widespread hostile attitude of Christianity to other religions: "Although most Christians today are unwilling to take a totally negative attitude toward neighbors of other faiths, there seems to be a good deal of hesitation on the part of many to reexamine the basis of their exclusive claims on behalf of Christ. The place of Christ in a multireligious society becomes, therefore, an important issue in the search for a new theology of religions."[5]

In his later main work *One Christ—Many Religions: Toward a Revised Christology*,[6] Samartha argues that christocentrism is applicable only to Christians, whereas it can never be considered as the only way to the mystery of the divine. Christocentrism cannot then be the norm by which the various religious traditions are valued. All various approaches to the divine have their validity.

Samartha observes that a process of rejecting exclusive claims and seeking new ways of understanding the relationship of Jesus Christ to God and humanity is already underway. There is a shift from the "normative exclusiveness" of Christ to what he calls the "relational distinctiveness" of Christ. The term "relational" refers to the fact that Christ does not remain unrelated to neighbors of other faiths, while "distinctive" denotes the recognition of the distinctiveness of the great religious traditions as different responses to the mystery of God.

Samartha argues that the Hindu and the Christian have their own particularly distinctive contributions to make to the common quest for truth. The problem of religious exclusivism (according to which only those who believe in Christ will be saved), is that it cannot explain why a God whose love and justice are universal would reveal the way of salvation only through one savior, one people and one book. Samartha wonders why the authority of one book should be thought binding for other faith communities with their own books, some of them even older than the New Testament. It is, rather, the limited view of Christians that argues for that kind of limitation in God's dealing with humankind he believes. The claim for the exclusive truth in Christianity means putting religion in the prison of history. According to Samartha, genuine pluralism does not relativize the truth; the only thing that can make the truth relative is the different responses by different people. The truth is no one's privilege. The goal of ecumenism and interreligious dialogue is to create a "truly universal community" that will cut across boundaries of nations and religions.

The drive behind the interreligious dialogue is not only the common search for the truth but also the changed situation in the world in which religions have found themselves caught up in a worldwide struggle against injustice. Interreligious dialogue must seek after truth not only for its own sake but also in order to promote justice, peace and equality. There can be no lasting justice, Samartha envisions, unless rooted in divine truth, and there is no authentic divine truth that does not produce the fruit of social justice.

3. The Sense of Mystery

In the context of India and many other Asian countries where there is a growing sense of religious tolerance but increased and intensified political and social intolerance, Samartha contends that there is a need for a Christology that is based on something other than clearly defined doctrinal formulations. He adds that in order for Christology to take root in Asian soil, the specific nature of the Asian mindset has to be taken into consideration. This is where the concept of "Mystery" is introduced into his theological discourse. Any attempt to formulate such a Christology should take into account at least two factors that have emerged out of Asia's long history of multireligious life. One is the acceptance of a sense of "Mystery" and the other the rejection of an exclusive attitude where ultimate matters are concerned. However, when it comes to the conception of mystery in Asian thought, it has to be noted that it does not denote something that fills the gaps in rational knowledge. Rather, Mystery provides the ontological basis for tolerance, which would otherwise run the risk of becoming uncritical friendliness.

> This Mystery, the Truth of the Truth (*Satyasya Satyam*), *is* the transcendent Center that remains always beyond and greater than apprehensions of it even in the sum total of those apprehensions. It is beyond cognitive knowledge (*tarka*) but it is open to vision (*dristi*) and intuition (*anubhava*). It is near yet far, knowable yet unknowable, intimate yet ultimate and, according to one particular Hindu view, cannot even be described as "one." It is "not-two" (*advaita*), indicating thereby that diversity is within the heart of Being itself and therefore may be intrinsic to human nature as well.[7]

The emphasis on Mystery is not meant as an escape from the need for rational inquiry, but it insists that the rational is not the only way to do theology. The mystical and the aesthetic also have their necessary contributions to theology. Samartha believes that Mystery lies beyond the dichotomy of theistic versus nontheistic. "Mystery is an ontological status to be accepted, nor an epistemological problem to be solved. Without a sense of Mystery, *Theos* [Greek term for god] cannot remain *Theos*, nor *Sat* [Hindi term for god] remain *Sat*, nor can Ultimate Reality remain ultimate."[8]

One strand of Hinduism, for example, has described this Mystery as *sat-cit-ananda*, "truth-consciousness-bliss." This is one way of responding to Mystery in a particular setting that differs from that of the early Christian centuries. The Christian doctrine of the Trinity with Jesus Christ as the self-revelation of God is a way of approaching the Mystery in a particular historical context. The terms *Sat* and *Theos* could be regarded as two responses to the same Mystery in two cultural settings concludes Samartha.

The nature of Mystery is such that any claim on the part of one religious community to have exclusive or unique knowledge becomes inadmissible. Samartha strongly believes that exclusive attitude erects a fence around the Mystery. Exclusiveness also creates dichotomies between different religious communities and leaves little room for the nonrational elements in religious life, such as the mystical, the aesthetic, meditation and rituals. Furthermore, exclusive claims isolate the community of faith from neighbors of other faiths, creating tensions and disturbing relationships within the larger community. But when the distinctiveness of a particular faith is stated in a manner that avoids open or hidden exclusiveness, then meaningful relationships between different communities becomes possible. As a consequence, Christianity in Asia need not be in competition with the whole range of Asian religions, but can instead foster cooperation in the common quest for fullness of life. The central effort of theology for Samartha is to acknowledge the mystery of Christ and explain the meaning of the person and work of Jesus Christ for theology and the church. Out of this commitment arises his theocentric pluralistic view of Christ.

4. Theocentric Pluralism

Samartha is a more moderate theologian of religion than many other pluralists. Like many of his colleagues, Samartha began with the open-minded Catholic view according to which the "cosmic Christ" is acknowledged by all religions of various kinds. Later in his theological and ecumenical career, however, he moved in the direction of Raimundo Panikkar and others. The Indian theologian Raymond (Raimundo) Panikkar, a Catholic priest from India, whose father was Hindu, spoke of *The Unknown Christ of Hinduism*.[9] In his earlier works, Panikkar still argued that in the historical Jesus the fullness of revelation had occurred even though not in an exclusive way. But in his revised version of *The Unknown Christ of Hinduism* in 1981, he had moved definitely towards a pluralistic version of Christology. In that book, he rejects all notions of the superiority or fulfillment of other religions in Christianity. The reason is simply that the world and our subjective experience of the world have radically changed since the Christian doctrine concerning Christ was first formulated. Along with the change of our experience of the world, our understanding should also be modified.

Another noted Asian theologian, the Chinese Choan-Seng Song from Taiwan, one of the leading Asian theologians, has attempted to establish bridges between Buddhist and Christian religions. The key to his theology in general is the term "transposition": it is a transposition from the Israel-centered view of history to the view that regards other nations as constructive parts of God's design of history. In that view, Israel's role as the "people of God" was symbolic, illustrating the way God would also deal redemptively with other nations. Asian nations have their own specific moments of salvation history parallel to Israel's exodus, giving of the law, captivity and so on. Furthermore, the savior figures of Asian religions parallel the savior figure of the Christian faith, Jesus Christ: "the expression of Buddha's compassion for the masses in his vows and the way he toiled unselfishly for their emancipation from pain and suffering are not without redemptive significance. Can we not say that Buddha's way is also a part of the drama of salvation which God has acted out fully in the person and work of Jesus Christ?"[10]

Consequently, the task of the proclamation of Christ on Asian soil is not so much one of conversion but of growing with Asians in the knowledge and experience of God's saving work in the world. The contribution of Christian mission is to inform the Asian spirituality of the love of God in Jesus Christ. This helps to transform Asian society towards freedom, justice and love.

Along with many other pluralists, Samartha became dissatisfied with the idea of the "anonymous Christianity" of Karl Rahner and similar ideas that still betray an assumption of the normativity of Christianity over other religions. Samartha has come to question the absolute finality and universal normativity of Christ. The reason for the shift in his thinking is his theocentric approach to theology in general and Christology in particular: before the total mystery of God, no religious figure or no single religion can call itself the final and full word. Samartha's reluctance to name Jesus Christ the final revelation is, interestingly enough, based on his understanding of God, and this makes his pluralism distinctive: "The Other [God as the Mysterious Other] relativizes everything else. In fact, the willingness to accept such relativization is probably the only real guarantee that one has encountered the Other as ultimately real."[11] In other words, those who recognize God alone as Absolute will recognize all religions as relative.

Clearly, for the mature Samartha, the incarnation is a symbol of the divine rather than a normative historical happening. Also, the death and resurrection of Christ, even though they are revelations of who God is, are not to be treated as a universally valid paradigm. Samartha has no problem in affirming the humanity and divinity of Jesus Christ, but he is not willing to affirm the orthodox teaching that Christ is God. The reason is simply that "an ontological equation of Jesus Christ and God would scarcely allow any serious discussion with neighbors of other faiths or with secular humanism."[12]

Samartha is also following Panikkar in that even though he relativizes all particular religious expressions and forms in history, the incarnation of Christ included, he is not willing to deny their necessity. The Mysterious Other must confront us through particular mediations. Therefore, Samartha is not naively assuming the equality of all religions. But he claims that each and every religion and its figures are limited: "a particular religion can claim to be decisive for some people, and some people can claim that a particular religion is decisive for them, but no religion is justified in claiming that it is decisive for all."[13]

For Samartha, classical theology runs the danger of "christomonism" in its insistence on the absolute finality of Jesus Christ. It turns Jesus into a kind of "cult figure" over and against other religious figures. Instead of a christomonistic approach to other religions, Samartha advocates a theocentric approach, which is more consistent with the God-centered message of Jesus of Nazareth. He tries to hold a dynamic between the normative significance of Christ as the revelation of God and the need for openness in relation to other faiths: [14]

> No one could have anticipated in advance the presence of God in the life and death of Jesus of Nazareth. There is an incomprehensible dimension to it. That Jesus is the Christ of God is a confession of faith by the Christian community. It does indeed remain normative to Christians everywhere, but to make it "absolutely singular" and to maintain that the meaning of the Mystery is disclosed *only* in one particular person at one particular point, and nowhere else, is to ignore one's neighbors of other faiths who have other points of reference. To make exclusive claims for our particular tradition is not the best way to love our neighbors as ourselves.

This kind of non-normative Christology, in Samartha's view, gives Christians an opportunity to hold their personal commitment to Christ and even their belief in his universal meaning although not in an exclusive way. For Christians, Christ represents the fulfillment of

God's promises. "But such an announcement will be an enthusiastic *witness* to their own revealer, *not* a denigrating *judgment* about other revealers."[15] Consequently, "whether it is in the attempts to redefine the goals of life or in the effort to meet human needs in the dust and heat of the plains, wherever two or three Hindus and Christians are gathered together in his name, there, one need not doubt the presence of the living Christ in the midst of them."[16]

5. Buddha, Rama and Krishna

As already mentioned, one of the main theological works of Samartha is the one in which he studied the interpretations of Christ in the Hindu Renaissance. He himself shows a clear preference for the *advaita* philosophy of Shankara. In an interesting analysis, he regards the Upanishads as Protestant movements within Hinduism, seeking to liberate the essence of religion from the authority of the church and old-fashioned modes and practices. Samartha sees a parallel to this in what happened with the early church as it struggled its way through the challenge of expressing the gospel in Greek thought forms. By the adoption of the categories of *advaita* in its classical and modern interpretations in the Hindu Renaissance, "Samartha wants to make room for faith in Jesus Christ in Indian pluralism and overcome the traditional claim of Christianity to absoluteness.... Christology and advaita are to be mutual correctives."[17]

In the Indian context, Samartha sees no way to avoid the comparison of Jesus Christ with the other savior figures of Hinduism and other religions of the area. Samartha cites Buddha, Rama and Krishna as examples and argues that no credible Christology can be constructed in an Asian context without relating Christ and these figures to each other. Many things unite these three saviors with Christ. In the life and work of each of them, revelation and liberation stand in a direct connection. Each of these savior figures experienced—according to their followers' interpretation—a development from original humanity to later deity.

Rama and Krishna are household words in India and are at the center of theistic *bhakti* (devotional religion), at times merging into the larger horizon of *advaita*. The question of the historicity of Rama and Krishna has always been a complex question, but Samartha does not want to give too much attention to that since the quest for the historical foundations of the founder of any religion is a recent phenomenon. The quest of the historical Jesus did not arise until the emergence of the

Enlightenment in the eighteenth century; before that the historicity of
Jesus of Nazareth was taken for granted.

Samartha believes that it is easier to talk about the Buddha and
Christ together, partly because the case for the historicity of each is
strong, and partly because both Buddhism and Christianity have
transcended their particularities and become universal in the sense that
they have found themselves at home in different counties and cultures.
For Samartha, the key to the similarities between Buddha and Christ
lies in their role as the liberators. During the past few centuries the life
and work of Jesus of Nazareth has provided both an inspiration and an
example for reformers working for the liberation of the poor and
oppressed in Asian society. In more recent years, it is the Buddha who
has provided both a shelter (*saranam*) and dynamic source of power to
missions of *Dalits* (the lowest class of people, the "class-less").
Millions of *Dalits* have adopted the religion of Buddhism in India and
rebelled against the ruling Hindu caste system. Christ can be an
inspiration for the followers of Buddha, Samartha argues, but a
"Christology of domination" is not good news for Buddhists. In this
context, Samartha quotes with approval Aloyis Pieris, who has argued
that an Asian theology of liberation evolves into a Christology that
does not compete with Buddhology but complements it by
acknowledging that the "one path of liberation of which Christians join
Buddhists in their *Gnostic detachment* (or the practice of voluntary
poverty) and Buddhists join Christians in their *agapaeic involvement* in
the struggle against forced poverty.... It is only at the end of the path, as
at Emmaus, that the path itself will be recognized by name (Luke
24:31)."[18]

With regard to his consideration of these four different savior
figures—Buddha, Krishna, Rama and Christ—Samartha argues that the
theory of multiple *avatara* (Hindu term for incarnated gods or other
significant persons) seems to be, theologically, the most
accommodating attitude in a pluralistic setting, one that permits
recognizing both the Mystery of God and the freedom of people to
respond to divine initiatives in different ways at different times.

6. Theses for an Evangelical Theology of Missions
in a Pluralistic Context

Stanley Samartha has done a service to Christian theology and
missiology by challenging its traditional exclusivism. He has both
taken notice of the changing, more tolerant atmosphere of the

contemporary world and the pressing need of religions to find a peaceful co-existence in a rapidly globalizing world. Through his extensive writings and wide ecumenical engagement, he has contributed significantly to the emergence of the discussion about plurality at the forefront of theology and religious studies.

However, there are serious theological and missiological problems in a pluralistic Christology such as his. It seems like this kind of pluralistic Christology emerged out of practical encounters with other religions rather than an extensive theological reflection. In response to the pluralistic Christology championed by Samartha and others, I will present theses for a responsible Evangelical theology of mission in the pluralistic context of Asia.

First, the "truth" question of religion cannot be compromised for the purposes of pluralism. No other modern theologian has argued more clearly for the necessity of the claim for truth in religions in general and Christology in particular than Wolfhart Pannenberg.[19] According to him, in all religions, beginning from the ancient religions and culminating in the plurality of contemporary religions, the dominant theme is the search for universal truth. Pannenberg rejects the older approach to the study of religions in which there was a search for a "common essence." For example, John Hick's view of a new, "pluralistic" religion that shares several elements from existing religions and at the same time cannot be identified with any of them is foreign to Pannenberg.[20] Instead, for Pannenberg religions represent rival conceptions of the ultimate truth. In this sense, his method takes the risk of placing all theological principles on the open market of public accountability.[21] "For a 'truth' that would be simply my truth and would not at least claim to be universal and valid for every human being could not remain true even for me. This consideration explains why Christians cannot but try to defend the claim of their faith to be true."[22] Denying the universal truth of religions' claims to truth would finally lead to the very denial of religions. It is the recent consensus among researchers of religion(s) that the essence of religion is to postulate some sort of absolute truth claim. Religion by its very nature deals with the ultimate issues of life and death and it might not be meaningful to talk about religion without such claims.[23]

> Without [this] element of truth claim, the teachings of religions would not make sense, since the question of the truth is an essential aspect of religions. If a religion does not talk about the ultimate things, but rather talks about the more superficial, that religion most probably cannot be regarded as a genuine religion. From the

perspective of metatheology, the conceptions of religions concerning the truth vary significantly, but still the right to present a truth claim is an irrevocable right for any religion.[24]

To argue with Samartha that the truth claim for Christ only applies to those inside the Christian household is a self-contradictory notion: truth cannot be true only to some people. It either is true or is not. It is a disservice to Christian mission *vis-à-vis* other religions to try to soften the encounter by a reference to a "partial" truth.

Even several Asian religions, such as Buddhism and Hinduism, while they have been more tolerant and pluralistic than Christianity and Islam, still regard themselves as the true religions. The mystical nature of many Eastern religions does not translate into an indifference to the truth question as pluralistic Christologies imply. Tolerance and denial of the truth claims of one's religion are not identical questions, but pluralism does not make a clear distinction between these two. Even though tolerance is a highly respected characteristic, there is no neutrality in religious claims. To deny the right to absolute truth claims would mean changing the concept of religions, as they are understood currently, and that most probably will not happen.

Second, the biblical testimony of Jesus' claim for a unique relationship to the Father and the coming of the kingdom has to be affirmed differently than does pluralism. The theocentric Christology of Samartha claims that Jesus of Nazareth shied away from accepting any claim for his uniqueness in his desire to serve God's kingdom. This is an old claim going back to Classical Liberalism's quest of the historical Jesus; it makes Jesus an honorable servant of God, but less than the unique savior. The problem is that, theologically, it makes the whole idea of the coming of God's kingdom dubious because in the New Testament, the coming of the kingdom is dependent on the person and work of Jesus of Nazareth. Jesus not only accepted the claim for a unique relationship to his Father; that claim finally led to his rejection by the religious authorities of his day. To eliminate this central teaching of the New Testament "demythologizes" the early Christian message into an ethical teaching without a claim to universal truth and saving force.

Third, while there are notable similarities between the savior figures of various religions, as Samartha and other Asian theologians have highlighted, it is not fair either with regard to Asian religions or Christianity to relativize their claims for uniqueness. Apparent similarities on the surface level do not necessarily validate the claim of the "common essence" of all religions that Arnold Toynbee and others have held in the past. One could argue either way: either that regardless of apparent differences on the surface level, the deep structure of religions is still the same ("common essence") or that while on the surface religions seem to be similar (e.g., they have similar types of prayers) the deep structures do differ considerably. A merely phenomenological survey of religions does not give us a definite answer here. The lesson is clear: the role of the savior figure in religions, for example Jesus Christ in Christianity, cannot be determined on the basis of apparent similarities or differences but on the basis of the theological structure of each religion. The claim of biblical and orthodox Christianity for the absolute uniqueness of Jesus Christ cannot be judged on the basis of phenomenological similarities between various savior figures.

Fourth, what one believes about Jesus Christ determines to a large extent one's beliefs about God. Classical Christianity argues for the knowledge of the Father only in the person and work of Jesus Christ. If one argues for a pluralistic Christology, as does for example John Hick, who moved from God-centered Christology finally to "Reality-centered pluralism" (according to which no God as such exists; what we call "god[s]" is the "Ultimate Reality"), one is left with a vague view of God. In Christian theology, access to the conception of God is in and through Jesus Christ. Pluralistic Christology sooner or later deprives us of the concept of God in the classical sense of the term or it leaves us with a merely formal concept of God as in the latest writings of Hick (the only thing you can say about "G/god" is that "G/god is," but you cannot identify any divine attributes or substance). When that development is taken to its extreme, one wonders if it still makes any sense to talk about "religion."[25]

Fifth, the concept of dialogue as used in pluralistic approaches needs a more nuanced definition. Dialogue does not necessarily mean giving up one's truth claims, nor should it. An honest dialogue with a predetermined idea of denying one's own and the counterpart's truth claim is not presuppositionless as is often believed. Here again Pannenberg's approach seems more relevant. Pannenberg comes to the dialogue table, as do the adherents of other religions, with a set of commitments, the most important of which is the conviction that there is one, unified, coherent truth to be searched for. Also, he contends that the Christian view of God is superior to the views of not only ancient religions but also of the living faiths of our day.[26] Unpromising as this kind of attitude might sound to most pluralists of our age, Pannenberg's theology of religion in fact does carry a lot of potential for a sustained dialogue. The purpose of the dialogue is not meant to soften the differences of religions and consequently to blur the importance of the search for a unified truth. Evangelical theology and mission enters the battlefield of religions with the humble, yet firm conviction that in Jesus Christ, the God who became human, divine revelation has come to us. He is the light that enlightens all men and women. Tolerance does not mean hiding one's conviction but honoring other religions and the adherents of other religions as honest seekers of truth. In the final analysis, "dialogue" and "mission" are not contradictory: genuine mission is always a dialogue, but a dialogue with certain convictions. Its aim is to present a truth claim for the consideration and affirmation of the other party. It cannot be, and it never is, without a certain agenda and presuppositions. Christian mission from the beginning has always survived best in the marketplace of competing religions as the person and work of Jesus Christ has been offered as the way, the truth and the life for all men and women. As Pannenberg has insisted, the history of religions is the arena in which competing truth claims finally show to what extent they are able to illumine our experience of the world. That religion which has the potential of offering an explanation of the experience of the world in the most satisfactory way will most probably prevail or at least offer itself as the most viable religion.

7. Concluding Reflections

Even when we are forced to offer criticism concerning some leading Asian theologies and Christologies, we need to affirm their basic intention, namely, to transplant the person and work of Jesus Christ in Asian soil. Much of Western theology is hopelessly useless for providing Asian Christians a solid foundation for presenting the case of Christ to Asians, who comprise more than half of the population of our globe. Song encourages Asians to write *Theology from the Womb of Asia.*[27] The "third-eye" type of Asian theology is tuned into seeing Christ through Chinese, Japanese and other Asian eyes; the "third-eye" refers to the Buddhist master who opens our eyes to see areas that have been unknown before. The goal of that kind of authentic Asian theology is "the freedom to encounter Jesus the savior in the depth of the spirituality that sustains Asians in their long march of suffering and hope."[28] Several Asian theologians talk about the "critical Asian principle" as the main guide to their theology. This principle seeks to identify what is distinctively Asian and uses this distinctiveness as a critical principle of judgment on matters dealing with the life and mission of the Christian church and theology. Nothing less should be our aim. Asia's struggle for humanization faces enormous challenges. Any authentic and genuine Asian Christology cannot help but delve deeply into the suffering and wounds of Asian people. Chi-Ha Kim, a Korean poet, wrote a play titled *The Gold-Crowned Jesus*. The scene plays in front of a Catholic church, where there is a statue of Jesus, made of cement. Christ is wearing a golden crown. Below the statue, on a cold winter day, beggars are lying. Looking at the gold-crowned Jesus, one of them wonders what might be the relevance of such a savior figure for a beggar with no place to go. And after all, how can a Jesus made of cement speak or feel anything? In the midst of his anguish, the beggar feels something wet, like small drops falling on his head. When he looks up, he sees the cement Jesus weeping. Noticing that the golden crown might be of value, the beggar is about to take it for himself, when he hears the voice of Jesus: "Take it, please! For too long a time have I been imprisoned in this cement. Eventually you have come and made me open my mouth. You have saved me."

It is the task of Asian Christology to free Jesus for the common people. Nothing less should be the goal of an Evangelical theology of mission for the Asian context.

---

[1] Kosuke Koyama, "Foreword by an Asian Theologian," in *Asian Christian Theology: Emerging Themes*, ed. Douglas J. Elwood (Philadelphia: Westminster, 1980), 13.

[2] The continent where more than half of the world's population currently lives is not easy to divide into manageable units regarding theological centers. However, for heuristic reasons that kind of classification might be helpful. Theologically, perhaps the most fertile soil has been India and Sri Lanka with the strong Hindu influence. Because of the long tradition of English-speaking education, these countries have contributed significantly to the emerging international theologizing. Another center of theological thinking is rising out of Korea where there is phenomenal church growth. There is a strong proliferation of Korean theology between, on the one hand, fairly conservative Evangelical theology that cuts across denominational boundaries and, on the other hand, a more liberal strand of Asian pluralism and Minung theology (to be discussed below). Then there is yet another cluster of Asian countries in which Buddhism has played a major role. Countries such as China, Taiwan, Thailand and Japan belong to this group. Some Japanese theologians, such as Kosuke Koyama, have made gateways into the international theological

academy, so also the Taiwanese C. S. Song and some others. The predominantly Catholic Philippines stands in its own category as does Indonesia, which is strongly influenced by Islam and in some areas by Hinduism and Buddhism also.

[3] Koyama, "Foreword by an Asian Theologian," 14.

[4] Jacques Dupuis, *Jesus Christ at the Encounter of World Religions* (Maryknoll, NY: Orbis, 1991), 15.

[5] Stanley J. Samartha, "The Cross and the Rainbow: Christ in a Multireligious Culture," in *Asian Faces of Jesus*, ed. R. S. Sugirtharajah (Maryknoll, NY: Orbis, 1995), 104.

[6] Stanley J. Samartha, *One Christ—Many Religions: Toward a Revised Christology* (Maryknoll, NY: Orbis, 1991).

[7] Samartha, "The Cross and the Rainbow," 110-11.

[8] Samartha, "The Cross and the Rainbow," 111. One of the distinctive features of Asian thinking is its reluctance to employ the Western "either-or" dialectic. Instead, most Asians would feel comfortable thinking in terms of the *"yin-yang"* inclusiveness. This term goes back to Taoism and Confucianism in their Chinese forms. According to that philosophy, the category of change is the interplay of *yin* and *yang*. These two terms, so crucial to much of Eastern thought (and which are expressed in different Asian languages and thought forms in varying terminology) means something like female [*yin*]-male [*yang*], weak-strong, light-dark, etc. But these poles are not to be thought of as opposites, but as complementary to each other. It is a matter of becoming rather than of being. One can easily imagine how this kind of inclusive thinking might affect one's Christology: "Jesus as the Christ, as both God and man, cannot really be understood in terms of either/or. How can man also be God? In the West we have to speak in terms of paradox or mystery in order to justify the reality of Christ. However, in *yin-yang* terms, he can be thought of as both God and man at the same time. In him God is not separated from man nor man from God. They are in complementary relationship. He is God because of man: he is man because of God." Jung Young Lee, "The Yin-Yang Way of Thinking," in *Asian Christian Theology: Emerging Themes*, ed. Douglas J. Elwood (Philadelphia: Westminster, 1980), 87.

[9] Raimundo Panikkar, *The Unknown Christ of Hinduism* (London: Darton, Longman & Todd, 1973).

[10] Choan-Seng Song, "From Israel to Asia: A Theological Leap," in *Mission Trends*, vol. 3, eds. Gerald H. Anderson and Thomas F. Stransky (New York: Paulist, 1976), 212.

[11] Stanley J. Samartha, *Courage for Dialogue: Ecumenical Issues in Inter-Religious Relationships* (Maryknoll, NY: Orbis, 1982), 151.

[12] Samartha, "The Cross and the Rainbow," 111.

[13] Samartha, *Courage for Dialogue*, 153.

[14] Samartha, "The Cross and the Rainbow," 112.

[15] Paul F. Knitter, *No Other Name? A Critical Survey of Christian Attitudes Toward the World Religions* (Maryknoll, NY: Orbis, 1986), 159

[16] Stanley J. Samartha, "Unbound Christ: Towards Christology in India Today," in *Asian Christian Theology: Emerging Themes*, ed. Douglas J. Elwood (Philadelphia: Westminster, 1980), 146.

[17] Volker Küster, *The Many Faces of Jesus Christ: Intercultural Christology* (Maryknoll, NY: Orbis, 2001), 89.

[18] Samartha, *One Christ—Many Religions*, 126.

[19] See W. Pannenberg, "Religious Pluralism and Conflicting Truth Claims," in *Christian Uniqueness Reconsidered*, ed. Gavin D'Costa (Maryknoll, NY: Orbis, 1990), 96-116.

[20] For an assessment of Hick's pluralistic proposal, see V.-M. Kärkkäinen, "'The Universe of Faiths': The Theological Challenges of John Hick's Pluralism," *Dharma Deepika* (forthcoming 2002).

[21] Carl E. Braaten, "The Place of Christianity Among the World Religions: Wolfhart Pannenberg's Theology of Religion and the History of Religions," in *The Theology of Wolfhart Pannenberg: Twelve American Critiques with an Autobiographical Response*, eds. Carl E. Braaten and Philip Clayton (Minneapolis: Augsburg, 1988), 287-312, esp. 294.

[22] W. Pannenberg, *Anthropology in Theological Perspective* (Philadelphia: Westminster, 1985), 15.

[23] See further W. Pannenberg, *Systematic Theology*, vol. 1 (Grand Rapids: Eerdmans, 1991), chs. 2 and 3 especially; see also Charles Taliaferro, *Contemporary Philosophy of Religion* (Malden, MA: Blackwell, 1998), 206, 236.

[24] Matti T. Amnell, *Uskontojen Universumi: John Hickin uskonnollisen pluralismin haaste ja siitä käyty keskustelu*, Suomalaisen Teologisen Kirjallisuusseuran Julkaisuja 217 (Helsinki: STK, 1999), 64-65, my translation.

[25] Some theologians of religion, for example Wilfred C. Smith, have in fact argued for the "end of religion"; instead of talking any more about "God," they prefer the term "Reality." This is a logical and unavoidable conclusion of extreme liberalism.

[26] I am well aware of the fact that Pannenberg is no Evangelical theologian. With all of his insistence on the claim for universal truth and "high"

Christology, he is convinced that even though salvation can be found only in Christ, salvation may be found outside the church (a typical inclusivist position that is championed both by the official teaching of the Roman Catholic Church after the Second Vatican Council and recently also by some Evangelical theologians, such as Clark Pinnock). The reasons for Pannenberg's openness to salvation outside the church are not to be found in pluralism but, among others, in his affirmation of the ancient view according to which Christ preached repentance to those in "hell."

[27] C. S. Song, *Theology from the Womb of Asia* (Maryknoll, NY: Orbis, 1986).

[28] Song, *Theology from the Womb of Asia*, 3.

"A CLOSE ENCOUNTER WITH THE TRANSCENDENTAL": PROCLAMATION AND MANIFESTATION IN PENTECOSTAL WORSHIP IN ASIAN CONTEXT

Julie C. Ma

1. Introduction

There has been an intense connection between proclamation and manifestation in the Pentecostal form of worship. Gathering together in the name of Christ is perhaps one of their favorite spiritual activities. Pentecostal worship helps believers experience the divine presence through hearing the word of God, praising, praying and other worship involvement. When one hundred and twenty disciples assembled together in one place, the Holy Spirit descended upon them and "all of them were filled with the Holy Spirit and began to speak in other tongues as the Spirit enabled them" (Acts 2:4). The "Gentile Pentecost" took place at Cornelius' home (Acts 10) in an amazing way when Peter spoke the word of God. The Holy Spirit was poured out upon them and they spoke in tongues.

In the same manner, Pentecostal mission is not complete if there has been neither active worship nor the exercise of spiritual gifts. This paper explores the relationship between the proclamation of the gospel and the manifestation of the Holy Spirit in Pentecostal worship and its implications to Pentecostal mission. Thus, this study consists of two aspects: proclamation and manifestation in worship and in mission. Throughout this discussion, my own experience in Asian churches and mission is reflected.

2. Proclamation

Expressions such as "Pentecostal preaching" or "Holy Ghost preaching" have been used in Pentecostal circles to characterize its distinct features in proclamation.[1] There are several elements in the preaching of the word, especially in its message and style of delivery.[2] As G. Duffield argues, all preaching begins with the preacher. A Pentecostal preacher is more than one with a loud voice, lots of energy, frequent movement around the platform, generous gestures, or someone preaching without written notes.[3] A true characterization of a Pentecostal preacher, instead, begins with his or her own distinct Pentecostal experience, which is commonly known as the baptism in the Spirit. In fact, only a Pentecostal preaches a Pentecostal sermon with corresponding conviction and dynamism.[4] In this section, three elements will be discussed: the Pentecostal use of scripture in preaching; contents of Pentecostal sermons; and aspects of Pentecostal proclamation.

2.1 Use of Scripture

In many ways, Pentecostals inherited the conservative approach to the scripture. Often higher criticism is an offense to the Pentecostal church. Scriptural records are accepted as fact unquestionably. In this sense, the Pentecostals have practiced a pre-critical literal reading similar to the Fundamentalists.[5] However, Pentecostals have more than an undivided loyalty to the authority of the word: they have unshakable confidence in God's power to repeat ancient miracles in the lives of present-day believers. Charles Parham's early sermon epitomizes this:

> Many teachers will at once admit that all the prophecies concerning Christ's first coming were literally fulfilled, but they spiritualize the prophesies of His second coming. So with teachers, concerning the promises of justification and sanctification, declaiming that they are possible of perfect realization today, and why not the promises of healing?[6]

Thus, the word of God and its authority become a pivotal emphasis in Pentecostal preaching in church and in the mission setting.[7] Another example of the Pentecostal use of the scriptures is observed in their understanding of interpretations of tongues and prophecy. Classical Pentecostals argue that their experience of tongues and prophecy must always "line up with" scripture and not contradict anything already directly revealed in the Bible. It is not, therefore, a "new revelation" in the sense of adding to biblical truth, but rather a special method of emphasizing a biblical truth, or of providing guidance (scriptural application) to real-life situations.

This timeless and universal application of God's word to contemporary settings has a direct implication to Pentecostal faith: the miracle-working God of ancient believers is the same God of today's believers and he is involved in mission work. In Pentecostal preaching, therefore, God's intervention is freely proclaimed and expected based on this non-dispensational approach to the scripture.[8]

Also unique in Pentecostal preaching is the frequent use of narrative material. This is not just for theological reasons although the narratives in Luke-Acts are used to substantiate the Pentecostal doctrine of the baptism in the Spirit. On a more existential level, figures in biblical narratives are often identified with one's own personal Christian life. This "narrative" theology becomes a favorite part of Pentecostal spirituality including the expression of their Pentecostal faith in the form of testimonies.

2.2 Sermons

When it comes to actual sermons, on the one hand, Pentecostal preachers have proclaimed standard Christian truth, which the historic church has upheld. On the other hand, there are features distinct and common to Pentecostal preaching. One should bear in mind that what was preached at the outbreak of the Pentecostal movement at the turn of the century will significantly differ from what is proclaimed in today's Pentecostal churches and mission field. In a similar way, today's Pentecostal sermons can vary from one socio-cultural environment to another. Several common topics are unique to today's Pentecostal preaching.

2.2.1 "Can do"

This contemporary Pentecostal approach has its roots at least in three elements. The first is the Pentecostal belief in God's intervention in human life. As discussed earlier, this has to do with the Pentecostal approach to the scripture. The second is a historical development during the rise of the charismatic movement in the 60s and 70s. Unlike the Classical Pentecostals, the second evolution of the Pentecostal movement brilliantly married the Pentecostal experience of a miracle working God and prosperity in local and overseas mission contexts.[9] The third is an upward mobility trend in the West as well as in some developing nations in the world (e.g., South America and Asia) which have traditionally suffered from chronic poverty. Majorities of non-Western Pentecostal churches as well as many contemporary Western Pentecostal churches have been impacted by this evolution of the movement. The impact was not only experienced in the churches but also in mission work. (Powerful messages by missionaries stirred the hearts of people and power manifestations occurred with proclamation.) For Sung-Hoon Myung, positive thinking preaching is a feature of Yonggi Cho's sermons.[10] One needs to remember that most non-Western Pentecostal churches began or grew during the 70s and on.

This phenomenon is not psychological escapism. In fact, Hughes describes it as a faith producing sermon.[11] It is "faith of an unusual nature, immediate faith, miracle faith"[12] produced as the word is proclaimed. In Pentecostal worship, one's faith is often challenged to believe in something humanly impossible.

Cho's "positive thinking" sermons made a striking contrast to traditional Korean Christianity which was predominantly influenced by the Presbyterian traditions. Until the 60s, Korean Christians had been hearing of God's presence in the midst of human suffering. Considering the church's short history during the Japanese persecution in its first half-century and Communist oppression during the Korean War in the 50s, God was viewed as a sustaining force in human suffering. Cho describes traditional preachers as setting "their pulpit in Mount Sinai to judge and condemn the souls."[13] In contrast, he labels his sermons as a message of hope. When Cho began to preach his characteristic "can do" sermons, he was severely criticized as propagating humanism, or even Shamanism.[14] In spite of these charges, Cho will be remembered as the one who reshaped the image of God among Korean Christians. His idea of God's blessing is holistic, encompassing spiritual well being, wealth and health based on 3 John 2. Cho obviously observed social context to present an appropriate and relevant gospel to touch the hearts of people. This contextualized message, in fact, played a role in lifting up souls in the society. Such "can-do" messages, preached with power, affected churches and the mission field.

2.2.2 "Experience God now"

In a Pentecostal's life, experience is a human dimension frequently emphasized. Through singing, testimonies and prayer, people are expected to "commune with God," that is, to experience God's presence. Preaching is a continuation of this expectation. Experiencing God can refer to anything from an emotionally charged state, the baptism in the Spirit, to physical healing. The transcendental God is viewed as the one who is immanent to his own people. In McGavran's words,

> Pentecostals...believe that God stands at our very elbows, knocking at the door of our hearts, speaking in our intuition and dreams. Pentecostals believe that God our Heavenly Father is instantly available, and powerful.... This common Christian doctrine is believed by all denominations but Pentecostals appear to believe it more than most others.[15]

God is experienced in Pentecostal worship in rather tangible ways. Consequently, many Pentecostal sermons deal with life-related issues such as illness, poverty, family problems, business, relationships, etc.[16] It is worth remembering that Pentecostal believers traditionally come from the lower end of the strata of a given society where missionaries work. They are often motivated to seek God's help more than the so-called mainline denominational believers whose socio-economic status is relatively higher.

This present-day orientation may be a contrast to the early Pentecostal mission movement, which understood itself as an eschatological reality.[17] Again, this could be a reflection of the second-generation evolution of the movement in the form of the Charismatic movement. This orientation towards life related issues is not only stressed in sermons, but also in the altar service after the proclamation. As an essential part of preaching, the altar service provides an opportunity for the audience to respond to the message. The most frequent invitation to the altar area is for salvation, healing, commitment/dedication, the baptism of the Spirit, praying over life's problems, blessing, business, children, marriage life, etc.

2.2.3 The baptism in the Spirit

The doctrine of baptism in the Spirit best characterizes Pentecostals. This is a "life-transforming event" subsequent to conversion.[18] In many ways, this pivotal belief is frequently reflected in

Pentecostal preaching. Since this makes one truly Pentecostal, many sermons end with an urgent admonition to seek this experience. Hence, even if Pentecostal theology books may say differently, a prevailing assumption among the congregation is that from the baptism in the Spirit, many other spiritual experiences flow.[19] As one is "empowered" through this experience, true Christian service takes place. For instance, when there is the baptism in the Spirit, people will begin to speak in tongues. Although this functions as the initial evidence of the Spirit baptism, this gift will remain and can be expressed in various ways such as a prayer language.

In many ways, this experience is a defining moment in a Pentecostal's life. My own experience testifies of suddenly heightened spiritual senses and awareness. Soon, I began to experience "listening" to God in various ways including a strong impression in mind, dreams, clear convictions coming through the scripture. Many experience spiritual gifts listed in the scripture.

It is also true that around this experience, many people encounter physical healing, emotional liberation from various bondages, answers to prayers, various kinds of miracles, a call to ministry especially for evangelism, and others. From an experiential viewpoint, the baptism in the Spirit is a doorway event. Even if a sermon has little to do with this particular topic, it is not unusual for the preacher to conclude his or her sermon by inviting people to pray for the baptism in the Spirit. This invitation also includes "old timers" wanting to experience the refilling in the Spirit.

2.2.4 "Soul-winning"

Pentecostal preaching is the missionary nature of the Pentecostal movement. Pentecostals have believed, from the very beginning that experiences of God's reality in the form of spirit-baptism are the very essence of Pentecostalism; and this experience is viewed as God's empowerment for witnessing (Acts 1:8). In other words, mission is the very reason for Pentecostal existence. This is one reason why preaching on the baptism in the Spirit is critical in Pentecostal churches. Dynamic and meaningful witnessing becomes possible only after one is empowered by the Spirit with speaking in tongues as the initial evidence. In the beginning, tongues attained a special significance as God's ultimate equipment for missionaries.[20]

In some non-Western Pentecostal churches, the original missionary zeal was not shared in its exact nature. For example, Yoido Full Gospel

Church has had relatively few cross-cultural missionaries. Most of its overseas work has been ministering among overseas Korean Christians. Nonetheless, an emphasis on soul winning has been consistent in preaching.[21] Cho's sermons have greatly challenged and motivated Christians to aggressively witness Christ to neighbors. Naturally, this emphasis produces church growth. For this, Wagner argues that Pentecostals believe not only in miracle power, but also in soul-winning power.[22]

2.3 Preaching

In the process of sermon delivery, Pentecostals also share several distinct features. These are not often found outside Pentecostal churches today.

Probably the most noticeable is the active participation of the audience during preaching. The audience of Pentecostal churches freely expresses their agreement by voicing an "amen" or "Hallelujah." This makes Pentecostal preaching a dialogue in a real sense. This element of making preaching extremely alive and responsive is viewed to have been influenced by black spirituality. Generous gestures and the lively tone of the preacher enhance this effect.[23] Pentecostal preaching in its content and form creates a sense of expectancy. God's immanent presence is often felt strongly in Pentecostal worship. Even a call for Christian service and ministry is made with urgency. Another general atmosphere in Pentecostal worship is a mood of celebration. With God's work in lives freely expressed through singing, testimonies and prayer, preaching often picks up this element and enhances the mood.

One can easily notice in Pentecostal preaching the frequent use of illustrations. They come from the scripture and contemporary lives. Sometimes, the entire sermon takes a narrative form. It is especially true in many mission fields where a narrative is a highly esteemed and familiar form of communication.

As spontaneity is an essential element of Pentecostal worship, preaching is not an exception. It is not uncommon to hear a Pentecostal preacher share his or her struggle as the Lord gives "another sermon just this morning." Many Pentecostal preachers may stand on the platform with a short sermon note, while others may not have anything but a Bible.

It is also noted frequently that the preacher deters from his or her original sermon outlines. In the middle of preaching, the service can easily break into a time of prayer. Pentecostal preachers will be sensitive to be "led by the Spirit" throughout the worship. Often "anointed" preaching is understood to mean a sermon prepared under the direction of the Holy Spirit, and delivered with strong conviction, and power.[24]

3. Manifestation

In Pentecostal worship, the high expectancy of God's intervention, or his immanent presence, often results in the manifestation of various spiritual gifts which are bestowed to edify the body (for instance, 1 Cor 12 and 14). There are two specific aspects of the gifts that affect the lives of believers.

First, the presence of the spiritual gifts themselves is a strong sign of God's presence and working among his people. The operation of the gifts brings a fresh recognition of God who still works among his people in the present day. Thus, charismatic spiritual gifts often bring a living immediacy and freshness to a congregation and to the lives of their individual members. The operation of charismata such as healing, casting out of demons and miracle working quickly brings one's attention to God. In this general way, God non-verbally communicates his existence and nature to his people.

Second, God, as the divine being, reveals and shows his will to his children through the manifestation of the gifts. God adapts to a specific individual and church and mission setting in which he reveals his specific will. The manifestation of the word gifts such as words of knowledge, words of wisdom, prophecy, speaking in tongues and interpretation fulfills this function of the gifts.

Although, it is an individual who experiences the manifestation of a gift, it is the entire congregation that is "edified," thus, underscoring the corporate nature of spiritual gifts. The manifestation of the gifts takes place, when God's people seek and desire them earnestly and are thus, a sign that the Holy Spirit comes upon a congregation in a personal and tangible way.

3.1 Healing

Throughout the Bible, healing is frequently used to manifest the presence, compassion and power of God (for instance, 2 Kings 20:3; Mark 1:29-34, 40-42; 2:1-12). This is a sign that the transcendental God is immanent in a specific human need, such as, sickness, weakness, or even death. Healing, therefore, is the manifestation of the supreme God who claims to be the Creator of all living things. Paul notes that healing is one of many gifts (1 Cor 14:9), which is intended to strengthen God's people. Healing is probably the most common manifestation of God's power among Pentecostal and Charismatic churches worldwide. The impact of healing manifestations in the mission fields of the Asian countries of Korea, Nepal, the Philippines, Singapore and Malaysia is particularly significant. It is because of their strong animistic orientations. Moreover, widespread poverty in many Asian nations causes supernatural healing to be favored. In fact, traditional healing is practiced through various spiritual means outside of Christianity. Therefore, Pentecostal mission workers freely exercise the spiritual gift of healing in worship services and informal fellowships. When a member needs the healing touch of God, he or she normally asks the congregation to pray for them before, or after, a service. I understand that many Pentecostal church pastors and missionaries pray for healing as a regular part of the service and this prayer takes place following the proclamation of the word. This not only reinforces the reality of God as just preached, but also affirms that the powerful God is also a God who cares for the needs of his children. People are encouraged to have total trust in the Lord and the prayer session provides the opportunity to practice what has been proclaimed. Many members grow in their faith through a personal healing experience or that of someone close to them. Consequently, the sick are encouraged to go to a solitary place to encounter the power of the Holy Spirit.

Many healings take place in the mission field. I remember an elder in one of the local churches in the Philippines where my husband and I were working as missionaries. He suffered from cancer, and medically had no hope of being cured. Knowing this, he put his hope totally in God. In this desperate situation, the role of his pastor was crucial. The pastor not only stood by to support him but also encouraged him to believe in God's healing power. At the same time, the whole congregation was requested to join in prayer. In the pastor's frequent house visits, he proclaimed God's love and power, and then always prayed for healing with the laying on of hands. This elder was healed and his healing became a great testimony to the congregation as well as to unbelievers who had been concerned about him.

In the Philippines, there are a good number of large Pentecostal-Charismatic churches. Since we have been working in this country for more than two decades, I have been able to do research regarding their growth factors. Such fellowships[25] like the Bread of Life, Cathedral of Praise, Asian Christian Charismatic Fellowship and other churches have regularly exercised the gift of healing in church services as well as in home meetings. The leadership of these churches strongly encourages their pastoral staff and lay leaders to actively pray for the sick.

Revival meetings are an annual event for many churches, especially in Korea. Regardless of denominational affiliations, during this special period, churches suddenly become very much like Pentecostal congregations. Often at the end of a revival meeting, the worship leader will invite the sick to the altar to receive prayer. At other times, the leader or the preacher will simply lay hands upon those who are seeking God's special touch. A common testimony is that while people are worshipping God, they feel a touch from the Holy Spirit and pain and illness often disappear. The senior pastor of Cathedral of Praise once shared that his wife was completely healed of tuberculosis in both lungs during a worship service. Mr. Chua, a member of Cathedral of Praise recounted that his wife, who had been suffering from a toxic goiter for many years and was expected by her doctors to die very soon, experienced the healing touch of God during a crusade. These living testimonies keep the church alive and expectant.

Kankana-eys, a tribal group in the northern Philippines, are a people group we have been working with. Most of them have come to Christ through the experience of miraculous healing. From 1950 to 1970, the manifestation of the healing gift was a regular feature in their worship services. The fact that Kankana-eys are basically animists and ancestor worshipers made it easy for them to believe in God's healing power. They have believed for centuries that the spirits of the deceased co-habit their houses and communities. Therefore, when God's healing power is manifested, especially to those who have exhausted all means of seeking help from the spirit world, people easily turn from their traditional religion to Christ. Whole families and entire communities have been known to turn to Christ as a result of divine healing. This "people's movement"[26] is often a result of God's miracle work, especially miraculous healing.

A classic example of this is an old man who had such a critical spinal problem that he could only crawl on his hands and knees like an animal. In 1958, his friends carried him to a neighboring village to attend a revival meeting by Elva Vanderbout.[27] At the end of the meeting, the man was instantly healed and he stood up and walked away. He gave his life to Christ. He stayed at the meeting place, telling everybody what God had done for him.

Reports of miraculous healings at Vanderbout services are numerous. At one service, an old man who had been deaf in both ears since he was a young man was instantly healed. At another, an old woman who had been blind in both eyes since 1942 was healed and could once again see out of both eyes. At still another, a paralyzed woman who has spent most of Sunday morning crawling to the service, was instantly healed during the worship service. She stood and walked through the aisle to the platform and testified of God's healing power. People in the meeting were amazed, and glorified the name of Jesus Christ.[28]

In 1961, Nepal had no churches and only about 25 Christians. A current report states that there are over 2,000 local churches today. Although this country is a Hindu kingdom, it is experiencing a spiritual harvest. People in the Himalayas are coming to Christ with an openness to the supernatural demonstration of God's power, especially through healing. Tamang's testimony is a good example. When his mother was ill, his father and the village priest prayed to their gods for her healing and sacrificed several goats and chickens, but she did not recover. The priest went to a nearby village to buy more animals to sacrifice, but the mother soon died. In his grief, Tamang went to a Buddhist lama and pleaded with him to restore his mother's life. The lama visited the house and chanted prayers for several hours, but with no result. Finally, Tamang decided to call a group of Christians from a nearby village, hearing that they had the power to heal the sick. The Christians came to Tamang's home and prayed for his mother, while the entire village watched. To Tamang's amazement and joy, his mother came back to life. And as a result, he and his family, along with 20 other households, totaling more than 160 people, accepted the Lord. Today Tamang leads 20 new fellowships in the Himalayas and is closely associated with Asian Outreach.[29]

Praying for healing is not confined to rural or tribal areas. Pentecostal churches in Singapore and Malaysia also actively engage in prayer for healing. As people seek the manifestation of supernatural healing, they experience it. This experience enhances their faith in Christ and enriches their Christian spiritual life.

Also, Pentecostals understand that often demons cause physical and mental disorders and sicknesses. For this reason, exorcism is a regular part of Pentecostal preaching as well as prayer after proclamation. It is Third Wavers who have further accentuated this element of "spiritual warfare."[30]

3.2 Speaking in Tongues

For Pentecostals, speaking in tongues has a critical significance; hence the common reference to them as tongue-speakers.[31] According to the Pentecostals, accounts in Acts and First Corinthians reveal more than one function for speaking in tongues. In Acts, glossolalia is viewed as the evidence of the baptism in the Holy Spirit. In 1 Corinthians speaking in tongues is seen as the gift (charisma) of tongues or the prayer language. Corinthian glossolalia occurred in a settled congregation and required the accompanying gift of interpretation to extend its usefulness beyond the speaker.[32]

Either way, speaking in tongues is common in Pentecostal worship. When the Holy Spirit comes upon a gathering of believers and the people are filled with the Holy Spirit, speaking in tongues normally takes place. Pentecostals hold to three distinct tongue phenomena.

First, when one receives the baptism in the Spirit (a popular Pentecostals term), it is regarded as an empowerment for service separate from regeneration (Act 1:8) and speaking in tongues is considered as the initial physical evidence. Because of the frequent link between the "empowering" nature of the baptism in the Spirit and speaking in tongues as the initial evidence, early Pentecostals once believed that tongues was a missionary gift of knowing a foreign language. [33] The baptism in the Spirit is normally considered a prerequisite for ministry within a Pentecostal setting. During the altar service, praying for the baptism in the Spirit with the sign of tongues is very common in a Pentecostal church.

Second, often during a time of reflection after a sermon, someone may speak in tongues publicly. This is believed to be the manifestation of the gift of tongues (1 Cor 14:7). This is not a sign of the baptism in the Spirit, although this gift is often found among those who have experienced the baptism in the Spirit. When the congregation is contemplating the message of the sermon just preached, they are expecting God to give an "utterance." According to Paul, this gift, just like other spiritual gifts, is given to edify the body of Christ. Hence, congregations are strongly encouraged to pray for the interpretation of the message delivered in tongues. Often, the person who spoke in tongues or even the interpreter, if different from the original tongue-speaker, is not aware of what he or she has said. This spontaneous and often ecstatic message often reaffirms the word just proclaimed. Third, tongues are also used as a private prayer language. Gordon Fee argues that the "groaning" of the Spirit in Rom 8:26-27 refers to speaking in tongues in private prayer.[34] Paul clearly alludes to this use of tongues in 1 Cor 14:14. That is, one prays in mind as well as in spirit. It is possible that the Corinthian Christians believed that this is the language of angels (1 Cor 13:1). During Pentecostal worship, there are long periods of prayer for various reasons; and during this time it is not unusual to hear the pastor urge people to pray in their "heavenly language." There is often a strong release of one's emotional or spiritual burden through praying in tongues. Logically, those who have experienced the baptism in the Spirit with speaking in tongues will also experience this type of intimate prayer. Whether all three tongues phenomena are one gift with three different uses or they are two or three different gifts altogether is a matter of debate.

Often, these three phenomena appear together in a public worship setting. Just recently, my husband and I made a trip to Bakun,[35] a municipality in northern Luzon in the Philippines. We held a Sunday service in a small tribal village. Sufficient time was given for various testimonies from members and then a typical Pentecostal sermon was preached with charged emotion and great expectancy of God's presence and work. Then, as is also typical of Pentecostal worship, the speaker urged the congregation to receive the baptism in the Spirit. He invited those who wanted the baptism in the Spirit to come forward and some young people came to the altar. While the whole congregation prayed for them, the preacher and other leaders laid their hands upon the young people and prayed for the baptism in the Holy Spirit. Soon they began to break out in tongues. One was weeping while another was lying flat on the floor. In the midst of prayer, one of them suddenly raised her voice and began to give out an "utterance." Everyone was aware that the Spirit was giving a message to the body and the congregation began to pray for an interpretation of the message. A few minutes later another lady who was standing beside them began to interpret the message and was extremely hesitant at first. She tried to speak out but the words did not come out smoothly in the form of a sentence. However, after a short while, the interpretation was made with highly charged emotion. The message was something like: "I love you. I will never forsake you. If you want to be baptized by the Holy Spirit, come forward. I will baptize you. Serve me continually...."

Since I was standing right behind her, I could closely observe her and listened to her interpretation. Then suddenly more hearts were opened and more people came forward for prayer. It was a tremendous spiritual encouragement to the congregation and this utterance reinforced the proclaimed message in a powerful way. There was a great move of the Holy Spirit among the members of that church and when the Holy Spirit touched them, they spoke in tongues, were slain in the spirit and they wept. The service continued for three hours.

3.3 Prophecy

Along with traditional Christianity, Pentecostals share the basic theological belief concerning the primacy of the written word as God's revelation. However, they also believe in God's direct communication through various other modes. As mentioned above, an utterance can be given in tongues with corresponding interpretation. The gift of prophecy functions in a similar way, although it can come through other means such as visions, audible messages and dreams as observed in the scripture. In Pentecostal worship, prophecy is often a declaration spontaneously given to the congregation in a public setting. Paul equates the value of messages in tongues accompanying an interpretation with that of prophecy for the building up of the body of Christ (1 Cor 14:14-20).

The Bible provides an ample amount of evidence that prophecy is a manifestation of the Holy Spirit. The Book of Acts records that people saw visions, and prophesied after the day of Pentecost. Having been baptized in the Holy Spirit, people spoke in tongues and prophesied (Act 8). Peter, by the Spirit, foretold the deaths of Ananias and Sapphira (Acts 5:1-10) and also saw a vision (Acts 10:9-16), which directly dealt with Peter's bias against the Gentiles and further substantiated revealed truth (v. 15).

As manifested in the book of Acts, Pentecostals and Charismatics experience the unfolding of God's will through dreams, visions, or personal messages, though God's written revelation functions as basic truth. However, in a real life setting, there are many situations that require decisions which have nothing to do with ethical or Christian principles. In these instances, "direct revelation" is sought, and the word gifts, such as prophecy, find their place.

Paul notes that prophecy is given for "strengthening, encouragement and comfort" (1 Cor 14:4). Often this reinforces the message just proclaimed, as a prophecy often appears during the post-proclamation prayer time. The message of God tends to alert the people to be faithful to strengthen their spiritual life. Also visions are seen during both private and public prayer times. In the case of a vision, an interpretation is required. However, for a prophecy, no interpretation is required. Instead, Paul urges the rest of the congregation to "weigh carefully what is said" (1 Cor 14:29).

3.4 Blessing

The Pentecostal understanding of blessing is not much different from that of traditional Christianity except in two distinct ways. First, Pentecostals believe that God, in fact, blesses them here and now; and second, God blesses not only the spiritual, but also the physical, material and relational dimensions of human life. In this sense, the Pentecostal understanding of God's blessing is close to the Old Testament concept of shalom. They believe that God intervenes tangibly when they ask, and specific blessings are expected. An expectant and experiential dimension in their relationship with God characterizes the Pentecostal belief.

The message of blessing is often proclaimed in the pulpit. It is based on God's character: his faithfulness (Lam 3:22), mercies, dependability (Deut 32:4; Ps 89:8; 1 Thess 5:23-24), goodness (Ps 100:5) and love. God lavishly also displays his love by providing rest and protection for his people (Deut 33:12).

The message about God's character encourages his people to anticipate God's blessings. Pentecostals believe that blessings are given when they trust God and earnestly seek for it. Because of this, people implore him to meet their needs and are sacrificially devout in prayer, setting aside certain days for this very thing.

A story is told about a woman who had been longing for a baby and decided to devote herself to dawn prayer for three months. She woke up early every morning and prayed. The last day of her three months of prayer, she went to a doctor for a check-up. She was pregnant. Some may say this was a shamanistic way of believing in God. On the surface, yes, it looked like she expected what she wanted; but on a deeper level, there was a fundamental difference. This woman truly believed in God not based on her devotion, but based upon who God is. God who "can-do" in his goodness and faithfulness was part of her belief. This is only one example. There are hundreds of thousands of people's testimonies of God's blessing. Magazines like Charisma and Pentecostal Evangel regularly publish stories of miraculous healing. *Shin-ang-gye* (World of Faith) which has been published by Yoido Full Gospel Church is the best-selling monthly magazine in Korea, and is full of testimonies of God's blessing in the form of healing, God's answers to prayer and miracles.

Secondly, many Christians believe in giving, and believe that it is a way of receiving his blessing. Often they give to God beyond their ability, trusting that God would be able to help them make up the difference. This certainly has a potential to promote a theological attitude to view God as a deity open for human control and even manipulation. One Korean church pledged to erect thirteen church buildings in the northern Philippines. It is a collaborative work of thirteen individual deacons and elders. Even one church would have been difficult enough to build but their faith and dedication enabled them to do so. In Pentecostal preaching, dedication and God's blessing are among the favorite topics.

The expectation of God's blessing has as its basis God's own character, which is exhibited in his relationship with his people. God promises his blessing to his people based on the divine integrity. His blessing is intended for his people's experience in daily life. This experience is meant not only to be transcendent but also to be immanent, tangible and empirical as well. For this reason, Pentecostals do not hesitate to seek such blessings from God. Experiences enhance their relationship with God as they are drawn closer to him, and this leads them into deeper faith.

4. Conclusion

Pentecostal worship, like Pentecostal theology, continues in most of the elements of historic Christianity. At the same time, differences characterize Pentecostal preaching in the church and in mission work. The distinctive of the Pentecostal faith is the combination of God's supreme reality and its intimate relevancy. The platform where this combination is experienced is our everyday life! Pentecostals have a constant immanent encounter with the ultimate transcendental. The catalyst of this uneasy combination is a unique Pentecostal experience called the baptism in the Spirit.

Pentecostal preaching in the mission field is one of several effective avenues where this unique Pentecostal combination is taught, proclaimed, reinforced and elaborated. Although in the popular preaching of some televangelists, health and wealth receive disproportionate attention, all the blessings are perceived as a means, or part of the empowerment to be an effective witness for Christ. This makes Pentecostal worship and life dynamic and alive. Preaching communicates this element not only in its content but also in its form of delivery.

As Pentecostals expect the manifestation of God's reality in everyday life, preaching becomes a vehicle of affirmation. There are various gifts through which one experiences God's presence and power in public Pentecostal worship. Pentecostals believe that these gifts, common in the early church, are intended for today as well. As indicated in the Book of Acts, these gifts brought renewal and strength to a believer's faith, and revival upon the church. The same result is observed in the Pentecostal mission field when God's power and love are manifested in worship. God's overwhelming presence becomes real. God is never miniaturized but remains a powerful and ultimate transcendental. God becomes immanent and tangible in human experiences through the intimate worship and fellowship in the believer's life.

---

[1] Guy P. Duffield, *Pentecostal Preaching: The L.I.F.E. Bible College Alumni Association Lectureship on Preaching for 1956* (New York: Vantage, 1957), 23.

[2] H. Vinson Synan, "Preaching, A Pentecostal Perspective," *Dictionary of Pentecostal and Charismatic Movements*, eds. Stanley M. Burgess and Gary B. McGee (Grand Rapids, MI: Zondervan, 1988), 722.

[3] Duffield, 24.

[4] Duffield, 26. The impact of spiritual experiences of Pentecostal leaders in a tribal setting is compared with leaders in the ancient Israelite society in Wonsuk Ma, "The Spirit of God upon Leaders of the Ancient Israelite Society and Igorot Tribal Churches," in *Pentecostalism in Context: Essays in Honor of William W. Menzies*, Journal of Pentecostal Theology Supplement Series 11 (Sheffield: Sheffield Academic Press, 1997), 291-316.

[5] William W. Menzies, "Non-Wesleyan Origins of Pentecostal Movement," in *Aspects of Pentecostal-Charismatic Origins*, edited by Vinson Synan (Plainfield, NJ: Logos, 1975), 85 detects the Pentecostal's "strong sense of kinship with fundamentalism."

[6] Charles F. Parham, *The Sermons of Charles F. Parham* (New York/London: Garland, 1985), 42.

[7] For instance, Duffield, 38-58; Ray H. Hughes, "The Uniqueness of Pentecostal Preaching," in *Azusa Street and Beyond: Pentecostal Missions and Church Growth in the Twentieth Century*, ed. L. Grant McClung, Jr. (South Plainfield, NJ: Bridge, 1986), 91. Sung-Hoon Myung, "Spiritual Dimensions of Church Growth as Applied in the

Yoido Full Gospel Church" (Ph.D. dissertation, Fuller Theological Seminary, 1990), 206 characterizes Yonggi Cho's preaching as first of all "Bible-based preaching,"

[8] John Goldingay, *Approaches to Old Testament Interpretation*, updated edition (Downer Grove, IL: Inter-Varsity, 1990), 66-96 terms this method as reading the scripture "as the story of salvation."

[9] Cheryl Bridges Johns, *Pentecostal Formation: A Pedagogy among the Oppressed*, Journal of Pentecostal Theological Supplement Series 2 (Sheffield: Sheffield Academic Press, 1993), 79.

[10] Myung, 206.

[11] Hughes, 93.

[12] Hughes, 93.

[13] Paul Yonggi Cho, "The Secret Behind the World's Biggest Church," in *Azusa Street and Beyond*, 102.

[14] Harvey Cox, *Fire from Heaven: The Rise of Pentecostal Spirituality and the Reshaping of Religion in the Twenty-first Century* (Reading, MA: Addison-Wesley, 1995), 224-6 argues for a strong link between Cho's sermons and traditional Shamanism in Korea.

[15] Donald A. McGavran, "What Makes Pentecostal Churches Grow?" in *Azusa Street and Beyond*, 122.

[16] Another characterization of Cho's sermons is "life-related" preaching, Myung, 206.

[17] The collection of Parham's sermons in the Garland Series, *The Sermons of Charles F. Parham*, includes twenty sermons and about one half of them deal with eschatological subjects such as "Future of Nations," "United States in Prophecy," "The Bride," "The Millennial Age," "The Judgment Age," etc.

[18] Grant Wacker, "Wild Theories and Mad Excitement," in *Pentecostals from the Inside Out*, ed. Harold B. Smith, Christianity Today Series (Wheaton: Victor, 1990), 21.

[19] This popular Pentecostal notion on the relationship between the baptism in the Spirit and the operation of spiritual gifts was recently challenged by Robert P. Menzies, "Spirit-baptism and Spiritual Gifts," in *Pentecostalism in Context*, 48-59. He concluded that the "spirit baptism is the 'gateway' to a special cluster of gifts" which he refers to more supernatural prophetic speech gifts (58-9).

[20] "New tongues missionaries" was probably the earliest term, which signifies the link between tongues and missionary work, *Apostolic Faith*, November, 1906, 2.

[21] Myung, p. 206 terms this as "mission-oriented preaching."

[22] C. Peter Wagner, "Characteristics of Pentecostal Church Growth," in *Azusa Street and Beyond*, 129.

[23] A comment during the Dialogue by a Pentecostal delegate represents this, "If Reformers have a problem with noise, we Pentecostals have a problem with silence" (Cecil M. Robeck, Jr. on May 13, 1997 in Chicago).

[24] Synan, "Preaching," 722.

[25] There are nearly twenty mega-churches in Manila, Philippines with over 2,000 members.

[26] Alan Tippet, *People Movements in Southern Polynesia* (Chicago: Moody, 1971), 6.

[27] She was a single American missionary and was the key person God used to reach the Kankana-ey tribe.

[28] Julie Ma, "Ministry of the Assemblies of God among the Kankana-ey Tribe in the Northern Philippines: A History of a Theological Encounter" (Ph.D. Dissertation, Fuller Theological Seminary, 1996), 89-90.

[29] "A Miracle for Tamang," *Asian Report* 222 (March, 1997), 8-9.

[30] For example, Charles H. Kraft and Mark H. While, eds., *Behind Enemy Lines: An Advanced Guide to Spiritual Warfare* (Ann Arbor, MI: Vine, 1994).

[31] This popular notion is reflected in Gordon L. Anderson, "Pentecostals Believe in More Than Tongues," in *Pentecostals from the Inside Out*, 53-64.

[32] Russell P. Spittler, "Glossolalia," *Dictionary of Pentecostal and Charismatic Movements*, 338-339.

[33] Charles Parham's initial belief in tongues as xenoglossa is discussed by James R. Goff, Jr., "Initial Tongues in the Theology of Charles Fox Parham," in *Initial Evidence: Historical and Biblical Perspectives on the Pentecostal Doctrine of Spirit Baptism*, edited by Gary B. McGee (Peabody, MA: Hendrickson, 1991), 57-71, especially 64.

[34] Gordon D. Fee, "Toward a Pauline Theology of Glossolalia," in *Pentecostalism in Context*, 24-37.

[35] The Assemblies of God has concentrated most of its mountain ministry in this area, and has established many churches.

THE MISSION OF THE CHURCH IN A RELIGIOUS PLURALISTIC SOCIETY WITH SPECIAL REFERENCE TO THE NEPALESE CONTEXT

Bal Krishna Sharma

1. Introduction

Asia is the mother of all the living religions of the world.[1] Christian missions in Asia have a long and cherished history, and Christians have lived alongside people of other faiths as a small, powerless and often persecuted minority.[2] Christianity was born in the pluralistic Greco-Roman world of the Mediterranean. The disciples of Christ went to the Greco-Roman world with the gospel message of Christ. The Bible, both the Old and New Testament, was written in a religious pluralistic context with emphasis on the uniqueness of the one true God.

Asia has long been noted for its pluralism of religions, cultures and systems of thought. Within the same religious system, we can observe important religious, social and organizational differences. Each religious system has developed its own religious traditions and Asian Christianity is no exception to this. Modern Asia is very complex with its old religions and new religious movements. It is colored by various cultures, traditions, social and economic diversities plus the influence of modern Western culture.

Among the Asian societies, India may be the most complex with great religious traditions mothering at least four living religions of the world and accommodating other living religions by granting them equal status. Constitutionally, India is declared a secular state where all religions can exist together with the "freedom of conscience, and free profession, practice and propagation of religion."[3] In spite of the constitutionally granted freedom of religion, there are social, economic, religious and political pressures that try to stop the mission of the Christian church on the Indian sub-continent. At various times in Indian history, different Commissions have brought bills against freedom of religion.[4] Such bills seek to prevent the conversion of the Hindus and the tribal groups to Christianity or Islam. Other religions, but specifically Christianity, are considered to be alien and are thought to be associated with European colonialism.

There is a strong notion in the Hindu mind that rationalizes the uselessness of a change of religion. Traditionally, a Hindu is born and not made. All religions are good enough for the people into which they are born. Liberal Christian theologians, who do not believe that people of various faiths have to be converted into Christianity, have expressed the above mentioned concept over the years. In the midst of the complex religious context in Asia and in other parts of the world, many Christian academics and church leaders have endorsed religious pluralism. They regard it not merely as a social fact but a new theological understanding of the relationship between the Christian faith and other faiths. Regarding the place of Christianity among the other faiths, there is a new turn represented by a pluralist model, which accepts the unitary pluralism model of American Catholic Paul Knitter. He asserted that "the world religions, in all their amazing differences, are more complementary than contradictory." He is of the opinion that each religion can contribute to the mutual growth of its adherents, the success of which would be measured in terms of "a Christian becoming 'a better Christian' and a Buddhist 'a better Buddhist' and a Hindu 'a better Hindu,'" and so on.[5]

Nepalese Christianity is a new expression in the Nepalese pluralistic context. Nepal is declared the only Hindu State in the world, but apart from Hinduism, other religions do exist in the nation. Indian Hinduism and traditions have a great influence upon Nepalese religious and social order. Christianity was introduced to Nepal in the eighteenth century by the Capuchin Fathers, but they were expelled along with the new converts. Even after 1951, Christian witness was strongly opposed by the government, and only after 1990 has the Christian church begun to exercise some freedom in worship; but there still exists prohibition in regards to propagation. In this religious, political and social context, the mission of the church has to be accomplished.[6] So far, the Nepalese church is Evangelical in its expression. It needs to prepare to face the challenges of pluralism both from liberalism and people of other faiths.

2. The Mission of the Church

2.1 What is the Mission of the Church?

The word mission comes from the Latin word *missio*, which means "sending," and it is used in the sense of "being sent." In the biblical narratives, it is understood as the mission of God (*missio Dei*). The thought of missions is related to God, because his very essence is the basis for missions today. Mission is not merely something God does and asks people to get involved in, rather it is the very nature of God himself. John R. W. Stott views mission as the very essence of God when he says, "All of us should be able to agree that mission arises primarily out of the nature not of the church but of God himself. The living God of the Bible is a sending God."[7] Ken Gnanakan highlights this concept clearly when he says, "mission begins with God himself, not merely is he the God of mission but his very character is mission."[8] Because mission is the very nature of God, he always gets involved in it and asks his redeemed to come along with him in order to accomplish it. God is actively fulfilling his will in the universe. He is, himself, mission through and through. Sending and being sent are integral parts of his nature.

The word church comes from the Greek word *ekklesia,* which is used at least seventy-three times in the New Testament. In ordinary usage, the word church denoted "the people as assembled" or "the public meeting."[9] The early Christians used the term *ekklesia* to express their consciousness that they were called together by the proclamation of the gospel for the purpose of belonging to God through Christ by the power of the Holy Spirit.

In order to indicate the mission of the church within the church and in the world, Jesus and the New Testament writers have used various metaphors.[10] Such images express what the church is and what the church should become. Such images call the members of the church to see themselves in a new light, challenging them to become more like the pictures offered. These images are metaphors of the church in mission. The church exists in the world as a living witness. The Bible talks of the church as the salt of the earth; the light of the world; the physical presence of Jesus in the world; a royal priesthood; and a priest for the Gentiles, who see the good works of the church and glorify God. It is expected of the church "to be the unifying, sanctifying, reconciling and proclaiming presence of Jesus Christ in the world, challenging local congregations to a transformed, purpose-driven life of mission in the world, locally and globally."[11]

The above discussions may throw some light on the issue of the mission of the church. The church exists in the world today for the mission of God, and if it does not fulfill God's mission, then there is no purpose for its existence. The church lives out its calling in the world through mission, finds its essential purpose in its participation in God's mission, and engages in a multitude of activities whose purpose is mission. If the church ceases to be a mission then it loses its own essential character.

Concerning the mission of the church, there are two major opposing views, although there may be other expressions, as well. The Uppsala General Assembly of World Council of Churches (WCC) in 1968 developed a thesis entitled *The Church for Others* that introduced a whole new vocabulary of mission. West European and North American task groups that developed the new vocabulary were given the task of discussing the missionary structure of the congregation. John Stott summarizes their discussion to indicate the position of WCC in regards to the understanding of mission.

> God is at work in the historical process, that the purpose of his mission, of the *missio Dei*, is the establishment of shalom (Hebrew for "peace") in the sense of social harmony, and that this shalom (which it was suggested is identical with the kingdom of God) is exemplified in "the emancipation of colored races, the concern for the humanization of industrial relations, various attempts at rural development, the quest for business and professional ethics, the concern for intellectual honesty and integrity."[12]

If mission is only understood in terms of social, political and economic improvement of a person or society then we are missing the very essence of mission. It is very easy to look at the physical aspect of a person with her/his needs and forget the broken relationship that person has with God almighty. This does not mean that the church does not have any social responsibility in the society where it exists. In fact, it has a greater responsibility in society because it exists there with the mission of God. The mission is to bring back a lost humanity to God through Jesus Christ and to help people realize that they are in need of forgiveness. God, through Jesus Christ, is waiting to accept them and remake them in his own image. Through his redeemed community, God wants to be known in this world. The mission of God starts with a spiritual transformation—reconciliation between God and a lost humanity. Every other social action has to be an expression of such reconciliation and love. We need to address social concerns in the light of God's mission rather than addressing God's mission in the light of social concerns. When we are committed to God's mission of reconciliation, we cannot but get involved in the social needs of the people. However, if we have no direction from God's mission then we will be wasting our time trying to change people who are not yet reconciled with God. Not everything done in the world in the name of development is "mission." Both theists and atheists can do such activities, and we can not call it God's mission. Mission concerns God's redeemed people, and what he sends them into the world to do. Therefore, the church has the tremendous responsibility of fulfilling God's mission in the world through its proclamation of reconciliation and its expression of love and concern.

2.2 When Did the Mission of the Church Begin?

Though God's concern is with the whole creation and all humanity, he chose to work with a particular group, which was revealed in his choice of Abraham, through whom his mission was to be accomplished. God chose Abraham to be a blessing for the nations. The election of Abraham was not for extra privilege but for greater responsibility of service. God chose Israel only as the channel for his blessings for the world. The privilege of being God's chosen people brings a greater responsibility to Israel, a responsibility involving the salvation of nations (Gen 26:4; Isa 42:6-7). God promised Abraham that he was going to bless him and bless the world through him if he obeyed. The promise of God to Abraham was seen in the lives of the Israelites in Exodus and the Promised Land. There was a historical progression of divine revelation given to the chosen race and at last "when the time has fully come, God sent forth His Son;" and after that the Father and the Son sent forth the Spirit on the Day of Pentecost (Gal 4:4-6; John 14:26; Acts 2:33).[13] This entrusted mission of the church is God's mission, "for it is he who sent his prophets, his Son and his Holy Spirit. Of these missions the mission of the Son is central, for it was the culmination of the ministry of the prophets, and it embraced within itself, as its climax, the sending of the Holy Spirit. And now the Son sends as he himself was sent."[14] Jesus, in his earthly ministry, sent apostles and other disciples as a kind of extension of his own preaching, teaching and healing ministry. Then after his death and resurrection, he commissioned every disciple to be a witness for him to the ends of the earth (Matt 28:18-20; Acts 1:8).

3. Religious Pluralism in the Asian Context

3.1 Definition of Religious Pluralism

Religious pluralism has been a reality throughout human history. Religious pluralism means that various religious aspirations are present in the world. The differing views on religious pluralism reflect different perspectives. Broadly speaking there are four distinct views that may be identified. One is an *exclusivist* view that emphasizes that salvation is to be found in Christ alone, and that salvation depends on an acknowledgment of Christ as Lord and Savior. The *inclusivist* view finds salvation somewhere in each religion. The *pluralist* view observes that the common root to all religions is precisely the salvific root. The pluralistic view emphasizes that there is no need to change religions. The purpose of a pluralist theologian must be to help others to realize and understand their own faith better. In other words, help the Hindus to become better Hindus; Buddhists, better Buddhists; Muslims, better Muslims and so on. A fourth view stresses that while salvation is necessarily based on Christ's passion, an overt knowledge of Christ is not essential to salvation.[15]

3.2 Development of a Religious Pluralism Trend

The pluralistic context is not a new phenomenon to biblical history. The Old Testament was written in a pluralistic context with full conviction that there is only one God and that he has made himself known as Yahweh. During the Old Testament period many religions of Egyptians, Babylonians and others existed. Going back to the history of the fall, we find that human beings were alienated from God because of sin. Because of human longing for supernatural powers, they started to submit themselves to nature and the demonic forces. Humans felt and experienced that the forces of nature and the evil forces were more powerful than they were. Therefore, they started to revere or worship nature and demonic forces. We cannot ignore the presence of evil forces that led towards the invention of religious pluralism. I am not trying to say that such evil forces were present only in the non-Jewish/non-Christian traditions. Such evil forces influenced even so-called Jewish/Christian communities. Because of this, prophets had to speak against such evil forces in the temple, synagogue, church, society, nation, etc.

The Old Testament Jews and the New Testament Christians were well aware of the presence of religious pluralism in their societies. It meant they were witnesses for Christ in their pluralistic societies. God wanted to convey his saving message through his redeemed people. God's call to Abraham was for a mission, to be a blessing for the nations. Not to despise these nations, but to transform them. Not to pass judgment on them but accept them as God accepts them. However, that did not mean compromising what God required of them. People are in need of forgiveness from the one, loving God. People need reconciliation with God, with others and with themselves.

3.3 Religious Pluralism in the Asian Context

As stated earlier, Asia is the mother of all living religions of the world. Living in a religious pluralistic society has always been a reality to the people of Asia. Even before the introduction of Christianity in Asia, there were people of many religious aspirations who lived side by side. Chinese and Japanese primal religions and other established religions existed together before the introduction of Christianity or Islam in that context. In these religions there always have been "give and take" principles adopted.

The Christian missionary movement of eighteenth century was started by William Carey, who is also known as the father of modern mission. The missionary movements in many parts of the world with their emphasis on education, learning, freedom, etc. brought forth the awakening of national consciousness in the nineteenth and twentieth century. Asian nations were considered to be the "mission fields" for Christianity. Now the situation is changing.

More and more, Eastern religious teachings are being exported to Western countries and there is a new awakening among the eastern people in regards to their own religious traditions. The Western scholars are now more interested in the study of eastern religions and eastern religious thought is being made available to the general public both in the east and the west. Many nations today accept Western scientific education minus Christian doctrine. People of various nations became aware of their so-called cultural heritage and efforts were made to revive it. Thus, the rising desire of people from every part of the world to develop themselves in their cultural surrounding has led to the acceptance of inevitable pluralism. The multi-religious society with all its religious thoughts and ways of living has become a current reality.[16] Christianity has a greater challenge to face in its mission endeavor. Because of the new awakenings of religions and traditions, Christianity is now considered only one religion among many. Such a strong presence of religious pluralism demands a new approach in communication in the mission endeavor.[17]

3.4 Religious Pluralism in the Indian Context

Indian society may be the most complex of Asian societies. Religious pluralism was already in existence prior to the Christian era. Most of all the major religions of the world have been present in India for a long time. Primal religions, as well as Hinduism, Buddhism, Jainism and some other religions existed in India before Christianity was introduced in the first century, A.D. Religions of India originating from Hinduism competed with one another, although they were co-existent.

Tradition has it that one of the disciples of Christ brought the gospel message to India in the first century. He was persecuted and killed. Such persecution in India and elsewhere was the sign that people were not eager to accept this new Christian faith which was preached to them. The nationalistic movements of the nineteenth and twentieth centuries with attendant cultural and religious awakenings tried to interpret religious pluralism, not from a mission mandate (i.e., salvation from sin through Christ alone), but from the perspective of the equality of all religions. It was believed by many theologians that "the world religions, in all their amazing differences, are more complementary than contradictory."[18] Among the Indian Christian theologians, Stanley Samartha has been a leading figure in ecumenical inter-faith relations. He is of the opinion that "while *Sat* (truth, being) is One, sages call it by various names."[19] Such views were expressed by most of the Hindu sages like Ramakrishna Paramhamsa and scholars like Radhakrishnan.

4. Mission of the Church in the Nepalese Context

4.1 The History of Christianity in Nepal

The earliest Christian contact with the land of Nepal took place in 1662, when the Italian Capuchin priests passed through Nepal en route to Tibet. After the return of these visitors to Europe, they encouraged the people to go to India, Nepal and Tibet to evangelize them. In 1703, the Capuchin fathers were assigned to go to North India, Nepal and Tibet. The first Roman Catholic missionary came to Nepal in 1707 for a brief period and in 1715 three priests came to reside in Kathmandu Valley. Over the span of 54 years of active mission work in the Nepal Valley, 29 Capuchin missionaries lived there. They pressed ahead with language learning, producing literature, preaching and teaching, conducting religious services, caring for converts and practicing medicine.[20] However, when the Gorkha king Prithvinarayan Shah conquered Nepal in 1769, he expelled the priests and the group of Newar Christians, who were living in Kathmandu valley, accusing them of being agents of European colonial power.[21]

From then until 1951, a firm Nepalese policy excluded all foreigners and Christians from entering the country. Such policy was formed on two main considerations: Independence from foreign power must be maintained, and the Hindu kingdom must be kept undefiled (i.e., the Hindu structure of society kept intact). Hence, foreign religions must be excluded. So the nation of Nepal was completely closed for almost two hundred years to any Christian mission. However, missionary work continued among the Nepalese living outside of Nepal. For two hundred years, many missionary agencies and individuals stood praying and waiting for the doors of Nepal to be opened once again. Finally in 1951, Christian missions were permitted to enter the land under certain conditions. The conditions were:

> They were to serve the people in such useful ways as should further the cause of nation building; they were to follow the rules of the department to which they were connected; they were to travel, and live only as their visas allowed; but they were not to propagate their religion or convert the people.[22]

With government restrictions, Christianity entered Nepal. Catholic Jesuit missions arrived in 1951 and boarding schools were opened. Other Protestant missions were allowed into the kingdom after 1951. Despite the condition that forbade proselytizing and in spite of persecution, Christians preached the gospel message and God was added to the church. In the early seventies, it was estimated that there were about 450 Christians scattered throughout the nation. At the close of the twentieth century, it was estimated that there were about 400,000 Christians throughout the nation. The young church of Nepal faces the greater challenge of discipling people who have committed themselves to Christ.

4.2 The Salient Features of the Religions in Nepal

The mission of God is being realized in the religious pluralistic context of Nepal. Nepal is the only Hindu state in the world[23] where other religions like Buddhism, Islam Christianity, Jainism and Sikhism also exist. The majority of the people are Hindu, but there are many similarities between the religions of Indian origin. Nepalese Hinduism has special features to adapt tribal religious beliefs and ancestor worship into its system, while tribal religions have similarly adapted Hindu beliefs. Chauhan asserts:

> The religion that emerged contained the elements of demonism, tantrism, Buddhism, and Hinduism. The basic trend and the form of this religion were, however, Hinduism but the basic spirit remained demonism. This is evidently manifested in all the major religious festivals that are observed in phases, encompassing various belief systems and rituals of different religious strands.[24]

The assimilation and the syncretism of demonism, tantrism and the worship of Hindu and Buddhist deities have shaped the Nepalese society in a peculiar manner. Both Buddhism and Hinduism, which came into contact with the indigenous people, reshaped themselves to suit the belief system of the people. The nature of Hinduism is accommodative, and it does not understand the need of changing religion. Every kind of belief and philosophy could be accommodated within Hinduism. Accepting Christ as one of the deities is not difficult to the Hindu mind. In fact, Hindus will be more than happy to do so. So it is in this religious pluralistic milieu the mission of God is to be accomplished. The church has a great challenge and opportunity to bring the kingdom of God into this context.

4.3 The Influence of Religious Pluralism in Nepal

Various religious groups and ideologies exist side by side in Nepal. Hinduism is the state religion and it is always against religious conversion, not because it is so hostile, but because it does not understand why religious faith has to be changed at all. Hindus in Nepal and India always feel that they have lost their people to Islam and Christianity and attempts have been made in the past to bring converted Hindus back with a purification ceremony. A majority of Hindus are of the opinion that any religious aspiration can lead a person to salvation, if adequately performed or realized. Buddhists also share similar views. Because of these dominating ideas in the Nepalese religious pluralistic society, preaching and conversion has been seen with great suspicion.

Though Nepal is a religious pluralistic society, Hinduism as the state religion, tries to dominate the religious, social and political atmosphere of the nation. From the beginning of Christianity until 1990, the political attitude toward Christianity was hostile. Many Christian leaders and believers were arrested and put in prison. Eastern religious accommodation and Western liberalism have influenced intellectual and elite groups. They see no logic behind any religious conversion.

4.4 The Evangelical Commitment of the Church in Nepal

The church in Nepal was established with the Evangelical commitment of the people who brought the gospel of Christ into the country. The Nepalese church, as a whole, is Evangelical in its expression. The church is strong in its conviction that the transformation of an individual, society and nation can happen only with the transforming power of the gospel. Evangelical Christians of Nepal have always emphasized the indispensable necessity of preaching the gospel for God has appointed his church to be the herald of the good news. The church in Nepal can identify with Martyn Lloyd-Jones who says:

> To me the work of preaching is the highest and the greatest and the most glorious calling to which anyone can ever be called. If you want something in addition to that I would say without any hesitation that the most urgent need in the Christian church today is true preaching, and as it is the greatest and most urgent need in the church, it is obviously the greatest need for the world also. Indeed, because man's essential trouble is his rebellion against God and his need of salvation, therefore preaching is the primary task of the church.[25]

There is no substitute for the preaching of the gospel, but the gospel has to be demonstrated in love. When Jesus began his ministry, he called people to repent, to be converted, to have a radically new mind-set, to be ready to face any kind of persecution (Matt 5:1-14). Such commitment was expected on the part of anyone who received and believed the gospel. But Jesus also helped the needy by meeting their physical needs. The Evangelical commitment of the church expresses holistic ministry by proclaiming the gospel as well as meeting social and physical needs in communities. But the social vision of the church should not replace the life transforming power of the gospel. The gospel has power to change the lives and mind-sets of the people. The Evangelical conviction of the church is the life of the church.

On the other hand, Evangelicals should not be arrogant in their presentation of the gospel. We should not detach ourselves from rest of the world. How important it is to identify ourselves with the people with whom we live and work. Emphasizing this aspect of identification, John Stott states:

> If we do nothing but proclaim the gospel to people from a distance, our personal authenticity is bound to be suspect. Who are we? Those listening to us do not know. For we are playing a role (that of the preacher) and for all they know may be wearing a mask. Beside, we are so far away from them, they can not even see us properly. But when we sit down alongside them, like Philip in the Ethiopian's chariot, or encounter them face to face, a personal relationship is established. Our defenses come down. We begin to be seen and known for what we are. It is recognized that we too are human beings, equally sinful, equally needy, equally dependent on the grace of which we speak.... He is a human being too, with sins and pains, and frustrations and convictions. We come to respect his convictions, to feel with him in his pain. We still want to share the good news with him, for we care about it deeply, but we also care now about him with whom we want share it.[26]

Again, true humility is essential in order to present the Evangelical conviction to the people. When we listen to another person and try to understand him or her, our respect for that person as a human being made in God's image grows. Our personal friendship will enhance clear communication and understanding with one another. We need to be honest and sensitive when we present the gospel to our friends. We need to deal with people not as belonging to some group or religion, but as our neighbors, our friends. Such tendencies will promote relationship and eventually the kingdom of God will be established.

4.5 The Mission Need for Adjustments

Christianity entered Nepal when preaching and conversion were considered illegal. Mission agencies from outside received entrance into the nation; obligated to follow the rules and regulations of the government of Nepal. Therefore, missions were engaged mainly with the national works of development. Officially they had no involvement in the growth of the church. Established missions were registered with the government of Nepal as international non-government organizations and they secured the official contract for five years with the understanding that they would adhere to the conditions set forth by the Nepalese government. Therefore, none of the established mission agencies attempted to do anything officially to promote Christianity and Christian gospel witness in Nepal. Today, many church leaders express the feeling that established mission agencies did not do anything for the church in Nepal. There was the expectation that these mission agencies should develop Christian manpower by educating doctors, engineers nurses and administrators, but those expectation were not fulfilled. They spent all their resources for the development of the nation and non-Christian manpower. These mission agencies have not developed Christian human resources for the churches and for their own mission agencies.

This criticism, as expressed by Nepalese church leaders, may contain truth. Christian mission agencies should have had a more visionary attitude from the beginning. They could have invested part of their resources to help develop Christian leaders for the church and the nation.

On the other hand, we have to consider the history of mission agencies in Nepal. Their entry occurred during a very difficult period. They had to sign an agreement with the government, which prohibited their direct involvement with the expected church activities. Many of the individual members of the mission agencies were involved in the mission of the church and engaged in the holistic ministry of the church. Indirectly, the involvement of these mission agencies has made a very positive contribution to the church in Nepal. The emerging church developed its own leadership because from the beginning there has been an emphasis on Nepalese churches being self-supporting, self-governing and self-propagating. Apart from a few exceptions, the Nepalese are the leaders in the Christian church, communicating to their religious pluralistic society that Christianity is *not* a foreign religion. But the church could not develop adequate Christian human resources to compete in the society. The non-Christians who were trained up by the Christian mission agencies became more hostile to Christianity than even other people. Majorities of their staff are non-Christians and the church is overlooked in the recruiting process of the staff. Human resources within the church have to be developed which could meet the need of the Christian mission agencies and have a Christian influence in the society and the nation. Deliberate strategy must have developed by the Christian mission agencies to work with the church in order to develop the Christian workers who could continue the ministry of the Lord

The church must have the mission of God in mind in order to fulfill God's desire. Ken R. Gnanakan emphasizes the intrinsic relationship between ecclesiology and missiology, when he says,

> The church without mission, ecclesiology without missiology, is only a static symbol of what God wants from his living body in witness to the world today.... While an ecclesiology without missiology is a hindrance to mission, an equally grave concern is missiology being worked out without a direct relationship to ecclesiology.... The traditional God-church-World sequence was said to be outdated and it was the God-World-church sequence that was to be seen as the direction of mission today. The church was being sidelined. What this amounts to is primarily an understanding of God's mission without any emphasis on the church-a missiology without ecclesiology.[27]

The Bible clearly indicates the central role the church is to play in relation to mission. Church is the people of God who are called to fulfill God's mission in the world. Every mission activity in the world has to be done through the church. Therefore, every church in Nepal should have mission activity and the mission agencies also should work through the church. Such a relationship will strengthen the church, and God's mission will be accomplished. God's mission is holistic, and gospel proclamation and social involvement need to come together for the transformation of an individual and society. The Christian mission agencies who have worked independent of the church need to realize that the mission of God needs to continue until Christ comes back. The church must continue its mission. There is no point of accusing one another. We must work together in order to accomplish God's mission. This is the priority. What happened in the past is past. The Christian mission agencies need to recover their mission mandate and start to work with the church to accomplish God's mission in Nepal. If they express that they are in Nepal not to work with the church, then they can remove their Christian identity and be like any other development agencies.

5. Conclusion

It is apparent that the mission of God has to be realized in religious pluralistic contexts. God's mandate has been entrusted to the church and he expects the church to accomplish his mission. God's mission is holistic and every aspect of human life has to be addressed. God's mission is not accomplished in isolation, but in the midst of people. In a religious pluralistic society, the challenges of mission increase everyday. New trends and concepts are being developed. In the midst of religious pluralism, secularism is also developing. Our holistic methods of mission presentation should meet the needs of the people with whom we are working. Here the holistic methods mean that every aspect of human needs has to be addressed. Our mission strategies need to be evaluated. Above all we need fervent prayers and the guidance of the Holy Spirit to accomplish God's mission. Our strategies and plans should be biblical and bring glory to our God.

---

[1] Hinduism, Buddhism, Jainism, Judaism, Christianity, Islam, Zoroastrianism, Taoism, Confucianism, Shintoism and Sikhism

[2] S. Moffett, *A History of Christianity in Asia*, vol. 1 (San Francisco: Harper San Francisco, 1992); Vinoth Ramachandra, *The Recovery of Mission* (London: Paternoster, 1996), viii.

[3] Ebe Sunder Raj, *The Confusion Called Conversion* (New Delhi: TRACI, 1998), 139.

[4] Raj, 133.

[5] P. Knitter, *No Other Name? A Critical Survey of Christian Attitudes towards the World Religions* (Maryknoll, NY: Orbis, 1985), 220-22; Ramachandra, *The Recovery of Mission*, ix.

[6] Bal Krishna Sharma, "A History of Pentecostal Movement in Nepal," *Asian Journal of Pentecostal Studies* 4:2 (July, 2001), 298.

[7] John R. W. Stott, *Christian Mission in the Modern World* (London: Church Pastoral Aid Society, 1977), 21.

[8] Ken Gnanakan, *Kingdom Concerns: A Biblical Exploration towards a Theology of Mission* (Bangalore: Theological Book Trust, 1993), 74.

[9] Charles van Engen, "Church," *Evangelical Dictionary of World Missions*, ed. Moreau, A. Scott (Grand Rapids, MI: Baker, 2000), 192.

[10] Paul Minear demonstrated that there are at least ninety-six different images of the church in the New Testament. Some of these are: body, temple, building, household, family, saints, new Israel, new creation, new branches of the vine, etc.

[11] Van Engen, 193.

[12] Stott, 17.

[13] Stott, 21.

[14] Stott, 22.

[15] Peter Cotterell, "Pluralism," *Evangelical Dictionary of World Missions*, ed. A. Scott Moreau (Grand Rapids, MI: Baker, 2000), 761.

[16] P. S. Jacob, "Mission and Pluralism: A Rediscovery," in *Doing Mission in Context*, eds. Sunand Sumithra and F. Hranghkuma (Bangalore, India: Theological Book Trust, 1995), 54.

[17] Secularism may be included in pluralism, because it is a developing trend all over the world.

[18] Ramachandra, *The Recovery of Mission*, ix.

[19] Ramachandra, *The Recovery of Mission*, 5.

[20] Jonathan Lindell, *Nepal and the Gospel of God* (Kathmandu: United Mission to Nepal and Pilgrims Book House, 1997), 17.

[21] Samuel R. Burgoyne and Jonathan Lindell, "Nepal," in *The Church in Asia*, ed. Donald Hoke (Chicago: Moody, 1975), 462.

[22] Burgoyne & Lindell, "Nepal," 464.

[23] National Planning Commission Secretariat, *Statistical Pocket Book Nepal 1990* (Kathmandu: Central Bureau of Statistics, 1990), 138.

[24] R. S. Chauhan, *Society and State Building in Nepal* (New Delhi: Sterling, 1989), 42.

[25] Stott, *Christian Mission*, 59.

[26] Stott, *Christian Mission*, 71.

[27] Ken Gnanakan, *Kingdom Concerns: A Biblical Exploration towards a Theology of Mission* (Bangalore, India: Theological Book Trust, 1993), 208, 211.

THREE TYPES OF ANCESTOR VENERATION IN ASIA:
AN ANTHROPOLOGICAL ANALYSIS

Wonsuk Ma

1. Introduction

The past several decades have witnessed a new self-awareness among Asian nations and this has resulted in a growing nationalistic emphasis. The emphasis takes different forms, like the emphasis of national languages instead of English in the Philippines, Malaysia, Myanmar and others, and the promotion of traditional culture (e.g., the emphasis of Confucianism in Singapore). In recent years, for instance, Sung-kyu Choi of Inchon Full Gospel Church has pioneered a creative contextualization to apply the traditional Korean cultural concept of *hyo* (孝, or filial tradition) to the reinterpretation of the scriptures.

Historically speaking, the church, as a social entity, has been in constant interaction with its given culture. Moreover it has not been exempted from the recent trend of self-awareness among Asian Christians. Ancestor practice in Asia is an example of such a struggle within the Asian church. Often how a church deals with this issue becomes an obvious indication of where one's Christian identity stands in relation to the given culture. Thus, this issue has become a showcase for contextualization.[1]

The present paper will attempt to view the issue of ancestor veneration from an Asian Evangelical perspective. A discussion will be devoted to the anthropological analysis of the ancestor practice in three types: religious, cultural (or ethical) and political. Various Christian approaches should be adopted depending on the type of ancestor veneration. Naturally, any firm solution or Christian alternative cannot be easily obtained. The paper, hence, hopes to encourage Asian theologians, pastors, evangelists and missionaries to engage themselves in a serious examination of the issue in the light of the "text" (the scripture) and the "context" (in this case, Asian culture). The reader should bear in mind the diversity of the Asian culture. Understandably, details of ancestor practice differ considerably from one location to another. Therefore, only general principles can be dealt with in the present discussion and any practical application to a specific setting will be left in the hands of those on the "front lines." Equally important is the fact that the current analysis of three types may not occur in reality. In most cases, ancestor practice in one locality may combine two or even three types rather than purely one type.

Before moving to the discussion, it will be in order to mention several relevant terms for the paper. "Ancestor worship" and "ancestor veneration" are two narrowly defined terms. The former has a strong religious emphasis while the latter is ethical in nature. "Filial piety" and "ancestor practice" are more broadly defined terms and generally refer to rites and practices that are associated with deceased ancestors. "Ancestor rites" may fall into a similar category.

2. Motives of Ancestor Practices

The subject has been a sensitive issue among Christians in Asia. Often, the subject becomes a showcase of contextualization where culture becomes a big issue. There are two basic elements that underlie the practices. Evidently both are uniquely non-Western.

2.1 Cultural Considerations: Asian Worldview

From an outsider's view point, the issue is simple and one is tempted to say, "What's your problem? Just stop this nonsense!" However, the root of the issue goes deep into the culture and the ancestor practice is only a response to what the culture demands. A culture is a mere reflection of one's worldview.

2.1.1 Concept of family system

The concept of family in Asia as the basic unit of society is much wider in its extent and deeper in its expectation from family members than perhaps in the West. A retirement plan is not known in this region and retirement homes are only for homeless and childless folk, or those deserted and abandoned by undutiful children. One pastor observes that the family name precedes the first name in Asia, suggesting that the individual exists for the family.[2] No elder person is called by the first name at all, and even younger people are generally called by their last names.[3]

Vertical solidarity in the Asian family is comparable to what we see in Scripture. It is not uncommon to see three or even four generations living under one roof, and eating from the same "pot." Often the old have the final say in family affairs. Proper respect toward them is taught and practiced at home. During meals the whole family waits until the grandfather picks up his chopsticks. In any social gathering, seniority gets priority. This results in consciousness of one's position in this vertical relationship. It is no wonder that in some Oriental languages, there are many different ways to address individuals depending on who is being spoken to. This vertical solidarity is extended even to the dead. The Bible exhibits the same cultural understanding. Amos recounts the saving act of God for ancient Israelites, but next moment, he includes his contemporaries in this experience of ancestors (Amos 2:9, 10, "you [eighth-century Judeans] were delivered"). However, the Asian culture stretches the concept further to accept the coexistence of the living and the spirits of the dead in the family system. The living are responsible to their dead ancestors, to ensure the continuity of the family existence, by bearing sons. Having a second wife when the first fails to bear sons is not only common but even desirable. The first wife remains a "sinner" who has failed to fulfill her obligation to the ancestors.

The horizontal solidarity in the Asian family is a sort of social security system. The extended family network ensures the welfare of its members. Everyone is obligated to exercise loyalty for the honor of the clan. If any one of the family becomes successful, by living in a big city like Manila, he is expected to accommodate relatives from his province. Sometimes, he is expected to help relatives' children go to school. If the eldest son does not take care of his parents, the second son will assume the responsibility. If there is no son to bear the responsibility, then a close relative like a niece of the old parents would look after them. Just as for the living parents, a close relative will carry out the responsibility to the deceased, if the spirit is not properly provided for by his or her son. A similar social security system is found in the Old Testament. The provision of kinsmen-redeemer (*go'el*) puts the case of an unfortunate member on the shoulders of the entire clan.

Christianity in Asia has been viewed with far more suspicion than it normally would, because of the West's strong emphasis on individuality. Individual decisions against the will of the family are regarded as a serious threat to cultural tradition. One's radical decision to take up a new lifestyle, contrary to what old family heads would dictate, is certainly seen as rebellion.

2.1.2 Awareness of the spiritual world

Historically, in the West, various religious experiences have been reduced to "abstract conceptualization" and this process is called "scientistic reductionism."[4] Christian theology became a child of the Age of Enlightenment. It is natural, in this intellectual environment, for the reality of the spiritual world to be played down, simply because it cannot be proven or *does not make sense* to the human mind. Christianity was reduced either to a set of religious rituals to lay people, or to dry intellectual exercises for theologians and religious leaders. The reality of God is so far removed (as expected in any "fully developed religion," like the Pharisaic Judaism of the first century, A.D.) that the immanent manifestation of God's power and his presence is just *remembered* but not often *expected*.

On the contrary, Asian culture is well aware of the reality of the spiritual world. Animistic belief prevails in most areas of Asia. Many times, deity is believed to be part of the natural world. Because of this "primitive" faith, one must obtain permission to "intrude" into the territory of a deity that is in charge of the locality. Religious rites are prepared to appease the deity, not only to keep it from intervening but also to obligate it to bless the offerer of the sacrifice. There is a give-and-take relationship between the divine and human world.

One clear example of spiritual consciousness is the various beliefs of an after-life among Asians. For instance, most Chinese, Japanese and Koreans believe that the present life activities continue beyond death, at least for a limited time. For this reason, one is very careful not to offend any deity during the funeral proceedings. Many Chinese believe that after death there is a journey and obstacles to be met that can only be overcome by the pious provision of the living. If not, the dead will remain on earth, causing much harm to the living members of the family. The deceased may also need things, sometimes to "bribe" the gate keepers of bridges, for the journey just as if he or she were in this world. For this purpose, a paper house, a car and even credit cards are made and burnt, so that the dead will receive and possess them. Food, wine and other things are also offered. It is also believed that the spirit of the deceased makes regular visits to the graveyard and the family altar on special festival days, as well as on the memorial day. Such a belief is not limited to the "folk-faith" but most religions that are practiced among Asians share similar concepts of immortality. For instance, Buddhists believes there is a cycle of incarnation after death.

2.1.3 Shame culture

In the "group first, individual next" setting, conformity is not only expected but also considered a virtue. One dresses not according to the weather but by imitating others. A sense of belonging has far reaching implications. Cultural tradition is a strong binding force and defines norms and obligations so that the individual remains within the security of the family or community network. *Utang-na-loob* (debt of gratitude) in the Philippines is closely related to the *hiya* (shame) concept and the idea of "smooth interpersonal relationship" gets high priority in one's life.

It is common for Asians to feel more comfortable when someone else makes a decision for them. In a coffee shop, when one is asked, "What would you like to have?" a response like "Anything is OK." is not uncommon at all. In his/her mind, there is a quick assessment of what is proper and accepted. In fact, many important decisions like marriage are made not by individuals, but by the family.

Bringing shame to the whole house, including the revered ancestors is a serious offense that a new Christian is likely to face. In Japan, committing suicide is sometimes considered far more honorable than remaining alive, and yet bringing shame to one's self and to the family.

2.2 Spiritual/Psychological Considerations

Having listed some cultural elements that underlie the ancestor issue, several human needs in the anthropological level contribute to the argument.

2.2.1 Anxiety for the unknown future

This worry is naturally based on the belief of the spiritual world. The problem is that many are misinformed. In their mind, a long journey is involved for the dead and provision for it is ensured by the living members of the family. The Igorot tribes in the Philippines prepare burial blankets to ensure that one's life after death will not be disturbed. The anxiety becomes real when one realizes that the destiny of the dead will one day be his or her own, and is in the hands of the descendants.

The Roman Catholic idea of purgatory is therefore an attractive approach to this psychological and spiritual need for Asians.

2.2.2 Fear of harm from the deceased

This fear is based on two beliefs: 1) the deceased spirit acquires the status of deity and has the ability to harm or bless the defendants; and 2) the spirit will seek revenge against the living members of the family for their mistreatment. Among the mountain tribes of the Philippines, almost all suffering such as sickness, accidents, bad crop and untimely death are attributed to the "claim" of the deceased. Retaliation is not only for the mistreatment done to the deceased while alive, but for the lack of proper provision after death.

Appeasing the spirit, therefore, is often to protect the living from any misfortune that the dead may bring, rather than to "honor" the deceased. This fear is the primary motive for the rigid and sophisticated preparation for burial and sacrifice. The recovery of the corpse from an accident site whether from the sea or mountain is a serious responsibility of the living, and does ensure that the lonely and hungry soul does not disturb others. Going through all the necessary procedures which will ensure the safety of the family is only possible if the corpse is available. A "spiritual marriage" is sometimes arranged for a deceased single man with a single woman who is also dead; but on rare occasions, a spiritual marriage between the dead and the living takes place. This will, according to the custom, enable the departed to "rest in peace" instead of wandering around disturbed and unsettled.

2.2.3 Desire for blessings from the spirits

There is a positive role that the deceased can play. Once satisfied, the spirits of the dead will be guardian angels protecting the family from misfortune. Since the spirit knows what a human does not, communication through a medium between the dead and the living is sought. Many fortune-tellers and mediums call upon the ancestral spirit for information. This is, in a sense, an expression of the present insecurity of the living.

It is also believed that by burying the dead facing the "right direction," and in the right location, the family will prosper. This belief is based on the *yin-yang* philosophy. Also by showing their veneration and loyalty to the dead, often expressed by using expensive items for the funeral, the descendants will be "rewarded" either by their ancestors or other deities.

3. Types of Ancestor Practices

The ancestor practice takes at least three different forms in Asia. Often they greatly overlap.[5]

3.1 Ancestor Worship: Religious Motif

This practice is purely religious and is usually found in areas of Asia where there is not much influence from Confucian ethics. Shamanism in Korea and animistic religion among the mountain tribes in the Philippines are typical cases.[6] A similar form is also found among the Chinese in rural and fishing areas where animism dominates popular thinking. A common belief is that the dead ancestor becomes a spirit (*kami* in Japanese; *hon* in Korean and *anito* in the Philippines), ranking among deities, with power to bless or to curse his/her family. As in many religions, the spiritual figure is not necessarily friendly, thus necessitating the need to appease the spirit so that the angry spirit will not curse the family. The deceased is an object of worship or fear, and the main goal of religious rites is to appease the spirit.

Among the Kankana-ey people in the Philippines, for instance, *cañao* is the most significant form of worship to the deceased. One who is "knowledgeable" of spiritual things among village elders becomes the "priest."[7] The sacrifice is prepared primarily for two reasons: 1) to remedy misfortune; and 2) to "please" the spirits so that blessings will be bestowed. In both cases, the priest "diagnoses" the misfortune, for example, sickness. It is normally attributed to a "disturbed" ancestor who is making a "claim" for the family member. A "prescription" will be made with the number of animals to be butchered and the specific date for the sacrifice. Normally, an Igorot dance precedes the butchering of the animal. In one instance, the number of pigs butchered reached to twenty five. This sacrifice will make the claim void. Yet, the "disturbing" element must be appeased. One time, according to the village priest in Lamut, La Trinidad, Benguet Province of the Philippines, an ancestor was disturbed because some roots penetrated his grave. After a big sacrifice, the family made another white cement grave and transferred the bones from the grave that had been invaded by the roots. The family claimed that their sick daughter recovered afterwards.

3.2 Ancestor Veneration: Cultural/Ethical Motif

This category is found among the places where Confucian ethic exerts a strong influence. Chinese, Korean and Japanese cultures fall in this bracket. These are the societies where strong emphasis is given to veneration to ancestors (孝), only next to loyalty to the emperor (忠). Historical surveys show that in China, the practices began by honoring heroes and emperors. The ancestor worship was added to it probably in the Chou Dynasty (1111-770, B.C.).[8] This is basically to compensate for what the children owe (*Bau*, 報) to the ancestors.[9] Traditionally, Confucianism teaches that "filiality is the foundation of virtue and the root of civilization."[10]

A Chinese pastor in Malaysia summarizes that filial piety is expressed among Chinese in five different ways: 1) by supporting and caring for parents; 2) reverence and obedience; 3) continuing the ancestral line; 4) glorifying the family name by bringing honor to one's parents; and 5) mourning and ancestral remembrance serving even after death.[11]

According to the teaching of Confucius, there are three stages of filial piety: 1) parents, when alive, should be served according to propriety; 2) when dead, they should be buried according to propriety, and 3) they should be sacrificed to according to propriety.[12] Confucianism even teaches that hurting or removing any part of the body is a serious offense against the parent. The ancestral sacrifice, according to the Confucian teaching is an expression of "remembrance" rather than act of "worship."

It is when Buddhism was introduced during the Han Dynasty under Emperor Ming (65-73, A.D.) that the rite acquired a religious significance. In particular, the ideas of heaven, hell, transmigration of souls and reincarnation resulted in various new practices being introduced, like burning paper objects.[13] Some practical elements of the rite began to gain religious meaning. For instance, candles were originally lit to light up the food since the rites took place at dawn. But later, this became an important part of the ancestor worship "to illuminate the food."[14] The wide spread understanding is that the spirit comes back to the world and visits the family during the memorial or festival days. Then the food and drink that are offered either before a picture or tablet of the deceased is not just a decoration, but a sacrifice to the spirit. In addition to that, many believe that the deceased ancestors have unusual "spiritual" power to influence the descendants. If these assumptions are the basis of the ancestor practice, then it is not just honoring or praising their virtues (德) as a filial expression, but worshipping as a religious act.

Of course it is often difficult, if not impossible, to draw a subtle line between veneration and worship, i.e., between the ethical and the religious act. Usually, surface arguments revolve around "honoring" rather than "worshipping," and, therefore, promoting cultural tradition rather than any "animistic religion." Yet it is obvious that the ancestor "respect" has a strong religious element.

3.3 Ancestor Veneration and Emperor Worship: Political Motif

This is the most complex type among the three patterns of ancestor veneration and is uniquely found in the Japanese tradition. By adding the political component, this appears to be the most developed form. However, a closer look reveals that a similar pattern is also found among tribal societies. A ritual that involves the entire village has a socio-political function to strengthen the solidarity of the community, while affirming the existing social order. Among the Igorots of the Philippines, a *cañao* is often prepared by a rich family for the whole village. This is also a time for a younger future leader (often a son of the rich family) to be introduced and affirmed by the community.

In Korea, during the Chosun Dynasty (1392-1910), Confucianism was formally adopted as the state religion. Thus, Confucian traditions and practices assumed political roles. As a consequence, any breach of these customs was considered an offense against the state. Historically, toward the fall of the Dynasty, Catholics were summarily persecuted not simply for ignoring cultural traditions, but for treason. Only when one recognizes the complexity of the religious, ethical and political nature, is it easily understood why the refusal of ancestor practices and cutting of long hair among men at the end of the Chosun Dynasty in Korea became the object of the state punishment. Because Confucianism was the state religion, its ethical traditions suddenly became political predicaments. Of course, this does not deny the religious role of the Confucian traditions.

The Japanese case of ancestor practices is the combination of the religious, ethical and political components. Through the medium of ancestor veneration, each family is connected to the state.[15] This pattern of solidarity was established among villages long before the advent of the centralized modern government system in Japan. Such a primitive link between individuals and a group was partly aided by the ancestor rites in the tribal society. Ancestor practices thus provided solidarity among large families and relatives which formed a community, and their loyalty to the society itself and its leadership.

In primitive Shintoism, before an elaborate theoretical system was formulated, the Japanese erected shrines for guardian ancestor deities/spirits for the families and the community. Around this Shinto shrine, group solidarity was achieved and through this process, their unique family tradition was transmitted to the next generation. The typical ancestor deity which the families and tribal communities worshipped was called Uji gami, and this became the center point for filial piety toward deceased ancestors and loyalty toward the tribal group.[16] Uji gami is not only the representative of all the ancestor spirits, but also the collection of them. According to Hori, once an ancestor dies, his or her spirit loses its individuality and joins Uji gami, the collection of all the ancestor spirits.[17] Today, the emperor is *the* Uji gami, thus uniting all the ancestor spirits. All these spirits become integral and essential parts of this complex Uji gami with the emperor as the apex of it. Thus, a complex system of ancestral practice has been developed to encompass the primitive religious worship, ethical veneration and now politically motivated solidarity and loyalty around the ancestral spirits.

4. Christian Responses

Historical records seem to show little evidence that Christian responses (particularly ones taught by Western missionaries) to the ancestral practices in Asia understood the various elements of Asian beliefs and practices. There have been two typical responses. Conservative Evangelicals either culturally labeled ancestral worship and veneration as anti-Christian superstition, or as idolatry, a breach of the Ten Commandments. Such crusader's mentality immediately brought a tension between the Asian society and Christians. On the contrary, the liberal wing of Korean Christianity has argued that filial piety (towards the living and the dead) is a traditional culture and practice (禮). The recent Vatican decision to repent of its historical sins and offenses prompted the Korean Catholic church to issue a formal penance. Two specific items are quoted here:

> 1. We, during the period of persecution against the Catholic Church in Korea when people knew very little of the world situation, sometimes tried to obtain the freedom of religion and protect the Church by depending on foreign powers, and experienced some cultural conflicts

on the way of the introduction of the Western culture. As it was shown in the events that caused sufferings and hurts to our people, we sometimes took part of unjust pressures of foreign countries.

7. We confess that we did not understand fully spiritual and cultural values, social and moral virtues within the other religions in our nation which forms a pluralistic society.[18]

The reference here is clearly to the traditional condemnation of the long-standing ancestor veneration as an idolatrous act as generally perceived among Evangelical Christians. A bloody period of persecution was the result of the "cultural conflicts."

Then it becomes clear how urgent it is to closely analyze various ancestral practices, their types and natures. Only after such an analysis, can Christians devise a proper response. It is, however, important to remind us, as mentioned earlier, that in reality there is no pure type of ancestral practice, but a delicate combination of various types. Therefore, in analysis, a careful look at each phenomenon according to the suggested types becomes important. The traditional Christian approaches are: Evangelicals insisting on the centrality of Christ's uniqueness for human salvation, while liberal churches being more generous toward traditional practices and beliefs. However, neither provides a satisfactory model for analysis, particularly if the complex nature of ancestor practice is ignored.

4.1 Religious Responses

For the religiously or spiritually motivated ancestor worship, Christian response can be rather simple. The Christian response should offer an alternative to the power of the ancestor spirits as an object of fear for their ability to curse, or as an object of worship for their ability and willingness to bless. God as the creator and Jesus as the only savior should be the base for the Christian response. A simple negation of the existence of gods and spirits by those who are not accustomed to the ancestor practices is not a solution. For instance, many funeral ceremonies in the Philippines contain both traditional and Catholic elements. Henry argues that Christianity has failed to offer an alternative by the simple denial of the spirit world. As a result, many folk beliefs and practices have persisted in daily life with their strong influences, while simply hiding themselves below the surface level.[19]

Such a syncretistic state of affairs can be traced to two fundamental oversights: 1) Christianity has been preached in Asia through a Western worldview and thought patterns, and 2) traditional Evangelical Christianity has tended to strongly negate the spiritual dimension of human life. For this reason, the Pentecostal movement of the twentieth century has challenged Christians to be aware of the reality of the spiritual world. Not many Asians would give up their deeply rooted beliefs in the existence of the ancestor spirits and their power by logical persuasion. Rather Christians should be able to communicate and demonstrate that God is more powerful and loving than ancestor spirits and other gods. At the same time, the Christians need to be able to prove that the so-called ancestor spirits are in fact either demonic elements or simply non-existent. For this very reason, many missiologists argue strongly for the need for exorcism or healing in the name of Christ.[20] Through power encounters, group conversion commonly called the "people movement" becomes possible and even an entire community becomes Christian.[21] That is, if the ancestor practice is based on religious and spiritual motive, Christian response also needs to present a religious and spiritual alternative.

4.2 Cultural and Ethical Response

The second is the cultural and ethical component of the ancestor practices. If one can successfully separate and remove all the religious and spiritual elements from the ancestor practices, continuing the cultural component would not pose a problem. However, the reality may not be that simple because forms are loaded with religious meanings, and they are integral in shaping the whole, and it becomes simply impossible to separate them. For example, instead of preparing food before the picture of the deceased ancestor and bowing toward it, a family can share a meal on the memorial day and remember the loved one's life and contribution. Although certain forms like a full bowl of food before a portrait of the deceased one can be problematic in the case of Korea, expressing one's love toward the deceased by placing a bouquet of flowers would be quite natural. And yet, if the intention is *not* religious but simply to remember the life and love of the deceased, even among unbelieving relatives, it could be easy to prepare a meal for the visiting relatives. At this time they may share their memories of the deceased one, thereby appropriately substituting other problematic elements such as setting a table for the deceased, placing a portrait before the table, bowing before it, and others. The bottom line is that the whole motif is not religious but simply cultural and ethical. The Korean Evangelical churches need to develop several viable models to express this aspect of the ancestor practices.

4.3 Socio-political Response

The ancestor practices with a political element added to other basic components are the most challenging and complex case. This unique and complex development of the ancestor practice may partly explain why Christianity has failed to make a significant inroad to the Japanese society. Some political variables may disappear as the society changes. However, there remains consistent continuity of this under girding principle evident from the tribal system to the modern centralized government.

Christianity needs to be extremely careful in devising its response, judging how a response would affect the nature and structure of a given society. For this reason, it may be worth paying attention to the people movement or group conversion as is often reported in the non-Western world. Also beneficial may be the study of the Catholic community system.

The impact and role of the ancestor practices in the society is also important. In almost all the cases, there is a clear social role that ancestor practices play. For instance, among the Igorots, their ancestral rituals enhance the solidarity of the community. As they have no other family or community festivals, such as Christmas, New Year and others, this role is critical. Some Christians, on the memorial day, butcher pigs as non-Christians do and feed the whole family or even the entire village. However, all the "pagan" elements are removed, such as the prayer of a pagan priest, the examination of the liver by the priest and others, and the void that creates is filled with a Christian substitute, such as singing praises, Christian prayer and even a short message. In this way, the primary purpose of honoring the deceased ancestor and the secondary social role are fulfilled. In addition, it provides a good evangelistic opportunity for the sake of other relatives and villagers.

5. Conclusion

This short study is intended to illustrate the need for a serious examination as to how individualistically-oriented Western Christianity has impacted Asia. At the same time, it also reveals that persistent denial and criticism of the Korean church without any serious analysis of

Korean ancestor practices has proven to be an inadequate approach. The question to be wrestled with is how Evangelical Christians and churches can proclaim the fullness of the Christian message while accurately segregating cultural elements and provide viable models that the church and society can easily adopt. This is not to deny various attempts made to bring Christian faith in the context of local cultures in various forms including memorial services. However, more proactive exploration is needed to bring the gospel and the given culture together.

---

[1] Ancestor veneration is one of the most urgent issues also among African Christians. For instance, Mathew Clark, "Asian Pentecostal Theology: A Perspective from Africa," *Asian Journal of Pentecostal Studies* 4:2 (July 2001), 182.

[2] Chi-Ping Yu, "Filial Piety and Chinese Pastoral Care," *Asia Journal of Theology* 4:1 (1990), 321.

[3] For instance, Wonsuk Ma, "Naming Names" (an unpublished reader for the New Student Orientation Manual of the Asia Pacific Theological Seminary, Baguio, Philippines, 2000).

[4] Chul-Ha Han, "A Critical Evaluation of Western Theology toward a Reappraisal of the Biblical Faith," in *Bible and Theology in Asian Contexts: An Evangelical Perspective on Asian Theology*, eds. Bong Rin Ro and Ruth Eshenaur (Taichung, Taiwan: Asia Theological Association, 1984), 41.

[5] Various forms of the ancestor practice in Asia are intensively discussed in *Christian Alternatives to Ancestor Practices*, ed. Bon Rin Ro (Taichung, Taiwan: Asia Theological Association, 1985), especially by Yuan-kwei Wei, "Historical Analysis of Ancestor Worship in Ancient China," 119-33; Lien-hwa Chow, "Christian Response to Filial Piety in Chinese Classical Literature," 135-46; Chi-ping Lin, "Ancestor Worship: The Reactions of Chinese Churches," 147-61; Myung-hyuk Kim, "Historical Analysis of Ancestor Worship in the Korean Church," 163-77. Also an excellent bibliography is found in this book.

[6] For various animistic rites and prayers, see Wasing D. Sacla, *Treasury of Beliefs and Home Rituals of Benguet* (Baguio, Philippines: BCF Printing, 1987).

[7] For the role of the priest, see Julie C. Ma, *When the Spirit Meets the Spirits: Pentecostal Ministry among the Kankana-ey Tribe in the Philippines* (Frankfurt am Main: Peter Lang, 2000), 114-15; Wonsuk Ma, "The Spirit of God among the Leaders of Ancient Israel and of Igorots Christians," in *Pentecostalism in Context: Essays in Honor of William W. Menzies*, eds. Wonsuk Ma and Robert P. Menzies (Sheffield: Sheffield Academic Press, 1999), 291-316.

[8] Wei, "Historical Analysis of Ancestor Worship in Ancient China," p. 125.

[9] Wei, "Historical Analysis of Ancestor Worship in Ancient China," p. 127.

[10] Chapter 1 of *Book of Filiality* (孝經).

[11] Yu, "Filial Piety and Chinese Pastoral Care," 317-18.

[12] *Analecta*, book II, V, 3.

[13] Wei, "Historical Analysis of Ancestor Worship in Ancient China," 130.

[14] Wei, "Historical Analysis of Ancestor Worship in Ancient China," 129.

[15] Kiyomi Morioka, "The Appearance of 'Ancestor Religion' in Modern Japan: The Year of Transition from the Meiji to the Taisho Periods," *Japanese Journal of Religious Studies* 4:2-3 (Jun-Sep, 1977), 185.

[16] Ichiro Hori, *Folk Religion in Japan: Continuity and Change* (Chicago and London: University of Chicago Press, 1968), 30.

[17] Hori, *Folk Religion in Japan*, p. 31.

[18] Catholic Bishops' Conference of Korea, "The Document 'Renewal and Reconciliation'" (http://www.cbck.or.kr/english/cbck/fr_en_cbck_index.htm, Dec 3, 2000), checked Aug 28, 2002.

[19] Rodney L. Henry, *Filipino Spirit World: A Challenge to the Church* (Mandaluyong, Philippines: OMF Literature, 1986), 2, 17-35.

[20] For the role of the supernatural work of the Holy Spirit among the Kankana-ey tribe in the Philippines, see Julie C. Ma, *When the Spirit Meets the Spirits: Pentecostal Ministry among the Kankana-ey Tribe in the Philippines* (Frankfurt am Main: Peter Lang, 2000). Also Gary B. McGee, "Miracles and Missions Revisited," *International Bulletin of Missionary Research* 25:4 (Oct 2001), 146-49.

[21] Allan Tippett, *Introduction to Missiology* (Pasadena, CA: William Carey Library, 1987), 253.

Part III

STRATEGIES

ISSUES IN THE SHORT-TERM MISSIONARY STRATEGY

Byung-yoon Kim

1. Introduction

Mission in the twenty-first century is as dynamic and healthy as it has ever been, but resistance to the gospel in some of the world's largest non-Christian religions seem to be growing more intense. The 1.21 billion Muslims around the world are unreached while 90% of India's population is still in castes and 300 million people continue to adhere to Buddhist beliefs. Thus, we need more missionaries who are motivated by a deep and abiding compassion for the lost and dedicated to the work of the ministry. We also need new methods which will be applicable in the new century's milieu in order to achieve the Great Commission.

We, however, live in a world different from any past era. The West has lost its dominant position in world missions while the two-thirds world missionaries are growing in numbers and ministries. At present, there are 1,540 global plans making progress such as Jesus film project which is now available in more than 630 translations, with more translations in progress. By the year 2000, the film had reached 4 billion people around the world.[1] The tools and resources needed for global evangelization are becoming more readily available. For instance, up-to-date resources on unreached peoples can be obtained from organizations such as the Adopt-A-People Clearinghouse and the Joshua Project II.[2]

2. Paradigm-changing Trends of Twenty-first Century Missions

2.1 A New Frontier: Unreached Peoples

Ralph Winter emphasized that today mission means going to peoples, not to places.[3] In the last century or so of missionary contact with peoples of the world, missionaries have become acutely aware of peoples and cultures. The modern science of anthropology owes much to the work of missionaries. The focus on ethnic groups and tribal languages has been carried on since the pioneering work of William Carey.

The "people group" concept has as its basis the assertion that reaching groups is faster and more effective than reaching individuals.[4] An unreached people group untouched by the traditional missionary presence will become a reached people group when Christians go and take the Good News of Jesus to them. When groups are reached, individual believers can fit into a group of their own kind and become firmly established in the faith. They will not be ostracized by and extracted from their communities. The "people group" idea also ensures the continuity of evangelism through the forming of indigenous Christian communities educated in the mission mandate. Mission will be carried on, not merely by individual efforts, but by the corporate, and therefore more powerful, efforts of the church.

2.2 Urban Missions: Cities as New Frontiers

If we are to reach the world of the twenty-first century, we must reach its cities and that will demand a new campaign of church planting.[5] The UN estimates that by the year 2025, urban areas are expected to be home to more than half of the world's people. At the onset of the third millennium, more than 280 cities exceeded one million inhabitants, and 14 of these are over 10 million. The numbers are expected to double by 2015.[6] The invisible, unreached peoples of the world's cities must be found. They are the poor, the industrial workers, the government employees and the new ethnic and tribal groups settling in urban areas. As the world becomes more urban, the emphasis on preparing missionaries to live and minister in urban centers grows. According to Roger Greenway, "the world of the twenty-first century will be urban, and so must be our mission."[7]

2.3 Non-Western Missionary Movement

Today, mission can no longer be viewed as one-way traffic, from the West to the Two-Thirds World. Paul Pierson notes the rapid growth of the non-Western Christian missionary movement as "the greatest new fact of our time." [8] The shift in dominance from Western missionaries to the co-existence and co-operation between missionaries from the West and the Two-Thirds World is a welcome change. Having non-Western missionaries in mission fields may represent a healthy corrective to the perception that Christianity is a Western religion. This decentralization is a significant step for world evangelization.

2.4 Partnerships and Networking

The buzzword in mission today is "partnership" (as opposed to "sponsorship" which suggests an unequal relationship). No single church, denomination or mission can fulfill our Lord's Great Commission. Neither can any one nation or continent. The Great Commission was given to the worldwide church to reach the world. Denominations, networks, missions, even individuals who are convinced that they know it all, have it all, and can do it all by themselves are the greatest hindrance to world evangelization today.[9] Mission in the new century will probably focus less on denominations.

For the most part, new century missionaries will be preparing for multi-ethnic and multi-lingual teamwork. Effective missionary teams of the future will flow with changing job and ministry opportunities. Interdependency (this is in contrast to independence, individualism and exclusiveness) and accountability, [10] however, are important in the partnership.

2.5 Cultural Pluralism

At the end of the twentieth century, the impact of the homogenizing pressures of modernization upon cultures could be witnessed worldwide. The pace of technological progress and the efficiency of global communications are imposing "sameness" on cultures everywhere. Mass culture is assaulting societies in an unprecedented fashion. Given such a scenario, Christianity has a role in helping people recover the riches of their own cultural heritages, or at least giving people a basis for critically assessing external (often Western) influences. Missionaries will have to allow new converts to develop a form of Christian belief and worship style appropriate and effective in their own culture.

2.6 Prayer as a Priority

A high premium on prayer is a characteristic of new century missions. This is especially needed in the restrictive and hazardous contexts where many Christians minister. Mission strategies today commonly incorporate detailed prayer programs and prayer mobilizations. "Prayer walk," together with people-group profiling, has become a regular aspect of pioneering work. Those prayer movements focus on world evangelization, not just on renewal of churches.

3. Wanted: Twenty-first Century Type Missionaries

3.1 Strategic-thinking Missionary

When I worked in Korea as a director of missions, one of my staff mentioned that there was a promo at a discount store in the city. If someone wins, she said, he or she can put anything they want into a cart, but they only have five minutes. "Wow! That's great!" was our immediate response, and we all hoped to win. While we were dreaming of winning, one of my colleagues told us that he would spend the first one minute and thirty seconds surveying the market. Five minutes, he said, is not long but if we made a market survey before putting merchandise into a cart, we may gather the better, more expensive items. This is strategic thinking!

Missionaries need to have this sort of strategic thinking also. It is not only a matter of how much time we work in the fields but also how we strategically use the time. Learning the language and culture of the host people and having some mission education or training might seem to be a waste of time but may produce better fruit in cross-cultural ministries. We need missionaries who can take one minute and thirty seconds from the five minutes for effective missions.

3.2 Creative Missionary

There are three eras in modern missions. William Carey started the first era along the coastal areas in India in 1792, and Hudson Taylor initiated the second era through pioneering work in interior China. Donald McGavran and Cameron Townsend became the forerunners of the third era through their focus on people groups. All the forerunners in missions in reality crossed the barriers of limitation. They were people who laughed at impossibilities! It is clear that it is hard to bring Muslims, Buddhists, Hindus and Japanese, among others, to Christ with the present methods. We need new and creative methods to reach them, even as the forerunners of modern missions did. Twenty-first century missionaries need to think differently! Twenty-first century mission is for creative missionaries who can laugh at impossibilities.

3.3 Professional Missionary

Unlike the secular business world, missionaries can survive even if they do not have enough support and do not produce good results. Thus, it is not a matter of how missionaries survive in the field but rather of growth and abundant fruitfulness throughout their ministry. Traditional mission approaches demand a significant financial resources and efforts to send and maintain the missionaries. On the contrary, professional missionaries who can not only meet some needs of the fields which are not often taken care of by traditional missionaries, but also they have financial flexibility and independency. The key question is: "Can such a missionary fulfill his/her assigned ministries effectively?" It is important for us to learn why missionaries spend two to three thousand dollars a month since their work could be done with less than one hundred dollars by local laborers in some cases. The missionary of the twenty-first century however, should have results-oriented concepts. They need to demonstrate excellence in ministry. We need to correct the paradigm of high cost/low efficiency with a low cost/high efficiency model.

4. Cross-cultural Missionary Formation

It is obvious that there needs to be flexibility in accepting missionary candidates so mission agencies are becoming more pragmatic about whom they will accept. Many are showing more and more interest in the actual competencies of their candidates than in their formal credentials or degrees. The mission field needs flexible, adaptable, teachable, purpose-driven and committed missionaries who display integrity in their lives and ministries. The following will be important in cross-cultural missionary formation.

4.1 Character-based Training

Mission agencies have recognized character as essential in effective leadership training. Christian and secular leaders alike have realized that a person's character, values and integrity between what they say and what they do, are important in any human endeavor. Ferris comments that the close linkage between character and training should not be overlooked. Character, unlike giftedness, is *not* a gift; it is trainable. We do not develop Christian character by providing and attending courses and seminars on Christian character. It is developed as a willing heart responds in obedience to the clear and systematic teaching of God's word under the Holy Spirit's influence.[11]

4.2 Language Acquisition and Cultural Adaptation

In order to have an effective cross-cultural ministry, missionaries must be students of language and culture (i.e., of the way a particular people organize their world). Culture is a system of beliefs (about God or reality or ultimate meaning), of values (about what is true, good, beautiful and normative), of customs (how to behave, relate to others, talk, pray, dress, work, play, trade, farm, eat, etc.) and of institutions which express these beliefs, values and customs (government, law courts, temples or churches, family, schools, hospitals, factories, shops, unions, clubs, etc.), which binds a society together and gives it a sense of identity, dignity, security and continuity.[12]

Since Jesus' missionary work included entering into the culture of the people and living with the inconveniences they had, his incarnational model (Phil 2:4-8) has to be the basic principle of cross-cultural mission even in the new century. Effective missionaries identify with the culture. Through an intimate knowledge of the people, missionaries see the world as the people see it and experience life as they do. We have no better example of this identification than Jesus Christ himself. He left his home in glory to become a vulnerable, dependent human infant. He knew hunger and thirst, poverty and oppression. He experienced rejection, anger and loss. He wept. His experience of human nature gave him tremendous insight. He manifested the above qualities during his earthly sojourn (Heb 2:17) and provided a relational platform for powerful ministry.

When we think of identification, the image of Hudson Taylor in native Chinese dress and a braided pigtail come to mind. Heart-to-heart identification however, is much more than adopting dress and customs. It is the result of a sequence of actions based on attitudes. Entering a culture with an open, trusting and accepting outlook is the first step. Responding to the inevitable cultural differences with humility, as a learner, is a second step.

4.3 Purpose-driven Missionary Training

Missionary training in the twenty-first century must equip candidates to work in teams composed of multi-cultural/international Christians from several nations, as well as to be able to take direction and counsel from leaders and co-workers from other countries. Servant leadership will be an essential quality and ministry skill to develop.[13] There are several purposes for training an individual to serve on the mission field.

(1) The first reason is to begin building a group of individuals into a team of missionaries with a common vision. Each individual joins the mission team with his/her own motives and goals. As the training phase progresses, each one should begin to take on the group's motives for service and desire to accomplish the goals of the group.

(2) The second purpose for training is to enable the missionaries to open their hearts to the culture and the people of their host country. This does not come naturally to people because we all have our own personal biases and preferences. An effective missionary is able to overlook personal preference (prejudice) in order to serve the needs of others. As the apostle Paul said, "Your attitude should be the same as that of Christ Jesus: Who, being in very nature God, did not consider equality with God something to be grasped, but made himself nothing, taking the very nature of a servant, being made in human likeness" (Phil 2:5-7). Being open to other cultures with a warm heart is essential for effective service.

(3) The third purpose for training is to develop experience. We want to be sure that missionaries will be trained in the areas in which they will serve. These areas may include, worship leading, directing games, teaching a Bible story, making a children's craft, sharing a testimony, or acting in a dramatic performance. This period of practice and honing of skills can make a big difference in building confidence and refining effectiveness.

(4) The fourth purpose is to provide an arena in which missionaries can worship Jesus Christ. After all, service should flow out of an attitude of worship. Time spent as a group in singing and other forms of worship can have a dramatic effect on the formation of spiritual values and attitudes.

(5) The fifth purpose is to discuss information concerning cross-cultural missions. It is important that missionaries know the specifics about cross-cultural missions to dispel unrealistic expectations. Questions should be answered, anxieties addressed and logistics discussed.

(6) The final purpose is to foster an attitude of understanding, service and learning toward other cultures. For many of the people who volunteer to go to the mission field, this will be their first exposure to another culture. Some time is needed to prepare these individuals for the things they will encounter.

5. Use of Short-term Missionaries for Cross-cultural Mission

The Mormons have experienced tremendous growth through using short-term missionaries.[14] From the founding of the Mormon Church, they were already known and characterized by their thriftiness, zeal and an admirable missionary spirit. During the Second World War, they had more than 2,000 missionaries actively working in many different countries around the world. And in keeping with the acceleration of cult propaganda everywhere, the Mormons have more than 30,000 missionaries (mostly, short-term) active today. Because most Mormon missionaries are young people, we personally noticed how aggressive they are to share their beliefs. They said that they make visitation to their prospects and members at least twice a week for discipleship and fellowship.

Among evangelicals, Youth With a Mission (YWAM) has supplied many workers to the mission field and most are short-term. Loren Cunningham believes that years of theological training do not necessarily qualify people to serve the Lord effectively. At the time when YWAM began, this was considered revolutionary. The idea of having relatively untrained young people doing missions was generally not considered, and was even seen as potentially disastrous. However over the years, while mistakes have of course been made, the concept of short-term missions has added huge numbers of people to the task of world evangelization. It is now accepted as a valid contribution to mission work.

Obviously, short-term missions has become a new pattern even in contemporary evangelical missions. Scott Bessenecker asserts that short-term mission endeavors, similar to those of the Apostle Paul in the book of Acts, are possible today. He presents five reasons for their viability. 1) English is the most widely spoken language in the world today as Greek was in the first century. 2) As travel along the Roman roads enabled Paul to reach vast areas, we are living in a world where we can freely and easily move from one country to another. 3) In Paul's day, Hellenistic culture was predominant in the world. In our age, Westernization of the world can help begin dialogue. 4) Mystery religions that indicated inward spiritual hunger in Paul's day are also seen in the New Age movement today. 5) Paul visited synagogues as a starting point. Likewise, the university campus is often an open door to a hostile environment today.[15]

5.1 Missionary Deployment and Field System

It seems that many Asian mission agencies lack effective strategies for missionary deployment. In the absence of effective strategies, missionaries usually move to the easiest ministry or country to enter at the expense of fulfilling the Great Commission. In contrast, the enlistment of Mormon young people into two years of missionary service can be a good model for every Christian local church to begin to enlist potential young people to do short-term missions. For effectiveness of short-term missionaries in cross-cultural missions, we may think about the following for mission dynamics: 1) actual redeployment of missionaries from resistant fields to harvest fields; 2) a shift from harvest field to hard fields, in contrast to above; for example, places within the 10/40 Window and unreached people groups; 3) a shift from mission fields to sending bases because missionaries are now being sent out from countries that formerly only received them; and 4) a shift from planting single churches to launching church planting movements (for instance, the Discipling A Whole Nation [DAWN] movement).[16]

It is possible for us to maximize the abilities of short-term missionaries by using them directly in church planting. As wartime soldiers, we can encourage short-term missionaries to adopt and practice a simple lifestyle. Since Asians are group-oriented, we need to develop team methodologies that are applicable to Asian missionaries.

Some Asian missionaries do not spend much time in ministry. There may be many reasons for this, but an inadequate system in the mission field may be the main one. Most Asian missions, unlike the Western missions, do not have proper field structures to implement mission endeavors. The remaining tasks are urgent and extensive so we need to develop an effective field system which fits well with Asian missionaries. Like Mormon missionaries and the secular business world, it is necessary for short-term missionaries to work at least eight hours a day and five days a week in their respective ministries. In this way, they can build relationships, visit homes and pray for the people. Church planting ministries could be multiplied through their full time ministry.

5.2 Missionary Care System

A missionary, in general, is expected to encounter difficulty in language learning and cultural adaptation. Kenneth Williams writes that from the day one enters the process of becoming a missionary, "spiritual, emotional, interpersonal and physical stresses begin to multiply, and these stresses usually continue unabated throughout one's career."[17] When stress builds unabated, missionary burnout is very likely. A poor missionary care system causes a dysfunctional team relationship in the field. Therefore, we need to develop better, more effective missionary care systems for Asian short-term missionaries.

6. Conclusion

The twenty-first century missions milieu is different from past centuries, and paradigm shifts in the world create crises in missions. A crisis, however, is not an impasse. From a divine perspective, a crisis may constitute a call from God for pioneering work to be done. Christian missionaries, however, are not called to cope with changes, even if these changes are global in character. They are called to judge changes from the perspective of God's revealed Word. They are asked to "reaffirm a biblical worldview that places Christ and his church above world trends, whether economic, political, cultural or religious."[18] It would be more effective if we could deploy and use short-term missionaries as teams. We also need to encourage those short-term missionaries to be strategic-thinking, creative and professional in their ministries. We may assign trained short-term missionaries in urban and unreached areas. Since more and more people are moving toward urban areas, there is a need to urbanize the missiological curriculum so as to provide tools for those preparing to minister in urban areas.[19] In order to achieve such goals, I suggest establishing more cross-cultural missionary training institutes in Asian contexts especially for short-term missionaries to make the paradigm shift.

---

[1] Rick Wood, "The Jesus Film Makes Astounding Progress," *Missions Frontiers* 23:1 (March 2001), 38.

[2] Joshua Project 2000 was launched in 1995 to develop an accurate body of data on unreached peoples. Joshua Project II is a continuation and expansion of the original project, with a special effort to highlight all the smaller and least-reached peoples of the world.

[3] Ralph Winter, "Editorial," *Mission Frontiers* 12:4-5 (April-May 1991), 2.

[4] Samuel Escobar, "Evangelical Missiology: Peering into the Future," in *Global Missiology for the 21st Century: The Iguasu Dialogue* (Grand Rapids, MI: Baker Academic, 2000), 109, however, calls "managerial missiology" the prevailing missiology trend today. It is characterized by the effort to reduce Christian mission to a manageable enterprise. Concepts such as "people groups," "unreached peoples groups," "10/40 Window," "adopt a people" and "territorial spirits" express the desire to use every available instrument to make the task achievable.

[5] James M. Phillips and Robert T. Coote, *Toward the 21st Century in Christian Mission* (Grand Rapids, MI: Eerdmans, 1993), 334.

[6] Harvie M. Conn, "Editorial: Refugees, the City, and Missions," *Urban Mission* 15:2 (December 1997), 3.

[7] Roger S. Greenway, "World Urbanization and Missiological Education," in *Missiological Education for the 21st Century: The Book, the Circle, and the Sandals* (Maryknoll, NY: Orbis, 1996), 145-46.

[8] Paul Pierson, "Non-Western Missions: The Great New Fact of Our Time," in *New Frontiers in Mission*, ed. Patrick Sookhdeo (Exter, UK: Paternoster, 1987), 9.

[9] Met Castillo and Katie Sisco, eds., *Into the 21st Century Asian Churches in Missions* (Singapore: Evangelical Fellowship of Asia, 1998), 96.

[10] Accountability is a preventive measure displayed by sturdy people who want to lead lives of growing godliness, and who know they cannot do it alone. It includes opening one's life to a few carefully selected, trusted, loyal confidants who speak the truth—who have been given the right to examine, to question, to appraise, and to give counsel. It means being regularly answerable to qualified people for each of the key areas of our lives. It means getting off each other's back and on each other's team. Accountability provides protection, growth, fellowship, and encouragement. We all have weak places and blind spots; we all have a tendency to rationalize and be defensive, to want to be

comfortable. Satan's attacks are subtle, and stress can be heavy. Without regular meetings for accountability and encouragement it is easy to become discouraged and to feel increasingly alone.

[11] Robert Ferris, ed., *Establishing Ministry Training: A Manual for Programme Developers* (Pasadena, CA: William Carey Library, 1995), 7.

[12] W. D. Reyburn, "Identification in the Missionary Task," in *Readings in Missionary Anthropology II*, ed. W. A. Smalley (Pasadena, CA: William Carey Library, 1978), 746-60.

[13] Stephen T. Hoke, "Paradigm Shifts and Trends in Missions Training: A Call to Servant-Teaching, A Ministry of Humility," *Evangelical Review of Theology* 23 (October 1999), 331.

[14] The Church of Jesus Christ of Latter-Day Saints, known also as the Mormon Church, known is one of the fastest growing religions in the world, and statistics add weight to that claim. In 1980, 578 converts were baptized daily, making the total of 211,000 for the year; not counting 65,000 baptisms of children who were raised as Mormons. At the time of their 151st anniversary, Mormons were dedicating about 1.5 church buildings per day all over the world.

[15] Scott Bessenecker, "Paul's Short-term Church Planting: Can It Happen Again?" *Evangelical Missions Quarterly* 33 (October 1997), 330-31.

[16] Hoke, 333-34.

[17] Kenneth Williams, "A Model for Mutual Care in Missions," in *Missionary Care: Continuing the Cost for the World Evangelization*, ed. Kelly O'Donnell (Pasadena, CA: William Carey Library, 1992), 47. See also Sally F. Dale, "Decreasing Fatigue and Illness in Field Work," *Missiology: An International Review* 2:1 (1974), 79-109.

[18] Araujo Alex, "Globalization and World Evangelization," in *Global Missiology for the 21st Century*, ed. William Taylor (Grand Rapids, MI: Baker Academic, 2000), 68.

[19] The following areas are important to the program: 1) a biblical theology of cities and of urban ministry; 2) urban anthropology, sociology and demographics; 3) conceptualization of the gospel in the urban environment; 4) history of urban mission and ministry; 5) nature of urban poverty and of community development; 6) urban political structures, social systems, and justice issues; 7) research techniques for urban evangelism and church growth; 8) effective methods and models of urban ministry; 9) physical and mental health in urban environments; 10) accessing urban resources, particularly through networking; 11) advocacy systems and empowerment in the city; 12) leadership development in diverse urban contexts; 13) communication

methods in the city; 14) non-Christian religions, cults and alternative world views; 15) principles of education and methodologies appropriate to various cultures and social contexts; and 16) urban spirituality and spiritual warfare in the city. See Greenway, 146-47.

THE CHALLENGES OF EMPOWERING PHILIPPINE CHURCHES FOR EFFECTIVE MISSIONS IN CHINA (AND BEYOND)

David S. Lim

1. Introduction

It has been almost two thousand years since our Lord Jesus gave his Great Commission to "make disciples of all nations" (Matt 28:19-20). We have to ask the question: where has Christian missiology and missionary practice gone wrong? With his full authority over heaven and earth, and with his promise to build his church without hindrance from the powers of hell (16:18-19), why has his church failed to finish the job? Why is one-third of the world's population still totally unreached? More specifically, why is the vast majority of the largest mission field today in China still unreached?[1] Although the most generous estimate counts about 100,000,000 Christians in China today,[2] this means that more than 1.1 billion remain unreached in that land alone.

This paper humbly ventures to suggest a possibility: the church has failed to faithfully move according to the intended (or original) plan that our Lord had for world evangelization! The challenge before us and our generation is to think, plan and work strategically under the guidance of the Holy Spirit. For the past two millennia, the church has been working on a self-defeating strategy, thereby disabling itself to mobilize the whole church to reach the whole world. The early church was doing quite well, but the next generations slowly shifted to the slow-paced mode of operation.[3] Especially since 313 AD when Constantine enforced Christianity as a state religion, the church has generally become dependent on "full-time missionaries" to reach the nations. It is no longer the whole church, but only a relatively few "called ones" who answer the Great Commission to be witnesses for Christ among the nations.

This paper assumes that before mobilizing churches to do mission, there needs to be a clarification of the mission paradigm. The discussion begins with a depiction of both the missiological vision (theology) and the missionary strategy (practice) that will be truly biblical and effective in mission to China (and elsewhere). It then proceeds to delineate and analyze the status of mission mobilization in the Philippines in empowering churches to do missions in China accordingly.

2. The Alternative Mission Paradigm

The thesis of this paper is that to finish the Great Commission the church should be in a total missions mobilization for church multiplication mode. In the early church, cross-cultural (and local) mission was done by almost all believers. Believers who scattered due to persecution in Jerusalem just used their homes to reach their neighbors and disciple them for Christ (Acts 8:1, 4; 11:19-21). As has been quoted in some circles, "Every heart with Christ is a missionary, and every heart without Christ is a mission-field." In this paradigm, cross-cultural mission comes naturally and is dependent on all believers (especially the so-called "laity") winning and discipling other (newer and/or younger) believers. Christians are also encouraged to migrate, work and study among the unreached peoples, mainly as tent-makers. Like the Apostle Paul, these bi-vocationals would not only be supporting themselves, but also subsidizing their co-workers and even helping the poor (Acts 20:34-35).

Better yet, global missions should be done mainly through sending *disciple-makers* to train Christians near the major unreached people groups (UPGs) to fulfill this "church multiplication strategy" or "church planting movement" (CPM). Each believer needs to aim to disciple just a few (perhaps a dozen, as our Lord Jesus did in His earthly ministry) "faithful people who will be able to disciple others also" (cf. 2 Tim 2:2). To go cross-cultural, these disciplers just have to focus on a few local contacts who are bi-lingual and/or bi-cultural. Upon conversion, these new believers can be discipled usually within a few months' time, to make new disciples among their compatriots through their natural "webs of relationships" (especially kin and friends)—almost always with greater effectivity, more cultural sensitivity and a faster "multiplier effect."

3. The Chinese Mission Paradigm

This is exactly the model of mission that the house churches in China have practiced for the past twenty years. They learned this "church multiplication" strategy mainly through experience, but not without the help of the ecclesiology of Watchman Nee, which prepared most Chinese Christians, particularly in his "Little Flock" churches, to cope with the state persecution that came upon China with the Communist takeover in 1949. Though most Chinese Christians will probably return to the traditional paradigm of church and mission if and when religious freedom is fully restored in China, it will be very hard to fully reinstitute the old mission paradigm there. After all, the house church Christians have shown full commitment and great success in evangelizing in this "new way," even at the cost of not being officially and legally recognized (and being considered members of cults, a major crime in China) by state authorities.[4]

The explosive church growth in China has been mentioned appreciatively in most missiological circles over the past 10 to 15 years. However, not much about their mission practice has been highlighted and adopted by the global church. Actually, the house churches have been the growing segment of the church in China, not just evangelistically in their immediate neighborhoods and among overseas Chinese, but also cross-culturally to the UPGs far and near them.[5] In contrast to the official government-sanctioned church (called the Chinese Christian Council/Three Self Patriotic Movement [CCC/TSPM],[6] which has been limited by the legal restrictions in religious practices, especially in evangelistic activities),[7] the unofficial house churches have been doing ministry and missions effectively without having to depend on government approval or foreign funding.

The main mission strategy among these house churches has been to send "short-term" (a maximum of two year terms) evangelists in pairs, who set out with simple provisions (often without return tickets) to plant churches along the way to their destinations. They normally do not stay long in a place, but appoint elders to take charge of the house churches before they leave, similar to the pattern of the first two missionary journeys of the Apostle Paul in Acts 13-18. Since the early

1980s, the house churches (mostly composed of rural farmers) have been sending young evangelists (some as young as 16 years old) two by two to plant churches and CPMs in surrounding villages. Several have also been sent to other regions, including the UPGs in Buddhist Tibet and Muslim Xinjiang. Various China-watchers have reported these outreaches over the years.[8] It is surprising that these strategies have not become a major influence in mainstream evangelical missiologies and missionary practice.

Their complementary mission strategy has been to send tent-makers, especially micro- and small entrepreneurs, into many unreached regions and gateway cities in China. They are active in Mongolia, Russia and Eastern Europe and most recently, in Latin America also. This has been the practice of the older house churches, especially from the Wenzhou area, since the mid-1980s. Admittedly, most of the churches that they plant are mostly Chinese, due mainly to their language limitations. The cross-cultural instances are almost all within China where the UPGs can understand Mandarin, the national/Chinese language.

With this "church multiplication" approach to missions, the challenge to overseas churches (including those in the Philippines) is to parallel and supplement this movement. Any less effective method will just slow the pace of the evangelization of China. To import traditional structures into China would just hinder growth and even retard the missions program of the churches there! Parenthetically, most house church supporters find that financial support that is being poured in to help the official CCC/TSPM is really counter-productive. Instead of helping in the CPM among the house church networks, these donations from overseas churches, especially overseas Chinese Christians are just adding more traditional Christendom structures that are preventing these government-approved churches from becoming truly self-supporting and self-propagating.

Simple church multiplication seems to also be the discovery of Christians in other restricted regions. Just as the house church Chinese have learned to say, "It is good to lead someone to Christ; it is better to plant a church; but it is best to plant a church planting movement," so other persecuted churches are learning the same paradigm. In India, they are saying, "Every Christian can plant a church; every house can become a church; and every church can become a Bible school."[9] Small churches called "Christ groups" are being multiplied in India, northeastern Thailand and rural Cambodia.[10] Similar CPMs under government and other pressures are also growing in Cuba, Vietnam, Nepal, Bhutan, etc.

4. The Converging Mission Paradigms

Now, there seems to be a convergence of confirmations from at least five streams or movements in the global church that point to this mission paradigm as the best way forward for global Christianity.[11] These are the mission mobilization movements, urban pastoral movements, biblical ecclesiology studies, student movements and holistic ministry movements.

First, as the most recent and closest to our concern, is the missions mobilization movement, led mainly by the International Mission Board of the Southern Baptist Convention (IMB-SBC). Since the mid-90s, it has become the main proponent of CPMs not just within their circles, but also in many mission circles especially those targeting UPGs and those associated with the DAWN Movement.[12] Their best findings are enumerated in the research and report of David Garrison (1999).

Their best model seems to be the POUCH strategy. One of their tentmakers in China discovered that to effectively do saturation evangelism among a UPG (of 6 million people in his case) the most effective strategy is that of church multiplication through planting *reproducible churches*. This means that each church should be able to plant another church within one year. In his case, 5,000 churches (each ministering to 1,200 people) were planted within 13.25 years. The key is to plant reproducible churches. When he implemented this strategy with his Chinese friends, they had 55,000 believers (from an original group of about 60) meeting in about 4,000 cells or house churches within 3 years. He left after a short time, and has been training other missionaries to do CPM since then.

The five characteristics of "reproducible churches" have been depicted with the acronym "POUCH": 1) *Participative* group meetings - the leader is a facilitator of discussion around God's Word, instead of a lecturer or preacher; 2) *Obedience*: the goal of meetings is to make disciples, to teach them to observe God's word; 3) *Unpaid* leaders: they found out that the most effective leaders were housewives who hardly finished Grade 3; 4) *Cells* or small groups: maximum size is 15 adults; before reaching that number, the church can start another church; and 5) *Houses* or venues that do not require rent or lot purchase.[13] With so few "overhead costs," believers can start new churches among their friends and contacts through simple witnessing for Christ, doing "friendship evangelism" in their hometowns and friends' facilities.

In a second stream belong the urban pastoral movements that may be best represented by Harvest Evangelism or the Prayer Evangelism of Ed Silvoso. The vision is to equip every Christian to be a minister/missionary, and mobilize every Christian home to be a church. All believers are trained to bless, befriend, serve, evangelize and then disciple their neighbors one by one in their homes (as "lighthouses" of prayer and evangelism).[14] This model is now being implemented in many parts of the world, especially in "Lighthouse Evangelism" in Singapore, and Mission America's "Lighthouse Movement" in the USA.[15]

In the next stream are the biblical theologians, especially of New Testament (NT) ecclesiology. There is a growing consensus that in the NT, *every Christian* is indeed expected to be a disciple-maker (a spiritually mature reproducing believer). After all, the NT teaches that every believer is a *prophet, priest and king* (*servant-leader*) in Christ, who is the only and unique Second Moses, High Priest and Royal Messiah (with no mediators in between). It is "upon all flesh" that the Spirit is poured out at Pentecost, so that *all* (not just professional evangelists) can declare God's words and works to the nations (Acts 2:17-18; 1 Pet 3:15). It is the "entire people of God" that functions as a priesthood (1 Pet 2:9-10; Rev 1:6 etc), so that all (not just ordained pastors and priests) can intercede for the people and offer sacrifices of praise and obedience to God (Heb 13:15-16; Rom 12:1-8). And it is the "whole body of Christ" that reigns with Christ in the heavenlies (Eph 2:6-7), so that all (not just "full-time" church workers) can work for the transformation of cultures and structures through the use of their spiritual gifts in loving service to all humankind (Matt 5:13-16; 2 Cor 10:3-5).[16]

I, as a New Testament theologian, suggest further that total mobilization was the original strategy of our Lord Jesus when he was on earth. To win the world to himself, he just used this simple disciple-making strategy:[17] he called 12 ordinary people (all rural folk, except for urbanite Judas!) After discipling them to do what he did (Mark 3:13-15), he sent them out two by two (that is six pairs) to make twelve disciples themselves (Matt 9:35-10:16). Therefore, when he sent out workers the second time, there were "72 others" (Luke 10:1, 17). If the "72 others" were sent out two by two, that is 36 pairs going forth to make 12 new disciples each, they would have made 432 new disciples in all. And in 1 Corinthians 15:6, Paul says that after the resurrection,

Jesus appeared to more than 500 brethren (11 + 72 + 432). If these 500 went forth in pairs, that is 250 making 12 new disciples each, they would be able to disciple exactly 3,000 new converts! That is probably what happened on the birthday of the church at Pentecost. All converts were *baptized immediately*, since the apostles knew they would all be followed up and discipled in at least 250 house churches in Jerusalem (from house to house, Acts 2:42, cf. vv. 41-47).[18]

In this NT ecclesiology, the role of church leaders who will serve more or less "full-time" is to serve as equippers (or teachers and *trainers*), not to monopolize the ministry, but to empower *all the saints* to do the ministry so that the whole church may be built up (Eph 4:11-13).[19] The ministry is therefore that of "making disciples," training a group of "faithful people" who will be able to disciple others also (2 Tim 2:2). The role of these servant-leaders is to model and train others to facilitate and coordinate the partnership and interdependence of believers in the house churches, as well as monitor and help enhance their qualitative and quantitative growth.

The fourth stream is the "cell multiplication" strategy which has been used by most of the student movements or campus ministries, particularly InterVarsity Christian Fellowship (IVCF), Campus Crusade for Christ (CCC) and the Navigators. They have been nurturing their constituencies through small groups, which actually are "disciple-making groups" (usually not more than 10 members each, so that the group does not lose the informal and intimate sharing of its body life) where they can participate actively and meaningfully. In the cells, they discover their calling as they use their spiritual gifts to serve and edify one another in love (cf. 1 Cor 14:26; Heb 10:24).[20] Students and young professionals are thereby empowered and sent out through such body life "into the world" (on the campus and beyond—without being subsidized) to be salt and light, making disciples wherever they go. To become a disciple-maker, every Christian student only needs to learn two basic skills: "friendship evangelism" and "leading cells."[21]

Each learns how to share the gospel and his/her personal testimony through "friendship evangelism." Students seek to lead others to Jesus *after* making a friendly approach to their non-Christian relatives, friends, colleagues and even strangers. They should be praying for a few non-believers among their contacts, and focus evangelistically on one or two of them at a time. Converts and potential converts are then brought to his/her cell group, or better, are encouraged to start an evangelistic cell at their convenient place and time. Then, they need to learn how to lead small group discussions (or inductive Bible studies) in their cells. This is where a leader can help all cell members participate in setting the agenda of their meetings, and seek the proper interpretation and application of God's word for the issues relevant to their personal lives and social contexts.[22] Equipping members in these skills has unfailingly produced effective leaders for ministry in the church and in the world.

Finally, the fifth stream is the holistic or transformational ministry movement. They empower communities for transformational development through the formation of core groups, which lead or guide the process called "community organizing" (CO). Using the CO approach, each group is given the freedom to manage their own body-life, according to their unique combinations of human and material resources in order to address the needs in their locality.[23] They should be able to collect funds for their own use (including about 10% for the support of the higher coordinating body in which their "servant-leaders" belong), as well as their own ministry or mission.[24]

Besides the convergence of these five streams, the marvel about this "church multiplication through total mobilization" strategy is that it has proven to be persecution-proof. In fact, it thrives under persecution, as in the case of China. This is especially significant since most, if not all UPGs (mainly Muslim, Hindu, Buddhist, Communist or animist) are warily (and often violently) opposed to any attempt to do overt evangelism among them. This low-key strategy may be the *best*, if not the *only* way to evangelize the vast unevangelized peoples of Asia, including China!

In fact, the rural house churches in China have also shown that this strategy is poverty-proof: poor churches can multiply this way without the need for external financial help. They have learned to *KISS* ("keep it simple and small") and *multiply*. In fact, it may be a disadvantage to be rich: rich churches usually fall into the trap of being inward-looking (or self-indulgent) and doing missions non-incarnationally (and non-holistically). They usually evangelize "from a distance" with their abundant cash and elaborate programs (which need a lot of time and energy for preparation), so that there is a lack of emphasis on spending time in building friendships, which is a prerequisite for effective disciple-making. Worse, they usually carry a patronizing and/or paternalistic attitude towards the target people. Such spiritual ineffectiveness comes from the degenerative effects of comfortable and luxurious living for the many who stay[25] (nicely called nowadays "senders").

5. The Philippine Church's Mission Paradigm

Hence, it seems that if Philippine churches are to do effective mission in China or elsewhere, they must be willing to adopt this mission paradigm, and thereby be equipped and empowered to do "church multiplication" effectively. They must learn to adhere to a simple doctrine ("priesthood of all believers") and a simple practice ("making disciples") in a simple structure ("house churches"). They have inherited a complex Christianity filled with man-made traditions, so that it will be hard for them to practice "basic Christianity" (prayer, Bible study, fellowship and witnessing) in basic Christian communities (small groups, called "household churches" in the NT). They have to unlearn the traditional paradigm that missions can be done only by experts or professionals (called "career missionaries") who are normally expected to plant (actually, to transplant) *their* (traditional/denominational) local church to other lands and cultures.

Providentially, the "relative poverty" situation of the Philippines and the Philippine church has been a big help for this paradigm shift.[26] In fact, the increasingly predominant missions thrust of the mainstream evangelical churches is pointed in this direction. All five converging streams are well represented in the Philippine church. Among the early advocates of this paradigm in the first stream are some of the active members of Philippine Missions Association (PMA), the Missions Commission of the Philippine Council of Evangelical Churches (PCEC), including: Asia Missions Network (AMNET), Asian Center for Missions (ACM), China Ministries International-Philippines (CMI-Phil), CrossTrain, Christ to the Orient Mission, Kairos Asia, New Tribes Mission-Philippines (NTMP), Philippine Challenge, Translators Association of the Philippines, etc. Several established local churches with strong missions programs are also among its membership, but they still have to make the mission paradigm shift; if and when they do- a "missions explosion" is in the offing!

In the second stream are charismatic churches that have been exposed to the Prayer Evangelism rallies of Ed Silvoso. They have formed the Philippine Prayer Evangelism Network (PPEN) presently led by Dan Balais, the National Chairman of Intercessors for the Philippines (IFP). Most interested in advancing this model is AMNET headed by Mario Albelda; they provide training in friendship evangelism, facilitating groups and church multiplication. Several ministerial fellowships that are moving towards becoming members of the Philippine Ministerial Fellowship Network (PMFN, led by Jonel Milan) are adopting the "every believer is a minister/missionary, and every Christian home is a church" model also.

The third stream consists of teacher-trainers in the missionary training schools, like ACM, CrossTrain, Great Commission Missionary Training Center (GCMTC), New Tribes Mission-Philippines (NTMP) and Penuel School of Theology. Some of the foremost advocates among them, also serving as faculty in seminaries, are: Eman Abrea, Valjun Apuzen, Robert Clark, Rey Corpuz, Corrie Acorda-DeBoer, Jun Escosar, Jun Gonzaga, David and Karen Lampinen, Jotique Lamigo, Jo Laville, Bob Lopez, Mel Luna, Peter Malvicini, Efren Roxas, Deng Samonte, Paul Stevens, Rey Taniajura, Emo Yanga and this writer.

In the fourth stream are the staff and members of various campus ministries like: Agape, Campus Crusade for Christ, InterVarsity Christian Fellowship-Philippines and Navigators. Most mega-churches and denominations also have "discipleship groups" or "cell groups" as part of their youth and young adults programs, which are not unlike those churches who are trying to become "cell churches."[27] However, these cells are still part of a centralized rather than decentralized structure, where the decision-making power devolves from the top (the pastor and the elders) rather than evolves from below (the cells).

In the final stream are the people involved in the Christian development organizations (CDOs), mostly affiliated with Alliance of Christian Development Agencies (ACDA) and National Coalition for Urban Transformation (NCUT). Among the leading CDOs who have applied the community organizing approach are: Buklod Biyayang Kristiyano (BBK), Center for Community Transformation (CCT), Christian Reformed World Relief Committee (CRWRC), Hosanna Christian Community, Institute of Studies in Asian Church and Culture (ISACC), Kaunlaran Sa Er-Ma Ministry, Kristiyanong Bayanihan Lingap sa Kabuhayan at Tagumpay (Kabalikat), Mission Ministries Philippines (MMP), REACH, Samaritana, Servants, Share An Opportunity Philippines (SAO), Ventures and Entrepreneurship Development Center in the Orient (VEDCOR), World Vision Development Foundation (WVDF), etc. There are also churches that have been transitioning into this approach to mission, like Alliance of Bible Christian Communities of the Philippines (ABCCOP), Christian Reformed Church (CRC) and Worldwide Church of God (WCG) in addition to all member-bodies of PCEC.

The constituencies of those who will be influenced by these five streams will provide the mission force for the missions delineated above. Like the house churches in China, though contextually different but perhaps more effective, the two major strategies of Philippine missions include: sending tent-making missionaries and sending short-term missionaries.

Through the Philippine Missions Association's Tentmakers Task Force (TTF), the Philippine church has adopted the vision of training and sending 200,000 tentmakers by 2010 AD. The Philippine economy will most probably maintain or even increase its export labor program in the next decade or so. With the presently estimated 6 to 8 million overseas Filipino workers (OFWs, now called OFIs as "investors"), there are possibly about 800,000 Christians among them. Many of them have been and are doing great mission work among their fellow compatriots overseas, and not a few are already doing effective cross-cultural disciple-making in their contexts (especially in the Middle East and Hong Kong). What is needed now is a coalescing of these efforts into a coordinated movement.

It is hoped that at least 1% (approximately 2,000) of these tentmakers will be serving in China. They can be English teachers, medical personnel, university professors, hotel and restaurant managers, agriculturists, entrepreneurs, students, etc. Among the mission agencies that are sending tentmakers into China today are: Asian Center for Missions-Philippines, Campus Crusade for Christ, China Ministries International-Philippines, Inc., Navigators, OMF-Philippine Home Council and Youth With A Mission. Most if not all of these missionaries in China today have been trained in the strategy outlined above. All of these agencies have a policy that their tentmakers must get the support of and be accountable to their churches as well.

The other strategy of sending short-term missionaries is particularly promising to Filipino Christians. Church leaders would bring some members (usually other church leaders) along with them on short term visits to other nations, not just do prayer-walk and Bible (and Christian literature) delivery, but also to provide practical training on various aspects of Christian ministries, mostly in the form of 2- or 3-day (usually simultaneous) seminars on discipleship, evangelism, children's and/or youth work, deliverance and healing, stewardship and church multiplication strategies. This has become a strategic goal of Asia Missions Network (AMNET) with its Project END (Empowering Nationals for Disciple-making). By 2010 AD, it aims to mobilize at least 2,000 of the best ministry practitioners (especially disciple-makers) in the Philippines to go on two-week mission trips. The purpose of these trips is to train at least 20,000 nationals to disciple their compatriots and UPGs (thereby doing saturation evangelization of their respective nations) more effectively.

So far, the mission groups that have facilitated the most effective short-term missions of this type are: CMI-Phil., Ethnos Asia, Open Doors Philippines (ODP), and most outstandingly, Tribes and Nations Outreach (TNO) led by Brother Joseph. Among the churches working in this mode are: Christ the Living Stone Fellowship (CLSF), Jesus Is Alive (JIA), Jesus Our Hope International Assemblies (JOHIA), Take the Nations for Jesus (TNJ) and most successfully, Warm Body of Christ (WBC) pastored by Andy Gaor. Only the mission groups noted above have ongoing programs for sending short-term trainers into China.

All of these mission groups and churches involved in praying and mobilizing for China belong to an inactive fellowship called China Network Philippines (CNP). The author serves as its convener, and plans to reactivate it in the summer of 2003, so that a more organized Filipino missions program to China can be developed.

6. Conclusion

So, it appears that the Philippine churches have started to become models and advocates of this mission paradigm, particularly in their mission to China. As shown above, a growing number of evangelical Protestant churches and mission groups have started to work in this mode already, albeit not in huge numbers at this time. Nevertheless, viable programs seem to have already been set in motion.[28]

Moreover, many of the Catholic Charismatic groups, especially Couples for Christ with its sister organizations, together with the Catholic Parish Renewal Experience (PREX), Basic Christian Community (BCC) and Basic Ecclesial Communities (BEC) movements have been forming small groups locally. They are also sending effective leaders to overseas assignments, mostly short-term training mission trips and a few as "lay missioners" (tent-makers).[29] Through the National Coalition for Urban Transformation (NCUT) and its member bodies, (especially World Vision), there are growing numbers of evangelical Protestant groups who feel comfortable and confident working in partnership with these evangelical Catholic groups. They are coming together to "finish the Great Commission in our generation."[30] This would increase the Filipino mission force greatly.

Philippine churches seem ready to stop *"playing* church (and mission)" and start *"being* church (and mission)." To stop maintaining "complex Churchianity" (which can hardly double in five years) and start spreading "simple Christianity" (which can easily multiply 2 or 3 times every year). Let them promote "church multiplication" and embark on church planting missions. May it match the rapid church multiplication in China. May the *whole church* in the Philippines be truly empowered to take the whole gospel to China and the whole world—quickly—"and then the end will come" (cf. Matt 24:14).

---

[1] An exhaustive study of unreached people groups (UPGs) in China is Paul Hattaway, *Operation China* (Pasadena: William Carey Library, 2000); a good summary of China's unreached cities is Paul Hattaway, *China's Unreached Cities*, vol. 1, *A Prayer Guide for 52 of China's Least Evangelized Cities* (Chiangmai: Asian Minorities Outreach, 1999).

[2] Tony Lambert, *China's Christian Millions* (London: Monarch, 1999), 37 has a conservative estimate of 30-50 million.

[3] This writer estimates that if we continue to do missions at this slow pace, which hardly copes with the world's population increase, we will not be able to evangelize the nations in another 500 years. Cf. David Barrett & Todd Johnson, "Annual Statistical Table on Global Mission: 2001," *International Bulletin of Missionary Research* 25:1 (January, 2001), 25 which shows that Christianity has decreased from 34.4% in 1900 to 33% in mid-2001, and will increase slightly to 33.4% in 2025, even when the global church has $15,500 billion of resources today, most probably more than enough to evangelize this world a hundred or even a thousand times over.

[4] For a detailed account of why they refuse to register as churches under state laws, read the "Official Statement of the Chinese House Church Attitude towards [sic] the Government, its Religious Policy, and the Three-Self Patriotic Movement" of 10 major house church networks issued in August 1998, in *China Prayer Letter,* No. 149 (November 1998-February 1999), 5-6; also in Lambert (1999), 55-68.

[5] For details on house church missions, cf. Lambert (1999), 43-177; Ross Paterson, *The Continuing Heartcry for China* (Tonbridge: Sovereign World, 1999), 208-21; and Raymond Fung, *Households of God on China's Soil* (Geneva: World Council of Churches, 1982).

[6] On CCC/TSPM, cf. Paterson (1999), 198-207; and Lambert (1999), 27-41.

[7] Prohibitions include: preaching may only take place in the registered building; ministry may be done only by approved pastors; evangelism by itinerant evangelists is strictly prohibited; no literature may be produced or distributed except the limited quantities provided by the CCC/TSPM; strictly no ministry among children and youth below age 18; etc.

[8] Most notable are the publications of the Chinese Church Research Centre and China Ministries International (both led by Jonathan Chao), Asian Outreach (Paul Kauffman & later David Wang), Open Doors (Brother Andrew), Overseas Missionary Fellowship and Friends of China (David Adeney, Tony Lambert, Elizabeth Lowe), Target Ministries and Christian Communications Ltd. (CCL).

[9] Reported by Steve Steele in *DAWN Ministries*, December 21, 2001.

[10] Cf., Tetsunao Yamamori, B. Myers, and D. Conner, eds., *Serving with the Poor in Asia* (Monrovia: MARC, 1995), 26-27, 53.

[11] This does not mean to claim that all five streams exist as single "movements," nor have they singly or corporately adopted this mission paradigm intentionally. Some are closer to the paradigm than others. This is just to show that there is a direction where all of their "best thinking" and "best practices" *can* converge.

[12] E.g., Wolfgang Simson, *Houses That Change the World* (Carlisle: OM Publishing/Paternoster, 2001).

[13] For more details, see David Lim, "The Fastest Way to World Evangelization: Church Multiplication" (Quezon City: CMI-Philippines, 1999), 1-4; and David Garrison, *Church Planting Movements* (Richmond, VA: International Mission Board of Southern Baptist Convention, 1999), 16-21.

[14] Cf. Ed Silvoso, *That None Should Perish* (Ventura: Regal, 1994); Jim Montgomery, *I'm Gonna Let It Shine!* (Pasadena: William Carey Library, 2001); and Jack Dennison, *City Reaching: On the Road to Community Transformation* (Pasadena: William Carey Library, 1999).

[15] For the USA story, see Montgomery (2001).

[16] Cf. Robert Banks, *Paul's Idea of Community* (Grand Rapids: Eerdmans, 1980), 91-107; Greg Ogden, *The New Reformation: Returning the Ministry to the People of God* (Grand Rapids: Zondervan, 1990); and David Lim, "The Servant Nature of the Church in the Pauline Corpus" (Ph.D. dissertation, Fuller Theological Seminary, 1987), 115-61.

[17] A most helpful book on how Jesus discipled the 12 is Robert Coleman, *The Master Plan of Evangelism* (Old Tappan, NJ: Revell, 1964); also cf. Leroy Eims, *The Lost Art of Disciple Making* (Colorado Springs, CO: NavPress, 1981).

[18] No wonder their numbers increased *daily.* It looks as though our Lord Jesus knew how to use the spiritual "network marketing" strategy quite effectively so long ago. Cf. Lim (1987), 219-269.

[19] Cf. Roland Allen, *Missionary Methods: St. Paul's or Ours?* (Grand Rapids: Eerdmans, 1962); R. Allan, *The Spontaneous Expansion of the Church* (Grand Rapids: Eerdmans, 1962); Banks (1982), 135-140; Fung (1984); and Lim (1987), 163-218.

[20] Note that ministry is repeatedly described as done to "one another" in mutual service and submission (1 Thess 5:12-22; Matt 18:15-20; James 5:16, etc.).

[21] E.g., Eims (1981); E. Griffin, *Getting Together: A Guide for Groups* (Downers Grove: IVP, 1982); Richard Peace, *Small Group Evangelism* (Downers Grove: IVP, 1985); and Petersen (1993).

[22] This *participative* approach is vital to ensure the authority of Scripture (and thus avoid dependency on the leader) and the development of *leaders* who can speak and think for themselves (and not of followers who remain immature and susceptible to false teachers).

[23] E.g., Bryant Myers, *Walking with the Poor* (Maryknoll: Orbis, 1999); Robert Linthicum, *Empowering the Poor* (Monrovia: MARC, 1991); and Yamamori, et al, (1995).

[24] Perhaps for house churches, at least 50% of their "common fund" can be used to subsidize their outreaches to non-Christians locally and internationally.

[25] The only antidote to this "comfort zone" lifestyle (and mission) is a "simple lifestyle" that is committed to sharing one's life and assets for missions, esp. among and with the poor (Matt 6:19-33; Luke 12:13-34; 14:25-33; 21:1-4; Acts 20:33-35; Eph 4:28; 1 Tim 6:6-10, 17-19).

[26] The author has labeled the traditional paradigm in the Philippines as "a third world church trying hard to do first world missions."

[27] "Cell churches" are patterned after the Faith Baptist Community Church pastored by Lawrence Khong, who has developed the two-winged model of the church (only "celebrations" on Sundays and "cells" on weekdays) set out in Ralph Neighbor, Jr., *Where Do We Go from Here?* (Houston, TX: Touch, 1990).

[28] Those who are interested to be trained in this mission strategy can get a simple 20-hour video/VCD training module produced by PMA's Tentmakers' Task Force (tel/fax: 63-2 533-6075). It consists of four 5-hour courses: Friendship Evangelism, Leading Rapid Church Planting Movements, Underground Spirituality and Contextualization (cross-cultural issues).

[29] On BCC and BEC, cf. Alvaro Barreiro, *Basic Ecclesial Communities* (Maryknoll: Orbis, 1982); Leonardo Boff, *Ecclesiogenesis: The Base*

Communities Reinvent the Church (Maryknoll, NY: Orbis, 1986); Stephen Clark, *Building Christian Communities: Strategy for Renewing the Church* (Notre Dame, IN: Ave Maria Press 1972); Keith Fournier, *Bringing Christ's Presence Into Your Home: Your Family as a Domestic Church* (Nashville, TN: Nelson, 1990); and James O'Halloran, *Living Cells: Developing Small Christian Communities* (Maryknoll: Orbis, 1982).

[30] See the author's unpublished monographs on "Riding the Next Wave of the Spirit" (2000) and "Consolidating 'Evangelicals and Catholics Together'" (2001).

A DESCRIPTIVE STUDY OF MISSION PROGRAMS OF SELECTED PHILIPPINE-CHINESE CHURCHES IN METRO MANILA: POLICIES, MOTIVES AND VIEWS OF MISSION

Chiu Eng Tan

1. Introduction

The theme of our mission symposium "Empowering Asian Churches for God's Mission" is appropriate to many Asian churches as we all enter the twenty-first century. We are glad that many presenters are indeed from our Asian churches, sharing with everyone what they have learned about mission. Allow me, then, to present an initial study of the mission programs of selected Chinese churches in Metro Manila. A brief introduction about the Chinese in the Philippines is in order.

First, the Chinese in the population is one of the smallest among the Diaspora Chinese in Southaast Asia. According to Kaisa Para Sa Kaunlaran, Inc. (KAISA), the Philippine-Chinese people constitute about 1.5% of the total population of the Philippines. [1] The 1.5% estimate may not be very precise and it ranges from 1% to 1.92% from previous studies. [2] While it is difficult to arrive at an exact number of Chinese in the Philippines, the 1.5% may suffice to give an overview. Currently, there are approximately one million Chinese, which is really a very small number in comparison to the 76 million Filipinos. The total population of the Philippines as of May 1, 2000 was 76,498,736. [3]

Second, there are primarily three groups of Chinese in the Philippines. The first is alien Chinese. These are Chinese who reside in the Philippines but are citizens of other countries. The new wave of immigrants from China in the last few years are engaged in business while some come as students studying in our local universities mostly concentrated in the Divisoria in the Chinatown area. Next are the ethnic Chinese. These are China-born Chinese mostly from the coastal Fujian province in southeastern China who immigrated to the Philippines and are residents and citizens of the Philippines. The China-born Chinese belong to the first and second generations or older generation of Philippine-Chinese, while the Philippine-born Chinese are locally born, raised and became citizens or permanent residents of the Philippines. The third and fourth generations or younger generation of Philippine-Chinese were born after the Second World War. They constitute 85% of the Philippine-Chinese in the Philippines.[4] The third group is the assimilated Chinese. They are the Filipinos with Chinese ancestry extending back to pre-Spanish times. This group, Filipino in culture, language and orientation, makes up about 10% of the Filipino population.[5] The terms "Chinese," "Filipino-Chinese," "Chinese-Filipino" or "Philippine-Chinese" used interchangeably in this paper refer to the second group of Chinese, i.e., the ethnic Chinese. The greatest numbers of ethnic Chinese reside in the Santa Cruz and Binondo area of Manila constituting 36% of the ethnic Chinese in the Philippines.[6]

Third in our overview is the fact that there are currently 78 Chinese churches in the Philippines, 33 of which are located in the Metro Manila area. The first Chinese church established in the Philippines is the St. Stephen's Parish Church (1903) and is located in the Chinatown, Santa Cruz, Binondo area of Manila. The second oldest Chinese church is Cebu Gospel Church (1916) is the largest Chinese church in Cebu City, Visayas, Central Philippines. The United Evangelical Church of the Philippines, also located right in the district of Santa Cruz, Binondo, Manila was founded in 1929. Some of the newer churches that were formed in the last fifteen years include Christian Bible Church of the Philippines (1987), Diamond Jubilee Evangelical Church (1989), Gerizim Evangelical Church (1990) and Glory Evangelical Church (1997). The Chinese church formed most recently is the New Millennium Evangelical Church founded in October 2000.[7] The Philippine-Chinese churches are self-governing, self-supporting and self-propagating.[8]

Finally, as far as I know, there has been no study on the mission programs of Philippine-Chinese churches. To encourage and mobilize Philippine-Chinese churches for God's mission, this exploratory study of the Philippine-Chinese churches chose only four churches in Metro

Manila for the purpose of this study of mission programs of Chinese churches. Due to time constraints, the criterion used to select these four churches was solely based on their annual mission budget or goal. The churches selected are the four Chinese churches that have the highest mission budgets or goals for 2001 or 2002 (or a fiscal year of twelve months).[9] Hopefully, a subsequent study will include other Chinese churches involved in mission in Metro Manila and other major cities in the Philippines.

This paper seeks to understand the mission involvement of Philippine-Chinese churches through the mission programs of the four selected Chinese churches in Metro Manila. In particular, we will look into their understanding of what mission is as reflected in their mission programs, the different mission involvement of the church members, the different kinds of mission ministries supported by these churches, and their motives in doing mission and policies of financial support of their missionaries. We seek to answer the following questions: What is their view of mission? Is their view of mission adequate to meet the challenges of the twenty-first century?

The author used the interview and questionnaire method to gather data, and also collected financial reports and other documents graciously provided by these four churches.[10] In each of the four churches the author interviewed the senior or mission pastor of the church (by interview) and chairpersons of mission boards (by questionnaire).[11] This paper seeks to show that the Evangelical conservative theology of the four Chinese churches interviewed influence their understanding of mission, i.e., mission is basically evangelism or the fulfilling of the Great Commission. Such an Evangelical view of mission is strongly reflected from the mission activities/programs, church mission handbooks and financial support of missionaries involved mostly in evangelism, church planting and the like.

2. The Mission Programs of Four Philippine-Chinese Churches in Metro Manila

This paper is divided into three parts: church mission involvement, financial policies of supporting missionaries, and views of mission. There are basically two approaches in what we call the mission programs of the four Philippine-Chinese churches. First, there are church activities that directly or indirectly promote mission awareness, fellowship programs that gain mission exposure and involvement with supported missionaries and/or mission organizations. Second, the mission board leads the church in setting mission goals and budget, promotion of mission awareness through mission exposure trips, financial support of missionaries and the like.

2.1 Church's Mission Involvement

The Philippine-Chinese churches, through individual church programs, promote mission awareness to let church members gain exposure and get involved in missions. First, the numerous church fellowships such as the men's fellowship, women's fellowship, young professional's fellowship and the like visit and participate in the mission ministries of the church's supported missionaries, whether in Metro Manila or in the provinces.[12] Churches formed regular/summer medical and dental mission teams to gain mission exposure and actual ministry experience by the church members. For example, the members of Grace Gospel Church who are doctors and dentists formed the Grace Evangelical Association Medical & Dental Team. They performed free medical services for the churches of their supported missionaries spread all over the Philippines, covering Antipolo, Bulacan, Caloocan City, Malabon, Novaliches, Pampanga, and as far as Baguio and Benguet.[13] PCC#1 plans ten summer teams for Year 2002.

Also PCC#1 has various outreach programs that are evangelistic in emphasis. The church has founded a Christian day school with an enrollment of 1,800 students from kindergarten to high school. 80% of PCC#1's numerical growth comes directly from the campus student ministries in this church-affiliated Christian school. Other outreach programs include the Evangelism Explosion Fellowship, outreach programs to senior citizens homes in two places, an outreach program to recent immigrants from China, and the church district fellowships. All of these programs focus on evangelism and share the gospel with their target group. Since 1991, PCC#1 has encouraged the church's young people, through its Youth Work Council, to get involved in holistic mission among the Filipinos, and has started holistic ministries through the various outreach evangelism ministries. They are ministering in orphanages, a jail ministry, helping the urban poor and battered children. Outreaches also include children feeding programs and evangelism to the juvenile youth in the Manila Youth Receptor Center. They are involved in the home for the aged, and distribution of goods and economic assistance to typhoon victims also.[14]

Second, these Philippine-Chinese churches also designate one Sunday per month as their evangelistic Sunday worship service, and church members invite their friends who are non-believers to attend that service. Usually the message has an intentional evangelistic thrust, making known the gospel message.[15] The same holds true for the other churches interviewed, churches in Metro Manila and various places in the Philippines.

Third, PCC#1, PCC#2 and PCC# 3 (and most Chinese churches) hold their annual mission week inviting speakers to expound on missions and several related subject matters such as support and care of missionaries.[16] A whole week is devoted to the teaching and preaching of mission, seminars and workshops designed for missionaries, fellowships between missionaries and church members, and missionaries speaking in different fellowships and teaching in Sunday school classes of the supporting church. Such week-long programs allow the church members and missionaries to know each other and also expose church members to first-hand reports of what their missionaries are doing in the field.[17]

Fourth, most Philippine-Chinese churches which have mission programs and an annual mission budget are organized under the leadership of the church's mission board. The members of the mission board are elders and deacons selected from the church council and mature lay leaders. The mission board is a separate entity distinct from the church council but is under the authority of the church council.[18] Second, all four churches are Evangelical in theology holding the divine inspiration of the Bible as having final authority on all matters of faith and practice.[19] Also, the task of evangelism is central to the life of the church and their mission programs.[20]

2.2 Financial Policies of Supporting Missionaries

From the inception of St. Stephen's Parish Church in 1903, the history of the Chinese church in the Philippines today is about 100 years.[21] Among the four selected Chinese churches, the earliest church was established in 1929 (now 72 years old), while the latest church was established in 1980 (about 20 years old). Table 1 shows basic information about the four Philippine-Chinese Churches. The total mission budget of these four churches for the year 2001/2002 is P26,188,791 (P=pesos) or roughly US$ 503,630.59 (using the rate of one U.S. dollar for 52 pesos, rate fluctuates between P51.00 to P52.00 in recent months).

Some simple procedures are normally taken when the mission boards of these Chinese churches support missionaries. Two principles are non-negotiable requirements before any missionaries turn in their applications.

First is the principle of Christian witness and the reputation of the mission organization and its missionaries. Normally, the Philippine-Chinese churches support missionaries affiliated with recognized mission organizations instead of directly supporting missionaries. Hence, the senior pastor or mission pastor has adequate knowledge regarding the reputation of the key leaders of the mission organizations. They are recognized for good reputations, Christian witness to the Christian community and their actual ministry involvement.[22] At times, some members of a church's mission board are also members of the Board of some locally recognized mission organizations. Hence, they recommend to the church qualified missionaries for possible support.[23]

Second is the principle of an Evangelical conservative theology. The mission organization's doctrinal stance, goals and objectives must be consistent with the Evangelical doctrinal position of the church. The theological requirement was strongly expressed by all four churches interviewed including the chairpersons of mission boards.[24] None of the churches expressed their desire to support non-evangelical mission organizations. Normally, when the first two requirements have been met, a missionary then turns in his/her application and the mission board reviews the application.

Third is the policy of partial support to foreign missionaries. The four churches all give partial financial support to missionaries serving in a foreign country. None of them could afford to give full financial support and find supporting foreign missionaries is significantly more expensive than local missionaries. For example, looking at the mission budget of PCC#2 from Table 3, it takes more money to support three missionaries in Taiwan (one couple doing church planting and one in office administration work), one foreign mission organization and one church in the US than to partially support ten local missionaries (involved in various ministries such as church planting, Bible translation, urban poor, student evangelism, tribes evangelism and church planting, theological education and Muslim work plus 10 local para-church organizations (Bible colleges and seminaries, other organizations doing children's ministry, counseling ministry, hospital ministry, radio ministry and student campus ministry).

This also holds true for PCC#3 and PCC#4. (See Tables 4 and 5.) It takes less money supporting nine missionaries of local Bible colleges and seminaries than supporting five foreign missionaries also involved in theological education (Table 4). PCC#1 only partially supports two foreign missionaries who take up 1% of their total budget. In fact, one of the churches has decided to decrease their support of foreign missionaries and end all partial support to foreign missionaries starting in the year 2003, due to the recent economic crises with the weakening peso, and the focus on China ministries.[25] One senior pastor expressed his observations of E3 mission:

> E3 mission is expensive and takes a long time before results can be seen. Our church leaders are businessmen by profession and hence are business-minded in their dealings. Their concerns include cost and practicality of intercultural mission. When comparing local and intercultural missionary work, it is obvious that local missionaries require less time and cost in their training. Our church leaders are inclined to consider supporting relatively inexpensive local/home mission than significantly more expensive E3 missionaries which require years of training but hardly promise good immediate results. Some of our supported missionaries are doing mission work in Panama, Taiwan and Australia. It is very expensive to provide full financial support. Therefore, we give partial support.[26]

Fourth is the policy of partial or full support to local missionaries. Three churches give partial support to local (Filipino and Philippine-Chinese) missionaries of a recognized mission organization or a monthly amount to support the operating cost of mission organizations, while PCC#3 gives full support. Full support here means full and adequate support of the monthly living expenses or "living needs."[27] Aside from the monthly support, PCC#3's financial support also includes "separation pay, thirteenth month bonuses, health insurance, limited calamity and funeral assistance, and retirement benefits for the missionary."[28]

Some churches such as PCC#3 provide allowance to the wives of supported missionaries. The wife of a supported missionary who is not employed and unable to help her husband receives an allowance of 50% of her husband's support. A wife who has children below 6 years old and hence is unable to help her husband receives a 70% allowance of her husband's support. And the wife who helps her husband full-time in the ministry receives an allowance of 75% of her husband's support. The wife of a missionary who is gainfully employed receives no allowance from PCC#3.[29]

Fifth is the policy of partnership. Acting as partners in the mission ministries of recognized mission organizations, the three other churches provide partial support or a monthly amount to missionaries or mission organizations. PCC#1 agrees to support a missionary and provides a monthly amount to the missionaries with the understanding that the mission organization shall match the same amount to support the missionary. Also, both PCC#1 (similarly with the other churches) and the mission organization agree to supervise, guide and monitor the missionary in the field.[30]

Sixth is the policy of multi-layer-support, i.e., financial support, ministry support and prayer support going together. Most missionaries are required to submit a monthly or bi-monthly report of their ministries. Supporting churches assign their Mission pastor to visit, guide, monitor and encourage supported missionaries in the field. PCC#3 prays for a missionary every Sunday morning during Sunday worship service.

The policy of priority of evangelism and church planting is seventh. Most of the financial support of the four churches goes to supporting local Filipino missionaries involved mostly in church-planting and to teachers and professors in local Bible colleges and seminaries. These are consistent with the goals and objectives of these churches. PCC#1 states, "The main tasks of a missionary are evangelism, discipleship and training." PCC#3 mission board's goal is "to give financial and prayer support to Evangelical Christians who are called to the mission field, particularly to do evangelism, discipleship and church planting." Bible colleges and seminaries are important in that they train and produce church leaders such as pastors and church-planters for the task of evangelism. Almost all are involved in E0/E1 ministries. This means that they are Filipino missionaries involved in urban and rural church planting all over the Philippines, Philippine-Chinese church leaders working among Philippine-Chinese churches all over the Philippines, Filipinos reaching their fellow-Filipinos or Filipino-Chinese reaching their fellow Filipino-Chinese.[31]

However, PCC#1, PCC#2, PCC#3 and PCC#4 also support missionaries directly doing E2/E3 missions. They are reaching out to tribes in the Philippines; the Aeta Negritoes, the Ilongots, the Dumagats, the Mananguas and the Muslims with a total of eighteen missionaries. One of the missionaries sent to the Muslims of PCC#3 is himself a converted Muslim and now evangelizing his fellow Muslims in Basilan Province. So far, since public preaching is prohibited in the Muslim area, pre-evangelism or sowing the word of God is what most missionaries are doing. To date, no converts have been won to Christ and no churches have been planted yet.[32]

Eighth is the principle of holistic evangelism. Whereas in the past the dichotomy between evangelism and social action was debated and even feared among some churches, the four Philippine-Chinese churches are involved in holistic mission work. These churches are directly involved with mission, particularly among the urban poor through raising up and sending their own medical and dental missions. They are also indirectly involved by supporting mission organizations who are doing mission work among the poor. Some of the ministries the churches support are: Mission Ministries Philippines (urban poor in Payatas), The Center for Community Transformation (urban poor in many parts of Metro Manila and other parts of the Philippines) and Integrity Sunday School Mission (urban poor children in Metro Manila). Some churches provide medical and dental services to nearby barangays, and even regular social work among youth and other depressed areas.[33]

In summary, the four Philippine-Chinese churches prioritize their financial support to local Filipino missionaries involved in evangelism and church planting. This is followed by leadership development through their support of teachers and professors of local Bible colleges and seminaries. Due to the expensive cost involved in supporting E3 or foreign missionaries, all E3s receive partial support. These churches may decrease their support as economic difficulties and the weakening peso continue.

3. View of Mission of Four Philippine-Chinese Churches

This section of the paper seeks to show that the Philippine-Chinese churches hold an evangelistic view of mission, i.e., evangelism is central to the task of mission. Direct evangelism is seen in church planting, sharing and preaching the gospel so that people may come to accept the gospel and Jesus Christ as Lord and Savior of their lives thus fulfilling the Great Commission.

What are the views of mission in the four Philippine-Chinese churches? What motivates them to have mission programs to get involved in mission and annual mission budgets to support missionaries involved in different kinds of ministries? Questions such as "Why does your church want to be involved in mission? Why do mission?" were asked of the senior pastors and chairpersons of the mission boards. Not only are these churches evangelical in doctrine, evangelism is a priority in their view of mission.[34]

First, a basic reason why a church is involved in mission is due to the strong leadership of a mission-minded minister who has brought the vision of mission to his church members. The whole church believes that mission is the function of the church and that a church should become a mission-minded church. The pastor of PCC#3 shared: "Thirty-five years ago, when the pastor and church leaders started our mission programs and organized our mission board, they impressed upon the hearts of all church members that 'the church exists to do mission.' Since then, our church members to this day understand that 'mission is the natural life of the church.'"[35]

Second, key words and phrases such as "the Great Commission," "evangelism," "to share the gospel" and the like repeatedly occurred in response to the questions asked.[36] One said, "Mission is implementing the Great Commission with a view to train believers to become disciples so that they in turn share and spread the gospel to others."[37] Another said to the same effect, "Mission is the spread of the gospel." The purpose statement of our church states that "we believe a great commitment to the great commandment and the great commission will grow a great church."[38] However, direct evangelism and the gospel are not the only meanings of mission. One pastor tried his best to widen church members' understanding of mission when he said:

> Our church members understand mission to be doing "direct evangelism" regardless who the target is. They also understand and know the traditional mission work, the traditional recognized ways of doing mission such as church planting, giving of gospel tracts, direct verbal sharing of the gospel. I am trying my best to widen their view of mission and let them understand that, for example, sports evangelism is another form of evangelism, and other concepts such as tentmakers and the like.[39]

The pastor of PCC#3 went on to add, "Mission involves evangelism but it is not just evangelism. There are always rooms for pre-evangelism which lays the ground for mission work. The traditional understanding of evangelism is an image of someone knocking at someone's door and directly sharing the gospel immediately." [40] Similarly, the pastor of PCC#4 shared, "There are two kinds of evangelism: evangelism in word and evangelism in deeds. Mission is evangelism and nurture. Moreover, mission involves not just evangelism but also pre-evangelism and post-evangelism. The goal of mission is not just conversion of souls but ideally the converted Christian should not stop at conversion but must be trained to lead others to Christ."[41]

Concepts such as life-style evangelism and establishing rapport should precede the actual verbal sharing of the gospel and are obviously understood by these pastors who in turn influence their church members. "Evangelism in deeds" includes extending help in times of crisis which becomes an effective pre-evangelism strategy to win the hearts and respect of non-believers before the gospel can be effectively shared and accepted.[42] Still, whatever strategy is employed in pre-evangelism, it is conversion, including training the newly converted to win others to Christ, thereby fulfilling the Great Commission, that constitutes mission.[43]

Third, the evangelistic view of mission is further seen in the mission statement of the mission board of PCC#1 which states, "We aim to positively respond to the Great Commission of our Lord Jesus Christ in going out to make disciples of the nations, baptizing them in the name of the Holy Trinity, and teaching them to obey His commandments. We will mobilize church resources, equip Christians through appropriate trainings, send them out into the mission fields, and reach the unreached for God by utilizing all suitable means, including networking with other organizations. Through these efforts and empowered by the Holy Spirit, we see men turning away from sin, receiving Jesus Christ as Savior and Lord."[44]

Related to this is the mission board policy of PCC#1 which defines the main task of a missionary to be "evangelism, discipleship and training."[45] PCC#3's Missionary Handbook states similarly: "The main purpose is to glorify God by fulfilling the Great Commission. Its goal is to give financial and prayer supports to Evangelical Christians who are called to the mission field, particularly to do evangelism, discipleship and church planting."[46] The main task in mission efforts concentrate on evangelism, discipleship, church planting and training.

Fourth, the evangelistic view of mission these four churches hold may be further seen in the missionaries they support and the kinds of ministries the missionaries are involved in. Tables 2, 3, 4 and 5 show the different kinds of ministries of missionaries supported by these four Philippine-Chinese churches. The four charts summarizing the mission budgets of each church interviewed and the different kinds of ministries they support show one significant trend consistent with their evangelistic view of mission. 18.32% of PCC#1's total mission budget goes to supporting missionaries directly doing church planting or pioneering work, i.e., sharing the gospel with a view to win converts in a prescribed period of time where there is no established church in a particular locality, whether urban or rural. Such a case is also true with PCC#3 (25.79% of total budget) which supports 22 missionaries involved in church-planting among the urban and rural places, among the tribes of Ilongots, Negritos and Dumagat and more recently among the Muslims in Mindanao.

4. Conclusion

We have fulfilled what the paper seeks to do. First, we have seen that the four Philippine-Chinese churches are themselves actively participating in missions through evangelistic outreaches to different target groups, by medical and dental teams, summer mission exposure trips and a host of other activities. Second, the mission boards of these four churches have their annual mission budgets which prioritize E0/E1 evangelism and church planting, and the support of Bible colleges and seminaries, training leaders and church-planters for the local churches in the Philippines. These churches give partial support to E2/E3 mission which is significantly more expensive than E0/E1 mission. Among all the missionaries supported, four Filipino-Chinese come from these four churches who are members or former members of these churches. The Philippine-Chinese population in the Philippines is indeed very small in comparison to the 76 million Filipinos. Aside from sharing their financial resources, how do we encourage more Filipino-Chinese young people to get involved full time in mission? Lastly, the Philippine-Chinese holds an evangelistic view of mission. Is this adequate to meet the challenges of the twenty-first century if we compare them with what David J. Bosch has suggested are the thirteen elements of a missionary paradigm?[47]

The results of this initial study of four Philippine-Chinese churches will be used to continue the author's study of other Philippine-Chinese churches which have mission programs, mission involvement and mission budgets. May God continue to use and challenge the Philippine-Chinese churches in the twenty-first century!

---

[1] For more details, check www.kaisa.org.ph. KAISA is an organization seeking to understand and study the Chinese in the Philippines and has many publications about the Chinese in the Philippines.

[2] See Hiroshi Maruyama, "The History and Religious Culture of the Chinese in the Philippines," in *Continuity and Change in Overseas Chinese Communities in the Pan-pacific Area: Proceedings of Symposium Held at the University of Tsukuba, June 19, 1990*, eds. Tsuneo Ayabe and Masaki (Tsukuba, Japan: Research Group for Overseas Chinese Studies, University of Tsukuba, 1993), 226 where he says that the ethnic Chinese in the Philippines in 1987 is 1.92% of the total Philippine population. Sylvia Palugod, *The Chinese in the Philippines: A Demographic and Socio-cultural Profile* (Manila: CCOWE Fellowship, Philippines, 1993), gives 650,00 Chinese in 1993 or about 1% of the total Philippine population. Bryant L. Meyers, *The New Context of World Mission* (Monrovia, CA: MARC, 1996), 21 in the section titled "The Population of Chinese Diaspora in South East Asia," the following figures are found: 7.2 million in Indonesia, 5.8 million in Thailand, 5.2 million in Malaysia (or about 32% of the total population), 2 million in Singapore (or 77% of the total population) and 1 million Chinese in Philippines.

[3] "Census 2000 on Total Population, Number of Households, Average Household Size, Population Growth Rate and Population Density by Region, Province and Highly Urbanized City: as of May 1,2000: Census 2000 Final Counts Summary of National Statistical Office."

[4] Palugod (1993), 2, 14.

[5] Ibid.

[6] Ibid.

[7] *Millennium Herald* 1:7 (September-October 2002), the official publication of the New Millennium Evangelical Church.

[8] Joseph T. Shao, "Heritage of the Chinese-Filipino Protestant Churches," *Journal of Asian Mission* 1:1 (1999), 94-95; also his "A Channel of Blessings in God's Hands," in *Chapters in Philippine Church History*, ed. Anne C. Kwantes (Manila: OMF Lit., 2001), 419-427. The self-propagating stage was most active from the 1930s to 1970s due to the outreach ministries of the Evangelistic Band of the United Evangelical Church of the Philippines, currently the largest Chinese church in country.

[9] The sensitive and confidential nature of financial reports graciously given by these four churches deserves total anonymity. When documentation relating to finances or sensitive issues are needed, the author wishes to preserve anonymity and chooses to use the names PCC#1, PCC#2, PCC#3 and PCC#4. Only when appropriate, the names of the Chinese churches may be used.

[10] See Tables 1 to Tables 7 for summaries of mission budgets and different kinds of ministries supported by these four Philippine-Chinese churches.

[11] A personal interview on December 18, 20, 2001 in Manila, Philippines.

[12] An interview with the senior pastor of PCC#4 on December 20, 2001, in Manila.

[13] An interview with the senior pastor of PCC#4 on December 2001, in Manila. Also PCC#1's *Church Mission Booklet Year 2001.* See "Medical & Dental Team Annual Report," in *Grace Gospel Church 35th Annual Missionary Conference 2001 Booklet*, 7.

[14] An interview with the mission pastor of PCC#1 on December 18, 2001 in Manila.

[15] An interview with the senior pastor of PCC#4 on December 20, 2001 in Manila. He also said "One of my church's key leaders is himself actively involved in evangelistic pulpit ministries supplemented by a drama team of church members. I believe this is one of the best ways to let our church members be aware of mission and also get involved in evangelism. We not only participate in mission through sharing of our financial resources, but we would like to "send" our own church members to be involved in evangelistic outreaches, get church members be aware of mission and get them involved in mission."

[16] See *UECP Mission Booklet for the 33rd Mission Week, 2001* with "Understanding Mission work...Becoming partners" as its main theme. Church members are encouraged to participate. It states, "Every member will actively participate in any of the above Mission Department ministries and give them financial and prayer support. You can participate in personal evangelization, short term mission trips or care for the various ministries of our missionaries. You can also dedicate to be full time missionaries. We hope that one day, our Lord can say to every member of our church, 'Well done, good and faithful servant, come and share your Master's happiness'" (p. 2).

[17] See *Grace Gospel Church 36th Annual Missionary Conference Programs* on November 17- November 25, 2001. Also, see UECP 33rd Mission Week Schedule on June 9-17, 2001 with the main theme: "GO and MULTIPLY the Great Commission."

[18] See *Operations Manual United Evangelical Church of the Philippines for the Organization and Ministries of the Mission Board*, 91-93. The mission board has four objectives: 1) to encourage church members to take up the responsibility of mission works, 2) to coordinate with all affiliated organizations in doing mission works, complementing each other in their ministries, 3) to send out missionaries to both national and international localities, and 4) to provide trainings for seminarians and missionaries, both national and international. See also *Grace Evangelical Association Missionary Handbook*, 1.

[19] PCC#3 *Missionary Handbook* states under the Doctrinal section: "The divine inspiration of the Scripture, both Old and New Testaments, that is the

highest standard for the church's conduct, and the ultimate authority in the life of the Christian." PCC#4's handbook for baptismal candidates states: "The Bible is God's Word to us. It was written by human authors, under the supernatural guidance of the Holy Spirit. It is the supreme source of truth for Christian beliefs and living. Because it is inspired by God, it is the truth without any mixture of error."

[20] Shao, "Heritage of the Filipino-Chinese Protestant Churches," 96.

[21] For a brief history of Chinese Protestant churches in the Philippines, see Shao "A Channel of Blessings in God's Hands," 413-28.

[22] An interview with the senior pastor of PCC#4 on December 20, 2001 in Manila.

[23] An interview with the mission pastor of PCC#2 on December 18, 2001 in Manila.

[24] All four pastors of PCC#1, PCC#2, PCC#3 and PCC# 4 were interviewed by author on December 18 and 20, 2001 in Manila. See also *Grace Evangelical Association Missionary Handbook*, p. 2.

[25] An interview with the senior pastor of PCC#3 on December 18, 2001 in Manila.

[26] An interview with the senior pastor of PCC#4 on December 20, 2001 in Manila.

[27] PCC #3 *Missionary Handbook*, 3.

[28] PCC#1 leaves the Social Security System, Medicare, Retirement and separation pay to the responsibility of the missionary's local church or mission organization. See Appendix 1, #8.

[29] Ibid.

[30] An interview with the mission pastor of PCC#1 on December 18, 2001 in Manila..

[31] Ralph D. Winter and Bruce A. Koch, "Finishing the Task: The Unreached Peoples Challenge," in *Perspectives on the World Christian Movement: A Reader*, 3rd ed. eds. Ralph D. Winter and Steven C. Hawthorne (Pasadena, CA: William Carey Library, 1999), 510-11.

[32] An interview with the senior pastor of PCC#3 on December 18, 2001 in Manila.

[33] Interviews with all the pastors of PCC#1, PCC#2, PCC# 3 and PCC#4 on December 18 and 20, 2001 in Manila.

[34] Arthur F. Glasser, "Evangelical Missions," in *Toward the Twenty-first Century in Christian Mission*, eds. James M. Philips & Robert T. Coote (Grand Rapids, MI: Eerdmans, 1993), 11.

[35] Ibid. A full treatment of this topic is the book by Charles van Engen, *God's Missionary People: Rethinking the Purpose of the Local Church* (Grand Rapids, MI: Baker, 1991), 30-33.

[36] A personal interview was conducted using both the Amoy dialect and English. The author took notes and translated all the questions and answers to English.

[37] An interview with the mission pastor of PCC#2 on December 18, 2001 in Manila.

[38] An interview with the senior pastor of PCC#4 on December 20, 2001 in Manila.

[39] An interview with the senior pastor of PCC#3 on December 18, 2001 in Manila.

[40] Ibid.

[41] An interview with the senior pastor of PCC#4 on December 20, 2001 in Manila.

[42] David J. Bosch, *Transforming Mission* (Maryknoll, NY: Orbis, 1991), 414.

[43] Such a view of mission is also reflected from the two chairpersons of mission boards. One says, "Mission is the gospel of Jesus Christ plus all activities that support, promote, further the end objective of leading all men and women to Jesus Christ as Savior and Lord." Another says, "Mission includes all activities that will cause people to know Christ, accept Christ as Lord and Savior, training believers to effectively fulfill the Great Commission."

[44] The mission statement of the Mission Board of PCC#1.

[45] See Appendix 1, PCC#1 Mission Board Policies on Missionary. This document is graciously given by the Mission pastor of PCC#1 on December 18, 2001.

[46] PCC#3's *Missionary Handbook*, 1.

[47] Bosch, *Transforming Mission*, 368-510.

Appendix 1: PCC#1's Mission Board Policies on Missionary

1. The main tasks of a missionary are evangelism, discipleship and training.
2. All support for missionaries shall be on a year-to-year basis (ending with the calendar year).
3. The minimum age requirement is 25 years old. The maximum age limit is 65.

4. Before the start of the calendar year, all missionaries are required to submit their personal, family and ministry goals for the coming year.
5. Thereafter, they shall be required to submit bi-monthly written reports on their ministries.
6. During the last quarter of every calendar year, the Committee on Missionary Affairs shall undertake the evaluation of all missionaries based among other things, on the goals and reports submitted.
7. PCC#1's Mission Board encourages ministry partnership with the planted local church in supporting the missionary. So whenever possible, our support for the missionary shall be gradually diminishing until he is fully independent.
8. PCC#1 aids monthly financial needs. SSS, Medicare, Retirement & separation pay is the responsibility of the missionary's local church or church organization. (PCC#1 benefit: birthday gift & 13th month allowance).

Table 1: Basic Information of Four Philippine-Chinese Churches:
Mission Budget/Goal of Year 2001/2002

Name of Church	PCC#1	PCC#2	PCC#3	PCC#4
Year Established	1929 (72nd year)	1968 (32nd year)	1952 (49th year)	1980 (20th year)
Year Mission Board Established	1968	1971	1965	1989
Church Budget 2001*	P21 million	Information Unavailable	P8.5 million	No fixed amount
Mission Budget 2001	P9,850,000 (for 2002)	P2,284,791	P10,454,000	P3,600,000
Total Church Budget	P30 million	Not applicable	P19 million	Not applicable
Regular Sunday Worshipers	1000-1200	400-500	400-500	250-300
Average offering per worshiper per year	P25,708 or P2,141 monthly	P4,569 year	P37,908 or P3,159 monthly	P12,000
Mission Budget (per month)	P684	P380	P1742	P1,000
Notes		Goal Attained	Goal (P9 million) for Mission offering exceeded	Goal attained

Table 2: Mission Budget and Ministry Supported by PCC#1

Ministries	Percentage of Total Budget (P9,850,000 for 2001)
Local Missionaries (52) including 43 in the field and 9 in process	55.13%
Para-Church Organizations (8)	12.48%
China Ministries	5.24%
Missionary Teachers (4)	5.14%
Short-Term Missions & Medical Outreaches	4.36%
Scholarships for Seminarians (6)	4.15%
1 Foreign Missionaries	2.00%
Others: Printing, Mission Week, Miscellaneous Expenses & Discretionary Fund	8.98%
Total	**97.48%**

Table 3: Mission Budget and Ministry Supported by PCC#2

Ministries	Percentage of Total Budget (P2,284,791 for 2001)
3 Missionaries in Taiwan	18.43%
Special Support to 1 Foreign Mission Organization with 1 Church in U.S. (one-time gift)	14.79%
10 Local Missionaries including 4 Urban & Rural Church Planting (1 Muslim ministry; 1 Bible school teacher; 1 translation worker; 1 in urban poor–children ministry; 1 in student evangelism ministry; 1 in tribal ministry)	17.06%
Local Para-church Organizations including 4 Bible Colleges, Seminaries & Training Institutes and Other Ministries (1 children's ministry; 1 counseling ministry; 1 hospital ministry; 1 radio ministry; 2 student campus ministry	13.13%
Scholarships for Seminarians	12.33%
Evangelistic Meetings	11.98%
Mission Exposure Trips	4.93%
Medical & Dental Outreaches	4.02%
Sports Fellowship & Sports Ministry	2.41%
Others: Love Gifts, Food Expenses, charity, subsidy for conference	0.79%
Total	**99.87%**

Table 4: Mission Budget and Ministry Supported by PCC#3

Ministries	Percentage of Total Budget (P10,454,000 for 2001)
Theological Education including Local Bible Colleges & Seminaries (9 missionaries); and Foreign Bible Colleges & Seminaries (5 missionaries)	39.82%
Mission Organizations including Church Planting (4 missionaries); Administration in Organizations (9); Urban & Rural Church Planting (6); Church Planting among 3 tribes (6); and Muslim Ministry	25.79%
China Ministries: Tribal work (2 missionaries); and medical ministry (2)	10.41%
E3 Intercultural Mission via SEND (2 missionaries in Spain)	8.08%
Foreign Mission Organization (1 missionary support)	4.54%
Evangelism & Discipleship (3 missionary supports)	3.34%
Student Campus Ministry (2 missionary support)	2.19%
Children's Ministry (supporting 2 missionaries)	2.19%
Christian Literature (supporting 2 missionaries)	1.88%
Sports Evangelism (supporting 2 missionaries)	1.29%
Total	**99.53%**

Table 5: Mission Budget and Ministry Supported by PCC#4

Ministries	Percentage of Total Budget (P3,600,000 for 2001)
Theological Education: local Bible colleges & Seminaries; 1 foreign seminary	20%
Support of 3 missionaries working in Panama, Taiwan and Australia	13%
Radio Ministry	11%
Church & Christian School Planting	9%
Support of 2 local missionaries in a student campus ministry organization	7%
Foreign Organization: training for short-term mission	6%
Evangelism & Training	5%
Urban Poor Ministry	5%
Foreign Organization: Evangelism	5%
Student Campus Ministry among Secular Schools	5%
Bible Translation Work	3%
Foreign Organization: Training of House Churches in China	3%
Support of a Filipino Church	3%
Foreign Mission Organization sending long-term, short-term or tent-making missionaries	3%
Local Mission Organization	1.67%
Total	**99.67%**

Table 6: Top Three Priorities of the Mission Budget Year 2001/Year 2002

Name of Church	PCC#1	PCC#2	PCC#3	PCC#4
Mission Budget	P9,850,000	P2,284,791	P10,454,000	P3,600,000
Priority 1 (% of Total Budget)	(55.13%) • Local Missionaries (52) • Church-planting: 18.32% • Theological Education: 15.58%	(18.43%) • 3 Missionaries in Taiwan (2 in Church Planting, 1 in administration)	(39.81%) • Theological Education • 14 missionaries (9 local missionaries [19.31%]; 5 foreign missionaries [20.5%])	(20%) • Theological Education (5 Bible Colleges & Seminaries)
Priority 2 (% of Total Budget)	(12.48%) • Local Para-Church Organizations : 7	(14.79%) • Special support of one foreign organization & one church	(25.79%) • Church Planting • 22 missionaries	(13%) • 3 foreign missionaries in Panama, Taiwan & Australia
Priority 3 (% of Total Budget)	(5.24%) • China Ministries	(17.06%) • 10 Local Missionaries	(10.41%) • China Ministries (4 missionaries)	(11%) • Radio Ministry
Notes	67% of total budget goes to E1 mission	• 33% goes to E2/E3 mission is expensive. • Partial support of 10 local missionaries is almost equal to partial support of 3 foreign missionaries.	• Development for local leaders is a priority. • E2/E3 missions is more expensive when comparing 25.79% (22) & 10.41% (4)	• Development for local leaders is a priority. • E2/E3 mission is expensive. • 13% of total budget goes to 3 missionaries who are partially supported.

Table 7: Summary of the Supported Ministries

Different Kinds of Ministries	Percentage of Total Mission Budget (P26 million)
Church Planting: PCC #4 includes Christian school planting, urban and rural church planting, Muslim ministry, tribal church planting (48 missionaries all over the Philippines)	30.94%
Theological Education: support of Bible colleges & seminaries (9 local and 4 foreign) and missionary-teachers.	23.97%
Support of Foreign Missionaries (21) and Foreign Organizations (6)	27.18%
China Ministries	6.96%
Others: Local Ministries including ministries to children, urban poor, Muslims and Bible translation.	10.95%

PROLEGOMENA TO A HISTORICAL PERSPECTIVE: THE USE OF EDUCATION AS A MISSION STRATEGY IN ASIA

Junias V. Venugopal

1. Introduction

Should general education be one of the strategies utilized by today's global Christian missionaries?[1] Is education a relic of the past that should be discarded?[2] Is the task of general education central to the missionary endeavor?

The intent of this paper is to initiate a process to begin to answer these questions, recognizing that a complete answer is beyond its scope. In fact, this paper will only begin to gather evidence from history and present some preliminary conclusions.[3] The plea is for discussion and dialogue to begin on the issues raised so that God's mission is accomplished and he is glorified.

Discussion of missionary strategy begins with articulation of the church's missionary task and recognition that the non-Christians to whom it was directed in the past were seen as "different" or as "other." This perception of the recipients of the gospel led to different strategies to evangelize this "other," including differing presuppositions when it came to educating them. The repercussions of these historical perceptions and educational approaches have implications for the continuing task of mission. Education has a vital role to play in the ministry of the church as all Christians seek to make disciples and be witnesses to every human being and bring glory to God.

1.1 The Missionary Task

Missionaries and missions have as their goal "the evangelization of the world in this generation." Taylor quotes Neill:[4]

> The slogan was based on an unexceptional theological principle—that each generation of Christians bears responsibility for the contemporary generation of non-Christians in the world, and that it is the business of each such generation of Christians to see to it, as far as lies within its power, that the gospel is clearly preached to every single non-Christian in the same generation.

Individual Christians have responded to the challenge of reaching their generation for Christ by traveling to different countries and cultures and presenting the gospel. These missionaries have used various strategies and adopted different tactics to accomplish the goal of world evangelization.

1.2 The Recipient of the Gospel Is the "Other"

However, the approach to accomplish this task, as evident even from the quote by Neill, has been that of "we" (Christians) reaching the "others" (non-Christians). At one time, however, "we" clearly meant European Christians and their descendants (U.S., Canadian, Australian and New Zealand) because they composed Christendom, while the "others" just as clearly meant Asians, Africans and South Americans, who formed the heathen peoples.

> [D]evelopments in Europe had brought about a virtual identification of "European" with "Christian."... Owing to a number of factors, not least the Muslim threat to Europe in the European Middle Ages and the experience of the Crusades against the enemies of Christianity, there emerged "the consciousness of a concrete territorial Christendom."[5] The weakening of the Christian communities of the Eastern Mediterranean, as well as their isolation from the active Christian centers of the Latin West, helped towards the identification of *Christianitas* with Europe.[6]

The British believed that their prominence as a world power was a result of their identity as a Protestant nation and because of their role as "the Guardian Angel of the Christian world."[7] Missionaries from America shared an equally lofty view that was "accepted by most Protestants since at least the Civil War, that the survival and expansion of the United States was part of the divine plan. 'God cannot afford to do without America,' a Methodist Episcopal bishop told a large crowd in 1864."[8]

Today, because of the spread of Christianity, the "we" is no longer confined to Caucasians, but includes Christians from every part of the earth. As Western countries have entered a post-Christian era, the identification of "we" and the "others" as specific ethnic peoples has to change. Paul Hiebert refers to Margaret Mead's comments at the American Anthropological Association.

> She noted that the first time she went to the South Pacific, she had to order her tea "native" or "Dutch." The former was black, the latter was with cream and sugar. But the word "native" soon became taboo. Twenty years later she went there, but now she had to order it "national" or "colonial." Then, the word "colonial" became a bad word. Twenty years later after this she went to the South Seas, but had to order her tea "indigenous" or "expatriate." If she were still alive, I suspect she would have to order the tea "contextualized" or "globalized."[9]

While the focus of this paper is not to address the inherent dangers of differentiating between Christian and non-Christian, the implications of this difference does affect how missions and missionaries approached education. At the time when "we" clearly meant Europeans and Westerners, it was also understood that these people were "the civilized." Meanwhile, the "others" just as clearly meant, at first,[10] "pagans" and "heathens," because they had "horrifying customs," and therefore needed two kinds of salvation. One was salvation from their culture and civilization and another was soteriological by grace through faith in the Son of God, Jesus Christ. The two kinds of salvation were not always clearly distinguished and the authors/speakers, when referring to the "other," meant both the non-Christian and the pagan/heathen. Later, with the coming of the Age of Enlightenment and a positivist mind set, the non-European "other" was always understood as a primitive.

It is in this context that Protestant mission began: the European missionary "we" going to share the gospel with the primitive non-European "others."

1.3 The Methods Used in the Missionary Task

Missionaries in Asia used a variety of methods to present the gospel. Often, if it was possible, missionaries preached and shared the gospel openly, but when that opportunity was not available, they used other methods to gain access to the local population. In Shandong province in China:

[O]pen-air services and the distribution of tracts, methods used in young mission fields throughout the world, brought little response here. Thus, in order to gain a basic hearing for the gospel, many missionaries turned to the running of primary schools and small hospitals and clinics.[11]

In India, missionaries entered the fields of education, medicine and civil action especially to address social ills. Their influence awakened the conscience of Hindu reformers and brought about an official ban on the practices of *sati*[12] and female infanticide, in addition to other actions uplifting the status of women.

In Japan,

[A]lthough the Japanese government was opposed to any contact with the Westerners, and though public clamor decried it, there were still many eager spirits, mostly among the young *samurai* who welcomed relations with the foreigners, and took great pains to get acquainted. They came aboard the ships, asked to be shown books, and received their first lessons in English; the commander of the ship himself sometimes doing the teaching. Some of these classes continued for weeks at a time. The Bible was often used as a textbook. In Nagasaki the governor sent a group of young officials to request instructions in English.[13]

The methods used in mission varied and all possible means were utilized to present the gospel to all people so that some may be persuaded to trust in Christ as their Savior.

2. Education in Mission

Of all the strategies, tactics and methods used in mission, education was primary, particularly because it was seen not only as a means of communicating the gospel, but also of educating the new Christian in the teachings of Scripture and the skills of ministry. "Education has never been simply an auxiliary to mission work—as, say, the medical work. It has always been an integral part of mission. This is in obedient response to the command of our Lord to 'teach all nations'."[14] But there were different approaches to education in mission depending on the worldview of the missionary and the mission society/organization, and on the particular method (tactic) which they thought would best advance the spread of the kingdom of God. The worldview of most missions and missionaries was based on their understanding of the "other," the recipient of the gospel message.

2.1 The Cultural Bias of the "We" Missionary

As Protestant mission got underway in a Western world affected by the Enlightenment, the secularist no longer considered sin as a matter of being evil, but of being ignorant. "The earlier distinction between refined-Christian vs. idolatrous-savage was replaced by the civilized-European vs. the superstitious-ignorant-primitive."[15] However, while Christian missionaries rejected the concept of evil as not being sin, they "bought deeply into the Enlightenment agenda of the West to educate and civilize the 'natives'."[16] Lamin Sanneh notes that the:

> [N]otions of Western cultural superiority found a congenial niche in the Western missionary enterprise where spiritual values were assumed to enshrine concrete Western cultural forms, so that the heathen who took the religious bait would, in fact, be taking it from the cultural hook.[17]

This concept of mission being directed from "we" civilized beings to "others"—superstitious-ignorant-primitive beings—led Hiebert to three conclusions: First, "this equation of the Gospel with Western civilization made the Gospel unnecessarily alien in other cultures.... Consequently, they [Christianized locals] were seen as foreigners in their own cultures."[18] Second, it assumes that the "other" culture is inherently evil and that nothing from it can be preserved. Hiebert, quotes John Pobee:

> [T]he historical churches by and large implemented the doctrine of *tabula rasa*,[19] i.e., the missionary doctrine that there is nothing in the non-Christian culture on which the Christian missionary can build and, therefore, every aspect of the traditional non-Christian culture had to be destroyed before Christianity could be built up.[20]

Third, Hiebert concluded that religious thought had evolved from the "other's" religion to a higher order, where "our" Christianity fulfills it.

It was, however, not until the arrival on the scene of the theory of evolution in the nineteenth century, the rise of liberal theology and the birth of the new discipline of comparative religion, that the stage was set for an approach according to which religions could be compared and graded in an ascending scale. In the Western world, there was no doubt, however, about which religion stood at the pinnacle. In almost every respect, every other religion—even if it might be termed a *praeparatio evangelica*—was deficient when compared with Christianity.[21]

These biases toward their own culture, were present to some degree in all missionaries, who were excused, for being a product of their times.[22]

2.2 Differing Perspectives

There are three general approaches when using education as a mission strategy. Although they were clearly utilized in India, not all were employed in every mission field in Asia. Although David Kopf[23] classified these three perspectives "under the headings of three 'parties'—Anglicists, Orientalists and vernacularists, though to describe each of these as a party dignifies them with a coherence which they did not in fact possess."[24]

The vernacularists studied and taught in the vernacular so "that they might more effectively propagate Christianity,"[25] and hence were involved in education as a specific mission strategy. The Orientalists valued the local culture, despite believing that the "other" was superstitious-ignorant-primitive while they, the "we," were civilized. Their mission was to educate the "other" to become "enlightened." The Anglicists wanted to share the gospel, but believed that the primitive "other" needed to be "civilized" first, so that they would be able to comprehend the gospel when it was presented to them.

2.2.1 The vernacularists' mission strategy

The vernacularists' approach was to learn and use contemporary local languages to translate the Bible and conduct open air preaching. Their involvement in education was initially to equip new Christians to do the work of ministry. However, those who became Christians (the new converts) as a result of this strategy recognized the benefits of education: that the educated were economically and socially privileged. They wanted to educate their children and themselves, so that they would "overcome their social disadvantages."[26] This led to the beginning of schools in vernacular languages. The "missionaries were also well aware that there were real economic obstacles to a self-sustaining church and that education could help to change this."[27]

General education was used because it would allow missionaries to reach the local population, otherwise inaccessible to the gospel. "The strategy was simple, gather them where they will assemble and teach them language, science, history, anything true and good, if thereby there be full opportunity to teach them of Christ."[28] This was true in the Philippines too:

> The missionaries usually insisted that these institutional (hospitals, dispensaries, orphanages, dormitories, schools, libraries, community centers, settlement houses and social clubs) ministries supplemented preaching. The ultimate end of missionary work, they insisted, remained individual salvation. "This must never be forgotten," said Bruce Kershner in 1908. "Educational, medical, literary or any other kind of work is carried on for the contribution it makes to this first end."[29]

There were three consequences of the use of education as a mission strategy. The first was that it was successful in presenting the gospel to those who would not have heard it otherwise. At the beginning of the twentieth century in Japan, the educational strategy was very successful because "nearly all the girls were Christian by the time of graduation"[30] in the forty or so schools for girls.

A second consequence was that people disagreed about the value of this strategy and saw the entrance into education as a dilution of the evangelistic effort. In China, when opposition developed to evangelistic preaching, the missionaries adopted the education strategy, but then ran into opposition from their home boards over this strategy. The home boards thought that the donations received for evangelism should be spent on that specific activity, i.e., preaching and not on education or medical clinics.[31]

The third consequence was that non-Christian teachers had to be hired at times to teach and this led to suspicions about the effectiveness of the strategy. In India, an inspection of village schools resulted in this report:

> I examined 45 of them and was astonished and delighted with their progress. All of them were perfect in their catechism, and had committed a great portion of Scripture to memory. Many of them were far advanced in reading, writing and arithmetic. It is to be regretted that they have been taught by a heathen.[32]

This embarrassment of having non-Christian teachers in a Christian school was acute since it diluted the strategy, but the defense was that "the mission would rather use non-Christian teachers in Christian schools than to leave the educational work to the secularized government schools which neglected the Bible altogether."[33]

2.2.2 The Orientalists: valuing the host culture

The Orientalists, who mostly served in the nineteenth century, saw value in India's past, but not in the *then* present. They noted problems in Hinduism, such as female infanticide and the practice of *sati*. "The model they invoked, however, was the Renaissance and medieval Europe. There, too, a culture had become moribund; but it had been invigorated precisely by means of recalling its splendid past."[34]

Instead of Scripture, the Orientalists believed that because of the Enlightenment and the recognition of the rational thought process, there existed a set of "universal values, such as reason, justice and truth."[35] "The perception of universal values meant that the educator was able to erect (or at the very least should strive to erect) a whole system of knowledge or a complete 'building of learning.'... Also it was a system built on reason rather than on experience."[36]

In the Philippines, the missionaries who held this viewpoint were not classified as Orientalists, but as having "secondary motivations." In addition to saving souls, the missionary often thought of him- or herself as an "advance agent of civilization" who spoke out against such remnants of barbarism as slavery, polygamy and cannibalism, and who taught the Horatio Alger virtues of honesty, sobriety, thriftiness, purity and industriousness. Such motives, according to Brown,[37] appealed to those who were cognitively oriented and considered the "intellectual type." The "emotional type" of person was more likely to exhibit another of the secondary motivations, the philanthropic (medical and educational endeavors). While such benevolent motivations were considered legitimate, the missionary leadership was distressed at the growing trend among missionaries to value these kinds of [secondary] motivations. The Presbyterians excelled in educational work, and while the salvation of souls no doubt remained an important premise of such undertakings, some missionaries placed increasing emphasis on good work itself. Kenneth P. MacDonald informed students who had inquired about enrolling in a Presbyterian dormitory that he was in the Philippines "not so much to convert the Filipinos to Protestantism as *to help them become the men and women that it is possible for them to be.*"[38]

Consequently, the Orientalists' blueprint for "the future of education in India" was rejected in favor of the Anglicists' position. The British enacted an education policy in India known as "Macaulay's minute,"[39] where Indian culture was devalued and English cultural values and perspectives were taught as part of progress in science and education. However, in both the Philippines and India, the effect of those who worked to enlighten the primitive continued and was adopted as *the* missionary strategy by many mainline denominations.

2.2.3 *The Anglicists' strategy: civilization as foundation for Christianity*

The Anglicist, like the Orientalist, believed that the effects of Enlightenment needed to be presented to the "other"—the primitive. The missionary whose name is synonymous with this position is Alexander Duff, who

> [W]as convinced that Western (Christian) culture was an inestimable boon which could be conferred through education on Indian society. The way forward was the replacement of Indian ways of thinking, which was based on "Hinduism" and steeped, as he believed, in error and superstition, by European culture based, again in his view, on the sure foundation of a Christian heritage. So he steadfastly insisted that in higher education at least, the medium of instruction should be English and the subjects taught should be, for example, English literature and "modern" science. Oriental languages were unfit for higher education, he felt. Sanskrit was barred from his College on the grounds that it was inextricably bound up with Hindu thought patterns.[40]

Those who held this view believed that those who are convinced by "enlightened" appeals to rationality and logic would accept Christianity. Since literature on logic and rationality were products of the modern English Western world, the students must learn English and equip themselves so as to understand reasoned discourse. This would enable them to accept the gospel.

In India, this position won over the ruling British government to enact a policy where English and Western education would be the curriculum in all the schools in India. A few British government officials were also interested in evangelism as evidenced by the remarks of Lord Macaulay, "It is my firm belief that, if our plans are followed up, there will not be a single idolater among the respectable classes of Bengal thirty years hence."[41] This remark was made in the middle of the nineteenth century. Lord Macaulay is remembered for his 1835 minute that set forth the British Indian government education policy as intending to create "a class of persons, Indian in blood and color, but English in taste, in opinions, in morals and in intellect.[42]" This class would serve as loyal bureaucrats to the British rulers.

This approach was criticized by Arthur Mayhew because of its presupposition that:

> All minds are alike and all minds that had no Western information were equally empty and receptive. What was "reasonable" in England, must be reasonable in India, and would, when forcibly presented, prevail. Get the right kind of information from England in sufficient quantities and the receptacles would soon be filled.[43]

2.3 Repercussions

The major repercussion of the Anglicist approach was that decolonization brought a backlash against Christianity because of its close identification with Western culture. The national religion of all Western colonial governments was (and is) Christianity,[44] and the colonial rulers publicly attended Christian churches, some of which would not allow Christians from the local population to attend church services in the colonies.[45] Christianity came to be branded as part of Western colonization.[46] Some of the association of Christianity and Western colonialism was based on the special treatment that was given to Christian churches and organizations by colonial powers in terms of land they were able to buy.[47] At other instances the link between colonialism and Christianity was clearer:

> [S]uch was the case in an era when an ardent imperialism was sweeping across Europe. Thomas Richardson, in the *Wesleyan Missionary Notices* of June 1890, declared, "We are under immense

obligations to India. I believe sincerely and religiously that it is our destiny to govern India, and I believe it is equally our destiny and providential call to Christianize it." For Wesleyans, generally, *enthusiasm for imperialism and for missions were two sides of the same coin,* and for nowhere did they feel that double-sided responsibility more keenly than for India.[48]

The "others" recognized that they were indeed different from the missionaries (who belonged to the Western "we") and the Western peoples. Christianity is viewed as a Western religion that was imposed by colonial powers on the countries they ruled. Political freedom is seen to include religious freedom. Today in India, despite its carefully secular constitution, the government is a coalition led by a fundamental Hindu organization. To be Indian is often synonymous with being a Hindu. Some fundamental Hindus discard the term Indian-Christian and urge Christians to refer to themselves as "Hindu-Christians"[49] as opposed to continuing as "Western-Christians," since the former includes identity with the national culture.

Not only do the "other" people belong to "other" religions, but they also see it as part of their culture and identity and take great pride in it. To be a Christian is actually seen as being "foreign" in many Asian countries. Islamic countries identify more closely with each other than with those that colonized them, in spite of the ministry of Christian missionaries for hundreds of years. The glue that holds the "we" and separates "us" from "them"—the "other" is religion:

> Of all the objective elements which define civilizations, however, *the most important usually is religion*, as the Athenians emphasized. To a very large degree, the major civilizations in human history have been closely identified with the world's great religions; and people who share ethnicity and language but differ in religion may slaughter each other, as happened in Lebanon, the former Yugoslavia and the Subcontinent.[50]

Some Christians in non-Western countries feel torn. On the one hand, they are Christians, believing in the deity of Jesus Christ and knowing that salvation is by faith in Jesus Christ, by his death on the cross at Calvary, which paid the penalty for personal sins. On the other hand, they do not identify with the national and political aspirations of Western countries, which is closely associated with their Christianity. Further, many Christians from other countries do not always agree with the policies of the fiscally conservative politicians and political parties, which many Western Evangelical Christians, particularly from the US, support.

Non-Western Christians clash with Western expatriate missionary leadership. "The rejection of colonialism by Asian and African Christians included rejecting Western missionary paternalism, with its Eurocentrism and moral superiority.... Churches around the world accused Western missionaries of paternalism, racism and cultural imperialism."[51] National Christians could cry, "Western Missionary, Go Home!" because they never "belonged" as part of the Western missionary endeavor—they were always the "other." Today that is changing, but the wounds of senior national leaders heal slowly and some missionaries continue to wound by invoking as superior, administrative methods from the West, without appropriately valuing local traditions and practices.

2.4 Modern Ramifications

Today, there are three ramifications of the earlier strategy to use education as missionary tool to reach the local population with the gospel. First, despite the Europeans' negative perceptions of the local peoples as primitive, Asians, Africans and South Americans did not reject Christianity, but have embraced it and their churches have grown, sometimes even under oppressive circumstances.[52] (Persecution and the ban on Western missionaries did not stop the Chinese church from growing.) Second, the national churches continue to run the schools left under their supervision when the missionaries departed. These schools continue to reach out to children from communities and families that are non-Christian by means of education. Third, today's missionaries and missions are not using education as a means to reach the local population with the gospel.[53] They overwhelmingly prefer to concentrate on the strategies of evangelism and church planting.

3. Lessons Learned

The strategy of approaching the non-Christian as an "other" who is either savage or primitive has caused deep wounds that need to be addressed. Evangelical churches today have defined mission as a more holistic enterprise and this has implications for utilizing education as a strategy in mission.

3.1 Eschewing the "We-Other" Approach

Paul Hiebert proposes that we view all people in three ways: First, we recognize that we are all human beings created as equals by God. "At the deepest level of our identity as humans, there are no others, there is only us."[54] Second, all who have trusted Christ are brothers and sisters in the same family and Jesus Christ is the head. "In the church there are no others; there are only us—members of the body of Christ."[55] Third, we share the gospel as sinners, as those who have been forgiven by the death of Christ, with those who have not yet trusted Christ.

In our ministry in the world, if we come as Christians to non-Christians, we are tempted to see ourselves as outsiders and superiors. If we identify with people in our common humanity, we come in humility, as one sinner inviting another to the salvation offered us all by Christ. Leslie Newbigin writes, "The real point of contact between Christian and non-Christian is not in the religion of the non-Christian, but in his humanity."[56]

But the church is not only called to identify with the world, but also to be a prophetic counter-cultural community calling people into the kingdom of God. This lies at the heart of mission. We cannot ignore the plight of our fellow humans, nor should we simply be content to sit and to commiserate with them in their miserable condition. We long to share the good news of salvation that was given to us, a salvation not based on who we are or what we have done, but on God. Therefore, we invite everyone to join us in that salvation which is open to all.[57]

Asian churches are now active in mission and their numbers multiply daily. Asian missionaries have already made some of the same mistakes related to ethnocentric approaches by treating those who need to hear the gospel as "others." In addition to the strategies of Hiebert enumerated above, more are proposed.

3.1.1 Recognize the ministry of the missionary

The service of the missionaries from European-Western people group, in leaving their home and traveling to distance lands, to share the gospel of Christ needs to be acknowledged and celebrated. They did this in obedience to their Lord and Savior Jesus Christ and are to be commended.

They lived with the people and often defended them against oppression from business and government. Moreover, by translating the Bible into native languages, communicating to them a universal gospel and baptizing the converts into the global church, the missionaries dignified the people and helped them more than other Westerners to preserve their cultural identities.[58]

Further it must be recognized that not all missionaries came with an attitude of superiority. "William Carey, foremost protagonist of the missionary enterprise, was one who held no belief in the religious superiority of Europeans."[59]

3.1.2 Acknowledge the pain caused by the attitude of "we-other"

There must be some attempt to recognize and acknowledge that the trading practices of Western commercial enterprises and the reasons European countries[60] colonized other parts of the world were selfish at best and destructively exploitive of resources and people at worst.[61] Their representatives led lives that ranged from righteous morality to immoral debauchery. Missionaries were caught in the middle to attempt to explain this behavior of the "civilized."

But having associated with them in the past, attempts to distance themselves from the misdeeds of their colonial governments and business countrymen are *in*appropriate. An acknowledgement would be far more beneficial.[62]

There are two aspects to this reconciliation between the "we" and the "other." The first is found between the "Christian—we" and the "non Christian—other," and the second is between the "Western/ European/North American missionary—we" and the "non-Western Christian—other."[63]

1) Apologize to the non-Christian

We Christians, whether from the West or from the East, have inherited the perceptions that non-Christians have about Christians. The recognition of offenses caused by our forefathers in the faith towards non-Christians, because of insensitive language and attitudes, is to acknowledge the hurt they suffer when they hear or read literary or historical accounts of those times. We tend to apologize for those who preceded us in the faith as being "a product of their times." But that is a failure to recognize the pain that was and is caused by the offense of being labeled, even by the "language of the time" as a "primitive-savage."[64] By standing up and apologizing for our predecessors we also acknowledge the common humanity we share with all human beings— of being fallible. Even today we do not know in what ways we are causing offense. We humbly hope our successors will acknowledge and repent for us. At the core of this rationale is the desire that no one is so offended that they cannot hear the message of the gospel. As Paul wrote, "I have become all things to all men so that by all possible means I might save some. I do all this for the sake of the gospel" (1 Cor 9:22b-23a).

2) Reconcile with the Christian

Evangelical mission organizations have already instituted processes that decry paternalistic attitudes and practices. However, some Christians from non-Western countries need to hear their brothers and sisters from the West acknowledge the mistakes of past generations. Partnership between Christians from different parts of the world is built upon a mutual foundation of respect and ability to contribute to the missionary enterprise. This is compounded by the fact that much of the financing for Christian missions and ministry comes from the West. The need to establish and maintain fiscal accountability structures may sometimes be misinterpreted as paternalism and the resulting fissure in the relationship feeds upon previous perceptions and practices of being treated as an "other"—who is still a "primitive-savage." Studies in Christian partnership between different ethnic and national groups will need to address this issue in greater depth.

3.2 Mission Is Holistic Christian Witness

Evangelicals are changing their perceptions about mission and missiology.

> As early or late as the Berlin World Evangelization Congress in 1966, EM [Evangelical Missiology] had a single focal point: evangelization of the world was what the purpose of mission was all about. After Lausanne, EM crossed the "Rubicon." Since then, at least camps have coexisted in Evangelical circles. Both are holistic in their approach. One camp stresses intentional equality between evangelism and social responsibility.... The other position has evangelization of the world as its primary focus.... The rest of Evangelicals will be found in between these two poles.[65]

One of the great benefits of the inclusion of a focus on social concern is that an increased number of ministries are reaching out in compassion to the economically poor and socially marginalized people. However, there is still a missing element when considering holistic ministry and mission. Engel and Dryness note that among the problems mission encounters is the fact that the church has made two great omissions in attempting to fulfill the Great Commission. The first is that it has divorced social transformation from evangelism and made itself, "privately engaging, socially irrelevant."[66] The second is that the church practices evangelism without discipleship.

The missing element is that discipleship is often limited to maturation in knowledge and practice in the spiritual arena only and not on growth and development as a witnessing Christian who makes a difference in society by being salt and light. "Spiritual development does not exclude any of the aspects of human personhood."[67]

Often when people are evangelized and discipled by a ministry, they are invited to join that specific ministry and do more of the same—participate in a commitment to the self-perpetuation of that particular ministry and focus on only the "spiritual" aspect of the persons to whom they minister. Churches and mission organizations fawn over people who have achieved success in various secular fields by inviting these rich and famous to share their testimony or serve on the boards of churches and ministries. However, these same churches, ministries and mission organizations rarely encourage or assist people within their sphere of influence to pursue those kinds of "secular" interests that achieve the success they celebrate. Christian organizations need to challenge their people to pursue nation building, education, research and other avenues so as to develop themselves to the fullest potential to which God has created and gifted them.

By creating a dichotomy between the secular and the sacred spheres of human existence, discipleship is often relegated to one part of their personhood, when it really should pervade all facets of a person's existence. God redeemed the complete human being, and people are responsible for all their actions (sacred and secular) as well as what that they have and have not done.

> If all that a believer does grows out of faith and is done for the glory of God, then all dualistic distinctions are demolished. There is no higher/lower, sacred/secular, perfect/permitted, contemplative/active, or first class/second class. Calling is the premise of Christian existence itself. Calling means that everyone, everywhere and in everything fulfills his or her (secondary) callings in response to God's (primary) calling. For Luther, the peasant and the merchant—for us, the business person, the teacher, the factory worker and the television anchor—can do God's work (or fail to do it) just as much as the minister and the missionary.[68]

Discipleship is God calling and gifting each person to fulfill God's purpose for God's kingdom and it seamlessly encompasses all aspects of life and vocation—whether sacred or spiritual. In *Chariots of Fire*, Eric Liddell, when confronted by his sister about spending too much time training for athletics states, "God made me and He made me fast. When I run fast, I feel the pleasure of God." Mission that is focused on fulfilling the Great Commission (Matt 28:18-20) enables all people to fulfill their fullest potential and in so doing "be my [Christ's] witnesses in Jerusalem, and in all Judea and Samaria and to the ends of the earth" (Acts 1:8).

Jim Plueddeman, president of the worldwide mission agency SIM International, states its agenda as one where, "lost people are invited to join them on the road to Christ, to involve them in a community of believers and help them to become all God intends them to be. They challenge them to follow the map of the word and to become life-long obedient students of Jesus."[69]

If ministry and mission encompasses more than evangelism and church planting and takes seriously the comprehensive and holistic view of discipleship, then

> [T]he goal of mission is not only to save individual human beings, but also to establish communities that worship the Lord and have a missionary responsibility. These quality communities will develop with a vision of the values of the kingdom of God and of their responsibility to serve Christ and their fellow human beings in *all fields* of human action.[70]

Holistic mission is discipleship ministry that can "never split the primary call ('by God, to God, for God') from the secondary call ('everyone, everywhere, in everything')."[71] Mission embraces a range of ministries that develops the complete human being in all areas of growth and service to the glory of God.

4. Education as Revealing the *Imago Dei*

The approaches to education as part of a missionary endeavor to educate the "uncivilized" primitives in rational thinking so that they can understand the gospel are not valid. It presupposes an Enlightenment paradigm that equates Western forms of knowing as essential to an understanding of the gospel. That premise would lead to the false conclusion that no one can be saved unless they have been educated to think in certain kinds of ways and that the Holy Spirit is unable to save anyone who has not been "civilized" by Western linear rationalistic thought. However, Scripture teaches that the Holy Spirit convicts human beings of sin (John 16:8) and that salvation is a gift of God that is available by grace (Eph 2:8, 9). All human beings, whether they have been educated or not, are capable of hearing and responding to the gospel of Christ.

While education is not a *praeparatio evangelica*, it is an important ingredient in discipleship and the establishment of a Christian witness:

> An individual's spiritual reality involves a composite of the whole person revealed in his natural abilities. In the new birth, a person is made alive spiritually, and he is thus a spiritual being invested in corporal substance. In general, spiritual development interacts with all that it means to be human, and at the same time spiritual development depends on conformity to the mind of Christ. Spiritual development is not equivalent to intellectual development, yet the appropriation of wisdom (making God-informed decisions about life) is basic (Prov 9:1-6).[72]

Education that allows the human being to develop and mature in every area of talent and gifting in wisdom is education with a Christian dimension.[73]

Christians should give priority to the tasks of education that will enable them to develop human beings to the maximum potential that each is created to reach. Christians believe that God created the world, that *all* human beings are created in the image of God, and that human nature reflects this image.[74] An education which respects each student as a creation of God and a bearer of his image will so mold itself to the gifts and talents of the individual, that every person will display the image of God to the fullest possible potential. Education plays its most sanctifying role in enhancing the display of the *imago Dei* in human beings and so brings glory to the creator God.

Such education is outside the mere natural, it is inherently Christian and needs to be provided by Christians as an alternative to modern enlightenment education that has classified the religious as myth, and lifted science as truth. Today's postmodern education, while respecting students, still does not elevate them to the status of bearers of the *imago Dei*. Education with a Christian dimension is part of the mission of the church as it seeks to glorify God on earth.

The curricular questions that need to be raised and discussed will have to address a host of different issues:[75]

- How will a neutral-faced education lead to evangelism and church building?
- How will we prepare Christians so that the Evangelical church impacts the culture in its country by the way Christians behave?
- How will we prepare Christian citizens who are patriots in their home countries and yet are firmly committed to a higher loyalty to Christ, the church and to human dignity in all countries?
- How will Christian values be integrated into programs to infuse nation building and economic development?
- How will programs lead the student to reflect on the material and to ask questions about its foundations and its application in real life situations?
- Will a Christian worldview supply the most adequate answers?
- Will Christian educators be able to design such programs?
- Will students who hear the gospel come to realize its value for their own lives, both personally and professionally?

5. Conclusion

Missionaries during the modern enlightenment era used education as a strategy to reach the unsaved with the gospel. They shared Christ in a world colonized by the West to people they believed were primitive and uncivilized. There were three kinds of educational strategies employed: One was a mechanistic use of education as a hook to get the people to read the Bible and hear the gospel. The second was as *praeparatio evangelica* to educate the people to a level where they would be able to logically understand the gospel. The third was to educate people until they cast aside their superstitions and attained modern enlightenment. The first two approaches led people to trust in Christ as their Savior.

As colonies became free, the differentiating of people into "we," the civilized, and the "other," the primitive-uncivilized, had repercussions. The barrier led the "others" to clearly express that Christianity is a Western, foreign religion and as such not native to their culture.

Christians are a forgiven people and as such can acknowledge their faults, seek to reconcile with their brothers, and seek forgiveness of those who were hurt by attitudes of superiority. Christians can approach fellow human beings as members of a common humanity, sinners forgiven by God, and thus appeal to all human beings to be reconciled to God (2 Cor 5:18-21).

God calls Christians to *make disciples* and *be witnesses*, and this task encompasses the total person—sacred and secular. The growth and maturation of the complete person is an educative task that can best be undertaken by the Christian who believes that God created all human beings in His image and likeness. It is this ministry of enhancing the *imago Dei* in human beings that makes education an effective strategy and a sanctifying service that gives all glory to God.

---

[1] *General* education extends beyond the specific curriculum followed by those in Christian ministry to provide Bible knowledge and enhance ministry skills to equip those that they hope will carry on their ministry goals and vision. The term *secular* education is not appropriate because general education includes information and skills presented through a grid that can be either Christian religious, non-Christian religious or non-religious.

[2] Some international cross-cultural mission organizations still run primary and secondary schools, while many "national" mission organizations are formed with the intent of providing general education. These *national* and *mission* bodies mostly tend to be involved in only the secondary (or lower) level of education. Few are formed with the intent of college and higher education. Where college and higher education is offered in missions today, they are organized as Bible colleges and seminaries, not towards granting a general or professional undergraduate degree.

[3] Hence, the word "prolegomena" in its title.

[4] S. Neill, *A History of Christian Missions* (New York: Penguin, 1986), 294.

[5] Denys Hay, *Europe: The Emergence of an Idea* (Edinburgh: Edinburgh University Press, 1957) quoted in Kwame Bediako, *Theology and Identity* (Oxford: Regnum, 1992), 35.

[6] Bediako, *Theology and Identity*, 228-29.

[7] Charles W. Iglehart, *A Century of Protestant Christianity in Japan* (Tokyo: Charles E. Tuttle, 1959), 4.

[8] Kenton J. Clymer, *Protestant Missionaries in the Philippines, 1898-1916: An Inquiry into the American Colonial Mentality* (Urbana, IL: University of Illinois Press, 1986), 153.

[9] Paul G. Hiebert, "DME 946: Religious Presuppositions" (Class notes, Trinity Evangelical Divinity School, Deerfield, IL., 1995), 1

[10] During the Age of Exploration when Europeans were seeking new trade routes to the East, the people they part in other parts of the world were considered to be *pagan* and less than "human," and it was only when Catholic missionaries were establishing churches, that Pope Paul III accorded humanity to Indians in declaring them to be "true men." See Paul G. Hiebert, "Critical Issues in the Social Sciences and Their Implications for Mission Studies," *Missiology: An International Review* 24:1 (January 1996), 67.

[11] Norman H. Cliff, "Building the Protestant Church in Shandong, China," *International Bulletin of Missionary Research* 22:2 (April 1998), 63.

[12] Sati is the practice where the widow is burned alive on the funeral pyre along with her dead husband, who is being cremated. Sati was officially banned in 1829.

[13] Iglehart, 30.

[14] Roger Kemp, "Education in Mission" (A paper presented at the International Council for Higher Education Triennial Assembly, Beatenberg, Switzerland, 2001), 1.

[15] Hiebert, "Critical Issues," 70.

[16] Hiebert, "Critical Issues," 72.

[17] Lamin Sanneh, *Encountering the West: Christianity and the Global Cultural Process* (Maryknoll, NY: Orbis, 1993), 22.

[18] Hiebert, "Critical Issues," 72.

[19] This doctrine of *tabula rasa* is described by Adrian Hastings, *Church and Mission in Modern Africa* (London: Burns and Oates, 1967), 60 as the desire to "treat everything pre-Christian in Africa as either harmful or at best valueless, and to consider the African once converted from paganism as a sort of *tabula rasa* on which a wholly new religious psychology was somehow to be imprinted.

[20] John Pobee, "Political Theology in the African Context," *African Theological Journal* 11, no. 168 (1982), 169.

[21] David Bosch, *Transforming Mission: Paradigm Shifts in Theology of Mission* (Maryknoll, NY: Orbis, 1991), 479.

[22] See below for alternatives to excusing *our* forefathers in the faith. Ultimately *we* (every human being who has trusted in Christ, including the author) are one in Christ and share in the corporate/communal culpability and benefits of those who precede us in the faith.

[23] See David Kopf, *British Orientalism and the Bengal Renaissance: The Dynamics of Indian Modernisation 1773-1835* (Berkley, CA: University of California Press, 1969).

[24] Ingleby, 13-14.

[25] Ingleby, 68.

[26] Ingleby, 79.

[27] Ingleby, 79.

[28] Ingleby, 94.

[29] Clymer, 18.

[30] Iglehart, 126.

[31] Cliff, 63.

[32] Ingleby, 76.

[33] Christi-An C. Bennett, "The Development of the Concept of Mission in British Wesleyan Thought, 1784-1914: Aims and Methods" (an unpublished paper written during Ph.D. studies, 1994), 75.

[34] Ingleby, 17.

[35] Ingleby, 34.

[36] Ingleby, 35.

[37] Arthur J. Brown was the secretary of the Presbyterian Mission Board.

[38] Clymer, 19-20. Emphases are mine.

[39] See below referenced by endnote 43.

[40] Ingleby, 19-20 n. 47.

[41] G. O. Trevelyan, *Life and Letters of Lord Macaulay*, vol. 1 (Oxford, UK: Oxford University Press, 1908), 328.

[42] M. K. Kuriakose, *History of Christianity in India: Source Materials* (Madras: Christian Literature Society, 1982), 50.

[43] Arthur Mayhew, *The Education in India: A Study of British Educational Policy 1835–1920* (London: Faber and Gwyer, 1926), 58.

[44] Except the US whose constitution clearly delineates the separation of church and state.

[45] There are numerous examples of this in India. The Scottish Presbyterian churches in the district of Darjeeling, West Bengal, India did not allow Indian Christians to attend until the 1950s, despite India having received its independence on August 15, 1947.

[46] American President McKinley connected US colonial, strategic, commercial and political interests to keep control of the Philippines with the desire to share the gospel. McKinley was reported to have said to a group of visiting Methodists, "there was nothing left for us to do but to take them all, and to *educate* the Filipinos, and *uplift* them and *civilize* and *Christianize* them, and by God's grace do the very best we could by them, as our

fellowmen for whom Christ also died" (Clymer, 3). The reasons, however, were far more self-serving to American interests than that, although even American secularists sought to justify it in noble, albeit paternalistic, terms: "Business interests noted the proximity of the Philippines to the 400 million potential Chinese customers. Humanitarians could not think of turning the islands back to "cruel" Spain. Diplomats argued that it would be silly for the US to withdraw as it would only lead to German, Japanese, or possibly British taking control. Politicians feared the consequences of lowering the flag. All agreed that the Filipinos could not govern themselves. There would be unstinting civil war for 50 years, if the Filipinos had no oversight" (Clymer, 3).

[47] Dana L. Robert, "Shifting Southward: Global Christianity since 1945," *International Bulletin of Missionary Research* 24:2 (April 2000), 50.

[48] Christi-an C. Bennett, "Seeking the Soul of India: Wesleyan Discussions 1886-1900," *Journal of Asian Mission* 4:2 (September 2002), 244. Emphases are mine.

[49] They also want the Muslims to become "Hindu-Muslims," since Islam is also considered foreign, because Muslim invaders came from over the Himalayas. They forget that Hinduism, too, is foreign to the sub-continent, having been brought by the Aryans, who also crossed the Himalayas to settle in the Indo-Gangetic plain.

[50] Samuel P. Huntington, *The Clash of Civilizations and the Remaking of World Order*, 1st ed. (New York: Touchstone, 1997), 42. Emphases are mine.

[51] Robert, 52.

[52] Proving the Bible teaching that people are saved by the ministry of the Holy Spirit and not by human tactics or persuasion.

[53] There are a few examples in Asia (Bangladesh, for one), but they are few.

[54] Hiebert, "Critical Issues," 77.

[55] Hiebert, "Critical Issues," 79.

[56] Leslie Newbigin, *One Body, One Gospel, One World* (London: International Missionary Council, 1958), 65.

[57] Hiebert, "Critical Issues," 79-80.

[58] Hiebert, "Critical Issues," 73.

[59] Bediako, 229.

[60] And the USA in the Philippines.

[61] Economic theory states that rational beings (colonizers and commercial entrepreneurs) maximize wealth (benefits/utility) *for themselves* at the lowest possible price.

[62] The acknowledgement may be similar to the apology of the Southern Baptist Convention for their racial practices and Caucasian pastors towards minority groups at the Pastors Promise Keepers in Atlanta in February 1996.

[63] Those who have accepted the gospel and placed their trust in Christ.

[64] The intensity of the emotion of one so affronted is expressed: "In the face of such *venomous calumny*, is it difficult to see why even as self-assured a person as Swami Vivekananda was driven to *rage*?" Arun Shourie, *Missionaries in India: Continuities, Changes, Dilemmas* (New Delhi: HarperCollins India, 1997), 130. Emphases mine.

[65] David Tai-Woong Lee, "A Two-Thirds World Evaluation of Contemporary Evangelical Missiology," in *Global Missiology for the 21st Century: The Iguassu Dialogue*, 137–138.

[66] James F. Engel and William A. Dryness, *Changing the Mind of Missions: Where Have We Gone Wrong* (Downers Grove, IL: InterVarsity, 2000).

[67] Ted W. Ward, "Evaluating Metaphors of Education: Part 3, Metaphors of Spiritual Reality," *Bibliotheca Sacra* 139 (October-December 1982), 291.

[68] Os Guinness, *The Call: Finding and Fulfilling the Central Purpose of Your Life* (Nashville, TN: Word, 1998), 34.

[69] Engel & Dryness, 98.

[70] Antonia Leonora van der Meer, "The Scriptures, the Church and Humanity: Who Should Do Mission and Why?" in *Global Missiology for the 21st Century: The Iguassu Dialogue*, 160. Emphases are mine.

[71] Guinness, 40.

[72] Ted W. Ward, "Botanical Metaphors of Development: Part 2, Metaphors of Spiritual Reality," *Bibliotheca Sacra* 139 (July-September 1982), 196.

[73] The International University-Vienna states it provides "Higher Education with a Christian Dimension." This statement is printed on various brochures and other material of that school.

[74] Millard J. Erickson, *Christian Theology*, 2nd ed. (Grand Rapids, MI: Baker, 1999), 532.

[75] These questions were asked by Stephen Franklin as his response to the proceedings on the Second International Council for Higher Education Triennial Assembly held on Nov. 28-29, 2001 at Beatenberg, Switzerland.

ASIAN MISSIONARIES AND TENT-MAKING

Elizabeth Ruth Peever

For too long now an emphasis in the world has been the belief that missions and missionary work is for people from rich, developed nations. Many people have thought that missions was mainly for Europeans or North Americans. They seem to think that they have a bigger budget, therefore, they are better able to go to mission fields around the world. However, in the book of Acts, on the day of Pentecost the Holy Spirit did not fall just on the rich and powerful of that day, but on all who were listening to Peter's sermon. Furthermore, *all* who were hungry to hear the truth of God were the ones to whom the Holy Spirit came and fell upon. Asians today are hungry for the word of God, willing to go with the message and best suited for this final hour of evangelism.

In this paper I will put forth my reasons why I believe this is the hour for Asian missionaries.

1. The Call of the Spirit

David Kensinger, an Assemblies of God missionary to Costa Rica, has said, "Since the beginning of modern missions with William Carey, two basic principles have been followed—those who are willing and obedient to the Spirit's call, *go* as missionaries; and those who have been willing and obedient *stay at home and financially support* those willing to go."[1] The Spirit's command to go is just not for a certain race of people but for *every believer, in every country* throughout the world to spread the gospel either by dedicating their lives or their finances to see that the lost are reached. As Brad Walz, a missionary to Argentina, says that "national missions is the awakening in every individual Christian his [or her] spiritual responsibility in reaching the lost, not only by testifying or preaching to those around him [or her] whom he [or she] is able to reach personally, but also to fulfill his [or her] responsibility of reaching the entire world by sending the gospel with his [or her] missionary offerings to those places in the world which he [or she] cannot reach personally."[2] Christians in every country of the world should be encouraged to either go and do missionary work using their talents and skills, either in long-term or short-term mission work, or to give to missions, supporting those who do go. We should not withhold the blessing of God from reaching our church members by denying them the chance to go or to give to missions.

2. The Message

If we look again at the Pentecostal message in Acts 1:8 we read Christ's words "But you shall receive power when the Holy Spirit has come upon you; and you shall be witnesses to me (or my witnesses) in Jerusalem and in all Judea and Samaria, and to the end of the earth."

Then in Luke 24:46-48, Christ said to his disciples: "Thus it is written, and thus it was necessary for the Christ to suffer and to rise from the dead the third day, "and that repentance and remission of sins should be preached in his name to *all nations*, beginning at Jerusalem. And you are witnesses of these things." Who? The ordinary men, fishermen, tax collectors and others who followed him for three and a half years and the millions of "fishers of men" who have followed him since that time.

3. Tentmakers from the Local Church

The local church in every country should promote and encourage all their people young, middle-aged and old to participate in mission work using the God-given skills they have. Some to go, some to stay at home and support and some to pray. My mother, a housewife, now in her 80s, feels that she is a world-missionary because she prays for missionaries in many countries around the world every day. Every person, in every church around the world, has his or her responsibility before God to be involved in some way or other in missions. It is not an option it is a command. The church in Asia is the fastest growing church in the world. The largest churches in the world are in Seoul, Korea. Peter Wagner states that in the year 2000, 60% of the world's Christians would be found in the third world.[3] Just think of the millions of Christians in these churches! If these people were trained and motivated to go with the gospel what an impact it would have on God's kingdom. Again, Peter Wagner says, "By the end of the century there will be at least as many missionaries from the third world out on the field as missionaries from the traditional Western nations."[4] Gerald Anderson at the Overseas Ministries Study Center estimates the number of Asian missionaries at 100,000 (Koreans alone, accounting for 11,500 of this number)[5] compared to 40,000 American missionaries.

4. Asian Missionary Potential

There are several important areas where Asian missionaries have unique advantage in comparison with Western counterparts. Some of these characteristics of Asian missionaries that I have observed are:

1) Language aptitude: Average Asians have the ability to speak several languages.
2) Cultural adaptation: As there are common cultural traits throughout Asia, less culture shock is expected.
3) Greater ability to identify with people.
4) Less expense to the church: Tentmaking is a part of the life style of many Asian missionaries.
5) Patient: They are more event-oriented than time-oriented.
6) Gentle: Asians are non-confrontational.
7) Not as noticeable in a crowd: Asians, unlike Westerners, can pass unnoticed.
8) Similar worldview: How they interpret things around them is quite similar among Asians, for example, the *yin-yang* system in interpreting people and things.
9) Similar spiritual problems: For example ancestral worship, Buddhism, Taoism and others.
10) Ability to dialogue: Due to similar thinking processes, e.g., with Hindus or Buddhists.

11) Fearless: For example, Chinese pastors in their evangelism or Fiji missionaries sent to New Guinea.

12) Intercessors: Asian Christians have developed intercessory tradition praying "with loud cries and tears..." (Heb 5:7).

5. "Fishing Evangelism"[6]

The greatest population in the world is found in Asia, which has over three billion people. Within this number are thousands of Christians who are professional in their fields—engineers, scientists, business people, nurses, agriculturists, computer technicians, teachers, doctors, media specialists and many more. With some training these people could integrate work and witness and be a mighty force for God in missions in the twenty-first century much like the Apostle Paul in the first century.

"Low-key *fishing evangelism* is most appropriate in spiritually hostile environments. Christians use bait to fish out the *seekers* from among the indifferent or hostile people around them. They live out the Gospel in an attractive, godly, non-judgmental way. They demonstrate the *joy* of knowing God and *hope* even in suffering. They practice *personal integrity,* do *quality work,* and develop *caring relationships*— all under unrelenting scrutiny. Because they are not perfect, they are quick to apologize and to admit that they are still learning to please God."[7]

6. Tentmaking

6.1 Who Are Tentmakers?

Tentmakers are missions-motivated professionals who support themselves doing secular work as they do cross-cultural evangelism on the job and in their free time. They may be business people or salaried professionals such as teachers, doctors and lawyers. They may be involved in exchange programs, funded research by a company or university or doing internship or study programs abroad. They are ordinary church members who love the Lord and have dedicated their lives to his use. Such people can be greatly used these days to enter countries that are closed to traditional missionaries. I think of the number of Christian businesspeople I have met in China who were reaching people from government leaders to managers of big companies. These tentmakers are no expense to the local church and do a great work in extending his kingdom.

Efraim M. Tendero, National Director of the Philippine Council of Evangelical Churches, said that the Philippine church would like to send out 200,000 tentmakers by the year 2010. With overseas Filipino workers in 181 countries of the world right now and many of them Christian believers, this would only add to the evangelistic work force.[8] I feel Filipinos make good tentmakers in that they speak fluent English, love to travel, are multicultural having Spanish, American and Asian cultural influences in their history and above all have a deep love for the Lord.

6.2 Tentmakers' Main Work: Evangelism on the Job.

A major misconception in mission circles is that tentmakers' jobs leave little time and energy for ministry. People may say, "Don't you find it frustrating to spend so many hours at a secular job and have little time left over for God and ministry?" But I believe that *all my time* belongs to God! How much did Paul work? In 1 Cor 9:6 it suggests that Paul and Barnabas, on their first missionary journey, already supported themselves in their travels through Cyprus and Galatia. In 2 Cor 11:12 on their second missionary journey it states that Paul worked "night and day," that is from early in the morning to late in the afternoon. In Corinth Paul's job-hunting resulted in working and lodging with Aquila and Priscilla (Acts 18:1-5) who were tentmakers by trade. In 1 Cor 4:11, 12, on his third missionary journey Paul wrote: "To this very hour we go hungry and thirsty, we are in rags, we are brutally treated, we are homeless. We work hard *with our own hands.*" In his farewell instructions to the Ephesian elders Paul says, "I have not coveted anyone's silver or gold or clothing. You yourselves know that *these hands of mine have supplied my own needs and the needs of my companions.* In everything I did, I showed you that by this kind of hard work we must help the weak..." (Acts 20:33-35).

6.3 Some Examples of Tentmakers

Dan taught linguistics in an Arab university and did a translation of the New Testament into the language of five million Muslims who had never had it before. He was unable to live in their homeland, so he got a job in a country where thousands of them were guest workers.[9]

Jim, an engineer, pastored the lay leaders of a dozen house churches in a very restrictive Arab country where Christians are not able to meet openly. He led them in preparing their weekly sermons and praying together.[10]

Ken, a high school science teacher, was invited to preach every third Sunday in a village church in Africa.[11]

Don, a graduate student of Hindu culture and religion in India, worked in a local church.[12]

Greg, a university English instructor, helped start a Christian publishing company in a Middle Eastern country.[13]

Mary taught writing and helped local Christians produce literature in East Asia.[14]

English teachers in China gave hours of care to children in a nearby orphanage.

Some tentmakers minister to businesspeople, women, children, slum dwellers or prisoners. Many do health care or family counseling.

An example from the past was in China in the 1200s. Genghis Khan the emperor of China asked Marco Polo for 100 Christian educators to come to China and teach his government leaders knowledge of math, science and religion. He was willing for the country to have the Christian religion, but Marco Polo could only find two monks who were willing to come. One died on the way and the other returned to Italy. As Christians, we lost a great opportunity to influence China with the Gospel at that time.

6.4 Tentmakers Work in Teams

Tentmakers should never work alone but in fellowship and accountability groups. They enlist friends and churches at home to pray. In their new host countries, they may work in tentmaker teams, with national churches, or as members of tentmaker sending agencies or regular mission agencies. Paul Pierson gave an example that illustrates this point: "Ahmed, seeking for the meaning of life, began listening to a Christian radio program, and wrote asking for a Bible correspondence course. This led to his meeting with a Christian worker (a tentmaker) living in his country, who led him to faith in Christ. Running his shop and caring for his family, he attended a night Bible course in another town and became part of a growing church fellowship. Five agencies coordinated their efforts over several years.... The radio broadcasters gave his name to the Bible correspondence people, who referred him to a Christian worker in the area, who passed his name to Bible teachers and national Christians. Clearly, these individual parts of the body of Christ combined to do something that none could have done alone. They needed each other to carry out the mission."[15]

6.5 Why Tentmaking Is Needed

The following quote from Ruth E. Siemens provides us with eight reasons why tentmaking is important if we wish to see the church of Jesus Christ planted in every people group.[16]

1) Tentmaking provides entry into hostile countries. About 80% of the world's population, including most unreached peoples, live in countries that do not allow Christians in as missionaries (and many of these countries are in Asia).

2) It provides natural, sustained contact with non-believers in restrictive and open countries. Tentmakers relate easily to their professional counterparts, e.g., Asian teachers with Asian teachers.

3) It conserves scarce mission funds for missionary ministries that must have full support. Tentmakers earn their own income.

4) It multiplies our personnel. Tentmaking is our best hope for an adequate missions force. There will never be enough paid religious workers. Professional lay people who witness in the workplace add a great resource to world evangelism, which was initially a lay movement.

5) It supplements Christian radio as the gospel must be seen as well as heard. The radio is widely used in Asian nations for spreading the gospel, e.g., China.

6) It legitimizes mission agencies. Mission agencies gain favor with governments when some of their citizens use their skills in secular institutions in foreign countries.

7) Tentmaking is ideal for emerging mission agencies in new sending countries. It is especially true for those who do not want to follow the Western model of donor support because they do not have the funds or cannot legally send funds abroad.

8) It makes use of today's vast global market. The global market is what God has engineered to help us finish world evangelization. We should not ignore hundreds of well-paid job openings worldwide while false religions and cults take advantage of them.

7. Conclusion

God used revival movements in England to bring the gospel to the South Pacific, but most of the real evangelistic thrust in the Pacific was done (and is being done) by people from the islands of Fiji, Tonga and Samoa. Over the years, more than 300 native missionaries have gone out from Fiji alone into the islands of the northwest.[17]

From Tonga, carpenters and wood carvers have carried the gospel as they sailed in their boats to other islands like Samoa and Fiji selling their merchandise and spreading the gospel at the same time. Allen Tippett tells how the first converts in Fiji were Tongans who were living there along the coast as fishermen. After twenty-five years, all the coastal people were converted and they began to spread the gospel inland to the Fijian people. It took nearly fifty years before the people inland were converted. When they were converted the newly established Fijian church asked, "When all of our people have turned from their old religion is, our missionary work finished? What do we do then?" Then the answer came, "We must go to other islands, because there are still many other islands which have never heard the Gospel." One time the Fijians planned a missionary trip, along with an Australian missionary, to New Guinea. They were all prepared to go when a disease called the measles hit the island killing 40,000. In one part of the island 200 Christian pastors and teachers died. So the question arose: "What about our mission? We have no pastors for our own churches, how can we send people to a foreign land if we can't look after our own home church?" The man leading the mission went to the seminary and asked the students if any of them would be willing to go with him or did they want to stay at home because of the great need in Fiji. He gave the students time to pray and think about it. The next day the 84 seminary students gathered and sat quietly. The principal of the school stood up and said, "Now I would like to know if anyone among you is willing to go to New Guinea with Dr. Brown. If so, will he please stand up." What do you think happened? Every one of the 84 stood up! The administrator of the country talked to them trying to tell them they did not have to go. He tried hard to discourage them and said things like, "Do you people want to die in a foreign land?" Then after some time one of the students stood up and said, "We have fully considered this matter and our minds are made up. No one has pressed us in any way. We have heard the call of God, we have given ourselves to God's work, and it is our mind to go to New Guinea. If we live, we live. If we die, we die." They went. Most of them died. But they planted the church, and that church is still there and alive today.[18]

Asians have shown from the past that they have great potential and a heart for mission work. The purpose of this paper has been to encourage all mission-minded Asians that with God and his Holy Spirit they can go and teach all nations the glorious gospel of our Lord and Savior.

---

[1] Brad Walz, "A Theology of Sending" (a paper presented for the Missionary Training Program at Asia Pacific Theological Seminary, Baguio City, Philippines, April-May, 2001).

[2] Ibid.

[3] C. Peter Wagner, *On the Crest of the Wave: Becoming a World Christian* (Ventura, CA: Regal, 1983), 163.

[4] Wagner, *On the Crest of the Wave*, 164.

[5] Paul C. Pierson, "The Church in Missions: Changing Contexts and Contemporary Challenges (A paper presented at Asia Pacific Theological Seminary for the 10th William Menzies Annual Lectureship, Baguio City, Philippines on Jan. 24, 2002).

[6] Dave Engish, "Missions for a New Millennium: Catching up with Paul" (www.globalopps.org/issue%20-%20New%20millennium.htm), 3.

[7] Ibid.

[8] In his keynote address at the International Symposium on Asian Mission in Manila on January 28, 2002.

[9] Engish, 2.

[10] Ibid.

[11] Ibid.

[12] Ibid.

[13] Ibid.

[14] Ibid.

[15] Pierson, "The Church in Missions."

[16] Engish, 4

[17] Allen R. Tippett, *The Deep-Sea Canoe* (South Pasadena, CA: William Carey Library, 1977), 13.

[18] Tippett, *The Deep-Sea Canoe*, 14-21.

CHURCH MULTIPLICATION COACHING NETWORKS

David A. White

Praise the Lord for the thousands of churches planted in the Philippines. In 1974 the DAWN 2000 movement began in the Philippines with about 5,000 churches. The aggressive goal was set to establish 50,000 churches by the year 2000. Praise the Lord, this goal was surpassed! In the final DAWN 2000 Congress last Sept. 18, 2001, it was reported that we have 51,600 churches in the Philippines!

In spite of these great successes, there are some concerns. A recent study showed that 91% of attempted church planting projects failed. This study was done among a denomination that is one of the best in the Philippines in church planting. Of the 13,000 churches planted in the Philippines in the 1990s, 6,000 died, and were not to be found by the year 2000!

What can be done to help church planting attempts succeed more frequently? And how can we help churches be planted in such a way that they will not only survive but be healthy? One thing that can help tremendously is Church Multiplication Coaching Networks (CMCNs).

1. What Is a Church Multiplication Coaching Network?

A CMCN is a training model designed to assist denominations and ministerial fellowships to increase their church multiplication capacity. It is specifically designed to help develop the necessary leaders for this to become a reality. The focus is upon developing the following leaders: national and regional denominational leaders; coaching network facilitators; coaches of church planters; church planters; and church planting team members

Networks consist of 3-10 church planters and their coaches. They all meet together for network meetings twice per month. One network meeting focuses on church planting skills. It includes practical training, coaching, sharing of lessons learned and prayer. The other monthly network meeting focuses on the spiritual life of the church planters.

Each planter has a coach. Coaches model ministry skills for planters at the church planting site. They also meet with planters monthly for planning, prayer and enhancing the personal development of the planter. The network ends when church planting projects are completed, usually within one year.

Philippine Challenge assists denominations and ministerial fellowships in implementing CMCNs.

2. Main Components

The main components are coaching appointments, network meetings and coaches' trainings.

2.1 Coaching Appointments

Each coach meets at least once per month with their respective planter to give personalized attention to the planter's personal development and progress in the church planting project. The following activities are engaged in during coaching appointments: 1) planning; 2) accountability; 3) evaluation; 4) encouragement; 5) problem solving; 6) resourcing; 7) personalized development plan; 8) spiritual life development; 9) modeling ministry skills on the job; and 10) prayer.

2.2 Network Meetings

Network meetings are held twice monthly. Some of the things done at network meetings are: 1) sharing successes; 2) problem solving together; 3) peer accountability; 4) skill training; 5) prayer for one another; and 6) spiritual life development

2.3 Coaches Training

Potential coaches are given the necessary training so that they might impart lessons they have learned to develop church planters. The fruit of the lives of coaches will be multiplied as they contribute to the development of others. Initial training is given to help coaches get started. Upgrading trainings are given when the coaches are ready to receive more.

3. Sample Schedule and Topics for Network Meetings

Topics for each monthly network meeting includes the following:

Month 1
- Why Plant Churches?
- How to Impart the Vision

Month 2
- How to Multiply Fruit through a Team
- How to Recruit and Train a Team
- How to Utilize the Spiritual Gifts on Your Team
- How to Mobilize Prayer Support

Month 3
- How to Set a Goal and Write Plans
- How to Select the Target Barangay in Which You Are Most Likely to Succeed
- Where to Get Funds for Church Planting

Month 4
- How to Utilize Spiritual Warfare in Church Planting
- How to Make Plenty of Contacts
- How to Make a Holistic Impact

Month 5
- Simple but Powerful Outreach Bible Studies

Month 6
- How to Lead Team Meetings
- How to Mobilize Your New Believers to Evangelize

Month 7
- How to Help New Believers Grow

- How to Free Satan's Captives

Month 8
- How to Produce Doers of the Word
- How to Find a Place to Meet

Month 9
- How to Form a Cell/Celebration Church
- How to Create Healthy Cell Group Life
- How to Baptize (with practice)

Month 10
- How to Prepare Expository Sermons
- How to Mobilize Members to Use Their Spiritual Gifts
- How to Have Inspiring Worship Services

Month 11
- How to Organize Your Church
- How to Multiply Cells
- How to Help Members Develop Loving Relationships

Month 12
- How to Develop Spiritual Passion in the New Church

4. Personnel to Be Developed through the Network

4.1 Church Planting Team Members

While it is true that many churches have been successfully planted by solo church planters, a church planting team is highly preferable. Three to twelve church members can be recruited to serve on the team. Although all team members are actually church planters, the team leader is given the title of "Church Planter." The development of the team members will be the responsibility of the church planter. The network training will equip the planter for this important task. Team members could come from any of the following: 1) The mother church; 2) Another church in the district (or beyond) that doesn't have its own church planting project; and 3) A large church in the district (or beyond) that has more than enough members to create a team for their own church planter.

4.2 Church Planters

Church planters should have sufficient experience as members of church planting teams before becoming a church planter and entering the network. There are several different types of church planters who may benefit from participation in the network:

4.2.1 Full-time

He or she could be a full-time church planter, coming from the mother church.

4.2.2 Part-time

The church planter could be a working person who is a member of the church planting team. Mobilizing this type of church planter is especially encouraged. The training can be adapted to accommodate this type of church planter. There are many more potential church planters of this type than those who have the potential to leave their jobs and become full-time church planters. Also, the financial responsibility upon the denomination and mother churches will be much less. Decreasing the financial obstacle can result in the mobilization of far more church planters. The field is ripe unto harvest. We only lack workers to reap the harvest. Greater mobilization of workers should produce much greater fruit!

4.2.3 The pastor

The pastor of the mother church could be the church planter. If so, he or she should concentrate much of his or her effort on developing a team member as the apprentice church planter.

4.2.4 Bible school student

Students could be encouraged to plant a church while studying. The network training could supplement the formal training received in the Bible school. If the student is young, he or she should be teamed with at least one older, more mature team member.

4.3 Coaches

Coaches should be veteran church planters or pastors who have mobilized their church to plant daughter churches. It is usually best for a coach to work with just one church planter. If the coach has plenty of time he or she may coach two planters. Here are a few possibilities regarding who might serve as coaches: 1) The pastor of the mother church; 2) A lay member of the church: This may work well if there is an older member who has good experience in church planting, but does not have the time to serve as team leader, and 3) Another pastor from within the district (or beyond).

4.4 Network Facilitator

The network facilitator has the responsibility of supervising the entire network. His or her main responsibilities will be to supervise the coaches and plan the network meetings. The facilitator could be one of the coaches.

4.5 Regional and National Leaders

Network facilitators develop and move on to holding positions of regional or national leadership to help facilitate their group's church multiplication movement.

Networks contribute to the multiplication and advancement of emerging leaders at all levels.

5. Features

There are several critical features for the network training to be successful. They are:

1) Timely training: All training will be given at the very time it is needed.
2) Practical training: All training received is applied in the church planting project.
3) Learning by experience: Much is learned in the context of actually planting a church.
4) Personalized development: Coaches give special attention to the development of each planter.
5) Spiritual life focus: Special emphasis is given to the spiritual lives of everyone in the network, especially the church planters.
6) Relationship-oriented: Relationships are built through interaction over studies, sharing, prayer and informal activities. Time is given to prayer for personal concerns and

developments in the church planting projects at all network meetings.

7) Available to lay people: Many who have excellent potential to plant a church are not able to leave their families and attend Bible school. This training program is especially well-suited for them. At the same time it can be an excellent complement to Bible school students and full-time planters.
8) Church-based: Local churches are mobilized to plant daughter churches.
9) Healthy churches: Training incorporates the principles from the book *Natural Church Development: A Guide to Eight Essential Qualities of Healthy Churches.*
10) Flexible: A denominations' distinctives or additional training can be easily included. Any other adaptations can also be made to fit various situations.

6. Multiplication

Denominations or ministerial fellowships should begin by establishing one quality network. If the first network is successful, it can be multiplied. Here is an ideal plan that could be followed:

6.1 Pilot Project (Year 1)

The denomination or ministerial fellowship will establish one initial pilot project of 6-10 churches. Coaches should be carefully selected as those who have the potential to become network facilitators the next year. It will be required that the denomination or ministerial fellowship not only provide a Facilitator, but also at least one apprentice-facilitator to help insure multiplication.

6.2 First Multiplication (Year 2)

The pilot network should multiply and produce one or more (hopefully several) new networks.

6.3 Further Multiplication (Years 3 and following)

6.4 Multiplication to Other Denominations or Ministerial Fellowships

Once the organization is well established in using coaching networks they can help others to set up their own networks. This provides opportunity for fruitful groups to expand their ministry by helping other groups.

7. Benefits to the Denomination or Ministerial Fellowship

Benefits can be gained in various levels of church life, but some of them are as follows:

1) Vision expanded
2) Productivity increased: Planters in coaching networks have proven to be eight times more fruitful than those working on their own.
3) Leadership development strengthened
4) Leadership multiplication increased: Multiplication of workers at all levels will be increased.
5) Lay development increased: Church members can develop into church planters through practical involvement on church planting teams.
6) Casualties minimized
7) Monitoring tightened: Church planting projects will be monitored very closely.
8) Relationships among sister churches strengthened
9) Expenses are minimal

This is my earnest prayer that the Lord may guide us to work strategically for a greater harvest!

SCRIPTURE INDEX

OLD TESTAMENT

Genesis
26:4   *151*
49:10   *108*

Deuteronomy
32:4   *141*
33:12   *141*

2 Kings
20:3   *135*

Psalms
2   *108*
16:8-11   *108*
22:1-18   *108*
45   *108*
72   *108*
89:8   *141*
100:5   *141*
110   *108*

Proverbs
9:1-6   *250*

Isaiah
42:6-7   *151*
52:13–53:12   *108*

Lamentations
3:22   *141*

Daniel
9:25-26   *108*

Amos
2:9,10   *165*

Micah
5:2   108

Zechariah
4:6   *87*
9–11   *108*
12:1–14:21   *108*

Malachi
3:1   *108*
4:5   *108*

NEW TESTAMENT

Matthew
5:1-14   *157*
5:13-16   *200*
5:17   *104*
9:35–10:16   *200*
11:10   *108*
16:15   *110*
16:18-19   *195*
27:4   *104*
28:18-20   *152, 249*
28:19-20   *50, 195*

Mark
1:27   *104*
1:29-34   *135*
1:40-42   *135*
2:1-12   *135*
3:13-15   *200*
15:39   *104*

Luke
10:1, 17   *200*
23:4, 14, 22   *104*
24:46-48   *258*

John
14:26   *151*
16:8   *250*
18:38   *104*

Acts
1:8   *132, 138, 152, 249, 258*
2:4   *124*
2:17-18   *200*
2:24   *105*
2:25-28   *108*
2:33   *151*
2:34   *108*
2:42   *201*
2:41-47   *201*
5:1-10   *140*
8   *140*
8:1,4   *196*
10   *124*
10:9-16   *140*
11:19-21   *196*
13:33   *108*
13–18   *197*
17:27b, 28   *106*
18:1-5   *261*
20:33-35   *261*
20:34-35   *196*

Romans
8:2   *101, 104*
8:26-27   *139*
12:1-8   *200*

1 Corinthians
3:6-7   *57*
4:11, 12   *261*
9:6   *261*
9:22b–23a   *247*
12   *134*
13:1   *139*
14   *134*
14:4   *141*
14:7   *138*

14:9   *135*
14:14   *139*
14:14-20   *140*
14:26   *201*
14:29   *141*
15:6   *200*

2 Corinthians
5:18-21   *252*
10:3-5   *200*
11:12   *261*

Galatians
4:4-6   *151*

Ephesians
2:6-7   *200*
2:8,9   *250*
4:11-13   *201*

Philippians
2:4-8   *186*
2:5-7   *187*
2:13   *87*

1 Thessalonians
5:23-24   *141*

2 Timothy
2:2   *196, 201*

Hebrews
2:17   *186*
5:7   *260*
10:24   *201*
13:15-16   *200*

1 Peter
2:9-10   *200*
3:15   *200*

Revelation
1:6   *200*

AUTHOR INDEX

Alberto Deiros, Pablo   76
Allan, R.   209
Allen, Roland   209
Alvarez, Miguel   77
Amnell, Matti T.   126
Anderson, Allan H.   88, 90
Anderson, Gerald H.   77
Anderson, Gordon L.   145
Anstein, Hans   89, 90
Antonio Nuñez, Emilio   77
Apilado, Mariano   40
Araujo, Alexandre   76, 192
Arrington, French L.   78

Banks, Robert   208, 209
Barreiro, Alvaro   209
Barrett, David   207
Bediako, Kwame   252, 255
Bennett, Christi-An C.   254, 255
Berg, Clayton   19, 28
Bergunder, Michael   82, 88, 89, 90
Berryman, Philip   19, 28
Bertuzzi, Federico   76
Bessenecker, Scott   188, 192
Boff, Leonardo   209
Bosch, David J.   222, 226, 253
Braaten, Carl E.   125
Braswell, George W., Jr.   93, 107
Brown, Arthur J.   240
Burgoyne, Samuel R.   162
Burnett, David   107
Bush, Luis   24, 50, 58, 72, 78
Butler, Keith   77
Butler, Phil   78

Carey, William   16, 153, 182
Castillo, Met   50, 51, 54, 58, 59,
    75, 191
Chauhan, R. S.   156, 162
Cho, Paul Yonggi   130, 144
Choi, Sung-kyu   163

Chow, Lien-hwa   176
Clark, Mathew   176
Clark, Stephen   210
Cliff, Norman H.   253, 254
Clifford, Mary Dorita   40
Clymer, Kenton J.   252, 254, 255
Coleman, Robert   208
Comiskey, Joel   19, 28
Conn, Harvie M.   191
Conner, D.   208
Cook, Guillermo   76
Coote, Robert T.   191, 225
Cotterell, Peter   162
Covar, Prospero   40
Cox, Harvey   144

Da Silva, Benedicta   78
Dale, Sally F.   192
De Mesa, Jose M.   30, 40, 75
Dennison, Jack   208
Duff, Alexander   241
Duffield, Guy P.   128, 143, 144
Dupuis, Jacques   124
Dussell, Enrique   76
Dyrness, William   247, 256

Edwards, Jonathan   35
Eims, Leroy   208, 209
Engel, James F.   247, 256
Engish, Dave   265
Erickson, Millard J.   256
Escobar, Samuel   76, 191

Fee, Gordon D.   145
Fernando, Ajith   75
Ferris, Robert   192
Fournier, Keith   210
Franklin, Stephen   256
Fung, Raymond   207, 209

Garrison, David   78, 199, 208
Girón, Rodolfo (Rudy)   76
Glasser, Arthur F.   225
Gnanakan, Ken R.   75, 149, 160,
    161, 162
Gnanapiragasam, John   75
Goff, James R., Jr.   145
Goldingay, John   144
Greenway, Roger S.   182, 191,
    193
Griffin, E.   209
Guinness, Os   256

Haas, Waltraud Ch.   89
Han, Chul-Ha   176
Harris, Murray J.   108
Hastings, Adrian   253
Hattaway, Paul   207
Hay, Denys   252
Henry, Rodney L.   173, 177
Hick, John   119, 121
Hiebert, Paul G.   235, 237, 238,
    245, 252, 253, 255
Hoke, Stephen T.   77, 192
Hong, Young-Gi   86, 89, 90
Hori, Ichiro   172, 177
Hughes, Ray H.   144
Huntington, Samuel P.   82, 83,
    84, 88, 89, 255

Iglehart, Charles W.   252, 253
Isley, William L., Jr.   75, 77

Jacob, P.S.   162
Jenkins, Philip   28
Jenkins, Paul   80, 88, 89
Johns, Cheryl Bridges   144
Johnson, Todd   207

Kärkkäinen, V. – M.   125
Kemp, Roger   253
Kensinger, David   257
Keyes, Lawrence   28

Kim, Chi-Ha   123
Kim, Myung-hyuk   176
Knitter, Paul F.   125, 148, 161
Koch, Bruce A.   225
Kopf, David   238, 253
Koyama, Kosuke   109, 110, 123,
    124
Kraft, Charles H.   145
Künster, Volker   125
Kuriakose, M. K.   254

Lambert, Tony   207
Larson, P.   28
Laubach, Frank   31, 40
Lawanson, Remi   28
Lee, David Tai-Woong   256
Lee Kuan Yew   84
Lee, Jung Young   125
Levine, Michael   95, 97, 107
Lim, David S.   75, 208, 209
Lin, Chi-ping   176
Lindell, Jonathan   162
Linthicum, Robert   209
Lloyd-Jones, Martyn   157
Lockyer, Herbert   108
Loong, Titus   75
López, Dario   76, 78
Lutz, L.   58

Ma, Julie C.   75, 145, 176
Ma, Wonsuk   63,75, 76, 144,
    176
MacDonald, Kenneth P.   241
Maggay, Melba P.   41, 75
Maruyama, Hiroshi   223
Mayhew, Arthur   242, 254
McClung, L. Grant, Jr.   77, 78,
    89
McGavran, Donald A.   16, 40,
    131, 144
McGee, Gary B.   177
Mead, Margaret   235
Menzies, Robert P.   145, 176

Menzies, William W.   *144*
Meyers, Bryant L.   *208, 208, 223*
Miller, Donald   *19, 22, 23, 28*
Minear, Paul   *162*
Moffett, S.   *161*
Montgomery, James   *40*
Montgomery, Jim   *208*
Morioka, Kiyomi   *177*
Myung, Sung-Hoon   *130, 144, 145*

Nacpil, Emerito P.   *75*
Neighbor, Ralph, Jr.   *209*
Neil, Stephen C.   *97*
Neill, S.   *234, 252*
Newbigin, Leslie   *25, 28, 245, 255*
Noss, David   *93, 107*
Noss, John   *93, 107*
Nye, Joseph   *83, 89*

O'Halloran, James   *210*
Ogden, Greg   *208*

Pace, Edward A.   *96, 107*
Padilla, C. R.   *76*
Padilla, C. René   *75, 76*
Palugod, Sylvia   *223*
Pannenberg, Wolfhart   *119, 122, 125, 126*
Pannikar, Raymond   *114, 116, 125*
Paramhasa, Ramakrishna   *154*
Parham, Charles F.   *128, 144, 145*
Park, Timothy Kiho   *28*
Pate, Larry   *28*
Paterson, Ross   *207*
Pentecost, E.   *28*
Phillips, James M.   *191, 225*
Pieris, Aloyis   *118*
Pierson, Paul C.   *183, 191, 262, 265*

Pinnock, Clark   *126*
Plueddeman, Jim   *249*
Pobee, John   *237, 253*
Pretiz, Paul   *19, 28*

Radhakrishnan   *154*
Rahner, Karl   *115*
Raj, Ebe Sunder   *161*
Ramachandra, Vinoth   *161, 162*
Reyburn, W. D.   *192*
Rheenan, Van   *97, 107*
Richardson, Thomas   *242*
Rivera, Juan A.   *40*
Ro, Bong Rin   *75*
Robeck, Cecil M., Jr.   *145*
Robert, Dana L.   *255*
Rodgers, James B.   *31, 40*
Rusling, James F.   *40*

Sacla, Wasing D.   *176*
Samartha, Stanley J.   *110, 111, 112, 113, 114, 116, 117, 118, 120, 124, 125, 154*
Sanneh, Lamin   *237, 253*
Schlitt, Richard   *59*
Shao, Joseph T.   *223, 225*
Sharma, Bal Krishna   *161*
Shibley, David   *77*
Shourie, Arun   *256*
Siemens, Ruth E.   *263*
Silvoso, Ed   *200, 203, 208*
Simson, Wolfgang   *208*
Sisco, Katie   *191*
Smith, Wilfred C.   *126*
Song, Choan-Seng   *75, 115, 124, 125, 126*
Spittler, Russell P.   *145*
Steele, Steve   *208*
Stott, John R. W.   *149, 158, 161*
Stuntz, Howard   *40*
Suico, Joseph R.   *75*
Synan, H. Vinson   *143, 145*

Taliaferro, Charles   *126*
Tano, Rodrigo D.   *75*
Taylor, William D.   *43, 58, 72,*
76, 77, 78, 234
Taylor, J. Hudson   *13, 16*
Tendero, Efraim   *261*
Tippett, Allen R.   *145, 177, 264,*
265
Townsend, Cameron   *16*
Toynbee, Arnold   *121*
Trevelyan, G. O.   *254*
Tucker, Ruth A.   *78*

Valea, Ernest   *107*
Van der Meer, Antonia Leonora
256
Van Engen, Charles   *161, 226*
Vanderbout, Elva   *137*
Veliz, Claudio   *76*

W. C.   *88*
Wacker, Grant   *144*
Wagner, C. Peter   *133, 145, 259,*
265
Walls, Andrew F.   *29, 40*
Walz, Brad   *258, 265*
Ward, Ted W.   *256*
Wei, Yuan-kwei   176, 177
While, Mark H.   145
Wilfred, Felix   *75*
Williams, Kenneth   *190, 192*
Winter, Ralph D.   *16, 28, 182,*
191, 225
Wong, J.   *28*
Wood, Rick   *191*

Yamamori, Tetsunao   ***208, 209***
Yu, Chi-Ping   *176, 177*
Yung, Hwa   *75*

266.0095
M1117
C.1

LINCOLN CHRISTIAN COLLEGE AND SEMINARY

106016

3 4711 00222 2489